CISTERCIAN STUDIES SERIES: NUMBER TWENTY-EIGHT

SAINT BERNARD OF CLAIRVAUX

THE SEAL OF SAINT BERNARD—1151

CISTERCIAN STUDIES SERIES: NUMBER TWENTY-EIGHT

SAINT BERNARD OF CLAIRVAUX

STUDIES COMMEMORATING THE EIGHTH CENTENARY OF HIS CANONIZATION

Edited by

M. Basil Pennington ocso

§

Cistercian Publications

Kalamazoo, Michigan

1977

CISTERCIAN STUDIES SERIES
Board of Editors

Ecclesiastical permission to publish this volume was received from Bernard J. Flanagan, Bishop of Worcester, 20 July 1973.

© 1977, Cistercian Publications Inc.
1749 West Michigan Avenue—WMU
Kalamazoo, MI 49008

Available in Europe and the Commonwealth through

A. R. Mowbray & Co Ltd
Osney Mead
Oxford OX2 0EG

ISBN 0 87907 828 6

Library of Congress Cataloging in Publication Data
Main entry under title:

Saint Bernard of Clairvaux

(Cistercian studies series: 28)
Bibliography: p.
1. Bernard de Clairvaux, 1091?-1153—Addresses, essays, lectures. I. Pennington, M. Basil. II. Title.
BX4700.B5S18   271'.12'024 [B]   77-4487
ISBN 0-87907-828-6

Library of Congress Catalogue Card Number: 77-4487

TABLE OF CONTENTS

INTRODUCTION

ON JANUARY 18, 1974 we mark the eight-hundredth anniversary of the actual canonization of Bernard of Clairvaux.[1] Those of us who through scholarship or spiritual affinity have come to know and love this "Last of the Fathers" would not want to let this occasion pass without taking the opportunity to offer him at least some small tribute.

The study of St Bernard and his writings began years before he died and was canonized, and it has never ceased. Fr Jean Leclercq, without doubt today's greatest Bernardine scholar and a man who is not ashamed to affirm publicly a deep personal love for the great and truly human Abbot of Clairvaux, brings us up to date here on the most recent developments in this field of study. At the same time Dr Adriaan H. Bredero, a geographical neighbor of Fr Leclercq and a scholar who has devoted many years to the classic *Life* of Bernard,[2] deftly and succinctly traces the path that has brought us where we are. As is most fitting on this occasion, Dr Bredero recounts in detail in a second article the complex history leading up to the actual canonization of Bernard.

1. Controversy concerning the year of Bernard's canonization seems to be a thing completely of the past now, with all scholars agreeing on 1174. For the documents of Alexander III promulgating this canonization, see the Appendix.

2. A. H. Bredero, "Etudes sur la *Vita prima* de Saint Bernard," ASOC 17 (1961) 1-72, 215-60; 18 (1962) 3-59.

As Dr Bredero has brought out in his first article, St Bernard has always been and will always be, first of all, a spiritual master, a theologian of the search for God. Professor William Paulsell of Atlantic Christian College continues the centuries-old labor of mining the immensely rich quarry of spiritual doctrine that Bernard left for us. It is not something altogether new for a non-Catholic to be joining in this labor. Dr Bredero has pointed to the work of Luther and his early followers.[3] But what perhaps is new and a sign of our times is how men like Professor Paulsell, coming from significantly divergent Christian backgrounds, now study Bernard not to use him as a weapon to defend their differences but to join in a common search to meet and share in the depths of the Christian life which the great White Doctor has known so well and revealed so beautifully.

Mr G. L. J. Smerillo of St Gregory's House, Oxford, turns his attention to a vein in this quarry whose potential we have only recently come to appreciate fully. As Fr Jean Leclercq went about his painstaking work of preparing the critical edition of the *Works* of St Bernard, he perceived clearly and brought to the attention of scholars the fact that the collections of the *Letters* of the Saint are not accidental accumulations but carefully constructed literary works.[4] Indeed, the earliest collections were put together by Bernard himself and, by their very precise order, give expression to his ecclesiology and theological outlook on the Church. Mr Smerillo turns his attention to the first significant section of the Bernardine collection, and explores the key concept to be found there: *caritas*.

If any one word were to be sought to sum up the life of St Bernard, it would be that word: *caritas*. Bernard was a man of love, loving God before all else, including himself, but

---

3. See below, p. 000. This study on the part of Lutherans has continued: See Carl Volz, "Martin Luther's Attitude toward Bernard of Clairvaux," *Studies in Medieval Cistercian History,* CS 13, ed. Joseph O'Callaghan (Spencer, Massachusetts: Cistercian Publications, 1971), pp. 186-204.

4. See J. Leclercq, "Lettres de S. Bernard: histoire ou littérature? " *Studi medievali* 12 (1971) 1-74.

loving God in all else, especially in his fellow men. And Bernard was human enough to find among his fellow men some who considered themselves his friends and others who considered themselves his enemies. My own brief contribution to this volume seeks to take one very small step further the fascinating question of the reciprocal literary and theological influence that existed between Bernard and the man who laid claim to being his dearest friend, William of St Thierry.

Dr Edward Little studies another, even more puzzling, "friendship". Over the past five years or more a very interesting public conversation has been going on between this eminent student of Peter Abelard and Fr Jean Leclercq.[5] The article here offered is the latest piece in the mosaic they are putting together which in the end will perhaps reveal to us the real picture of this very complex human relationship.

In his lead article, Fr Leclercq tells us that "the most original contribution"[6] in the field of the study of the intellectual history of St Bernard and his times has been made by Professor John R. Sommerfeldt, the Executive Director of the international Institute of Cistercian Studies. Professor Sommerfeldt offers here another contribution to this important study, one that makes us even more eager for the volume which we have been promised will follow shortly.

One of the areas that is certainly being profoundly effected in the present Cistercian and, indeed, Western Christian renewal, is the area of man's worship. The liturgical *aggiornamento* inaugurated by the Second Vatican Council has had repercussions far beyond the Roman communion. Fr Chrysogonus Waddell ocso, America's leading scholar in the field of Cistercian liturgy, makes a plea for the continuing significance of Bernard's directives in this area of Christian life.

Perhaps, though, the most significant and forward-looking contribution in this commemorative volume is that of Fr

5. Dr Little's significant study, *The "Heresies" of Peter Abelard*, will be published shortly by Librairie J. Vrin, Paris. He has published numerous articles on the subject.
6. See below, p. 000.

Joseph Chu-Công ocso. His paper is the first step in exploring an exciting new possibility opening up through contacts between the Cistercians and the East. Father is eminently prepared for the task he has undertaken, having spent many of his mature years as a spiritual guide in his native North Vietnam before entering a Western Cistercian Abbey in 1961.

There are many parallelisms that can be drawn between the times of St Bernard, the twelfth century, and our own rapidly passing twentieth century. For Western civilization both have been periods of considerable evolution and seeming turmoil, in the midst of which man was experiencing new freedom. In Bernard's time many an ordinary man was for the first time free to decide his own future, to stay on the land or to drift to the emerging city, to go off to military adventure or seek the greater adventure to be found within the peace of the cloister. Today, the young have unprecedented freedom to strike out on their own and do what they please. Along with this is greater self-consciousness or man-consciousness.[7] Man, finding himself as it were in his own hands, has a heightened curiosity about himself. Almost all the first great Cistercian writers of the twelfth-century have left us treatises on what we would call Christian anthropology.[8] Today the emphasis on the study of man, the behavioral sciences, is all-pervasive. We may smile at some of the rather rudimentary physiology found in the anthropological treatises of the Cistercian Fathers, but in the final analysis their studies have something that many of today's more sophisticated studies sadly lack, the ultimate key to the understanding of man, the realization that man has been

7. See Colin Morris, *The Discovery of the Individual:* 1050-1200, Church History Outlines 5 (London:SPCK, 1972).

8. See *Three Treatises on Man: A Cistercian Anthropology*, CF 24, ed. Bernard McGinn, (Washington, D.C.: Cistercian Publications, 1974). If Bernard left us no single treatise explicitly and specifically on this topic, the study of man is certainly not absent from his writings. See especially, *Grace and Free Will*, tr. Daniel O'Donavan with an Introduction by Bernard McGinn, in *The Works of Bernard of Clairvaux*, vol. 7, CF 19.

created and remains the *image* of God.[9] Man's search into himself, then as now, leads to the realization that he needs something, someone, beyond himself. And so the eleventh, leading into the twelfth, century was marked with much spiritual searching. New spiritually oriented communities of all types were springing up every where. Most were ephemeral, though some led to great spiritual traditions still alive today: the Camaldolese, the Carthusians, and the Cistercians. One does not have to comment here on the widespread spiritual awakening and searching of our times, nor on the many attempts at communal living. All the same elements are present.

But there is another factor that stirred and shaped the twelfth century and has its parallel today. That is the influence of new currents of thought from the East. Then it was the Near-East: the thought of early Christians and pagans alike, coming into the West through Arabs, traders and crusaders. Today, we are being challenged by the approach to thinking of the Far East. I do not think we have as yet even a suspicion of how profoundly this is going to influence our current Western outlook.

Somehow, in the midst of change, renewal and search, the early Cistercian leadership, possessing some of the answers men were seeking, found the way to communicate them and thus played a very significant role in the development of Western Christian culture and society. St Bernard's personal role stands out like a beacon, but it had solid foundations in the Cistercian Order. The extent to which the Cistercian

9. The theme of "image" is a very fundamental one in Cistercian theology and spirituality. See Maur Standaert, "La doctrine de l'image chez saint Bernard," *Ephemerides Theologicae Lovaniensis* 23 (1947) 70-129; Amédée Hallier, *The Monastic Theology of Aelred of Rievaulx*, CS 2 (Spencer, Massachusetts: Cistercian Publications, 1969), c. 1: "Man the Image of God," pp. 3-24; Robert Javelet, *Image et ressemblance au douzième siècle de saint Anselme à Alain de Lille* (Paris: Letouzey, 1967). Aelred has a very complete and concise presentation of the theme in his *Second Sermon for the Feast of Pentecost, In die Pentecosten*, ed. C. H. Talbot, *Sermones inediti B. Aelredi abbatis Rievallensis*, Series Scriptorum S. Ordinis Cisterciensis 1 (Rome:Editiones Cistercienses, 1952) pp. 107-9.

answer responded to the needs of the time can be gauged
from the fact that in 1113 there were some 13 men out in a
swamp. Forty years later, in 1153, their family had grown to
include over 340 monasteries[10] which dotted the map of
Europe and reached beyond, some of them housing communities of six or seven hundred men.[11]

Today, we are rapidly moving toward being, in fact, one
world. East and West must meet. But they can really meet
only on a spiritual level, for this is where the East truly is. If
it would only know itself, the West would say the same—
though unfortunately it has been trying hard to live on the
level of a superficial materialism. In the spirituality of
Cîteaux, expressed preeminently by St Bernard, but no less
truly by his friends and disciples, William of St Thierry,
Aelred of Rievaulx and Guerric of Igny among others, the
West has the expression of a spirit that is specifically its own,
and most deeply its own. Once again the Cistercian spirit
could play a very significant role in the renewal and on-going
development of Western Christian culture as it receives and
assimilates new currents from the East. It is a challenge which
underlies the undying relevance of Bernard of Clairvaux as we
pause to pay tribute to him on the anniversary of his canonization. Although eight hundred years have passed since he
was officially raised up as a teacher for the nations, Western
civilization has as much need of Bernard's spiritual doctrine
today as it had in the twelfth century. And in this teaching it
has something to bring to the meeting with the East that will
be recognized and appreciated.

I want to conclude this brief Introduction with an expres-

10. Due to the difficulty in dating some of the foundation charters and the
great rapidity with which new monasteries were being founded, it is not possible
to say with certainty how many Cistercian monasteries there were at any particular moment in these years of great expansion. For the terminal year we are
concerned with, see Leopoldus Janauschek, *Originum Cisterciensium* I (and there
was only one volume published) (Vienna: Hoelder, 1877) pp. 136-47.

11. Walter Daniel tells us that at Aelred's death in 1167 there were at Rievaulx
"one hundred and forty monks and five hundred *conversi* and laymen." *Walter
Daniel's Life of Ailred, Abbot of Rievaulx,* ed. and tr. F. M. Powicke (London,
New York: Nelson: 1950; Oxford University Press, 1951) p. 38.

sion of sincere gratitude to all those who have generously collaborated to make possible this humble tribute to our Father and Teacher. May this volume perhaps help some others to come to know and love him.

M. Basil Pennington ocso

Saint Joseph's Abbey
Spencer, Massachusetts

ST BERNARD IN OUR TIMES

IN 1953 WE CELEBRATED the eighthundredth centenary of the death of Bernard of Clairvaux. At the end
of the last of the congresses held in Bernard's native
Burgandy on this occasion, it occured to several of the scholars who had been brought together by the study of this
singularly attractive personality that it would be a good idea
to gather together again in his memory. Two more cente-
naries were then impending: first of all, in 1963, the introduction of Bernard's cult at Clairvaux—the equivalent of his
beatification—and secondly his canonization, in 1974. At the
first date the project remained but a dream, but in 1974 a
volume of studies on Bernard is being published and the project will to a certain extent be realized. This time the initiative has come from the United States. Although interest in St
Bernard is still very much alive in Europe, it has spread to
Australia and above all to America, to such an extent that we
shall soon perhaps be able to say: *America docet.*

If I have any right to confine myself to work which has
been undertaken during the last ten years, it is because in
1963 an inventory was made of all that had been done between the centenary of Bernard's death and that of the introduction of his cult to Clairvaux.[1] Since then work has by no

---

1. "Les études bernardines en 1963," *Bulletin de la Société internationale pour
l'étude de la philosophie médiévale* 5 (1963) 121-128. In the following pages, any
titles which are not preceded by the name of an author indicate publications
where I have dealt at greater length with subjects which can only be touched upon
here.

1

means come to a standstill; that much we can see from the
Bibliographie bernardine which has just been brought out by
Fr Eugene Manning. For the period in which we are interested it lists more than two hundred and twenty five publications, about one a month.[2] Even then the *Bibliographie* takes
into account only books or articles which deal either prin-
cipally or at least at some length with Bernard; those in
which he is merely mentioned are omitted. A tenth of these
works were written or published in the United States or
Canada. Lectures about St Bernard are being given regularly
at The Catholic University of America in Washington, while
the activities of the Institute of Cistercian Studies at Western
Michigan University (Kalamazoo) are bound to intensify
interest.

I shall not here be able to do more than mention a few of
the recent publications on St Bernard—their titles alone fill
up many pages. It is enough to sketch in the main areas in
which new discoveries either have been made or are likely to
be forthcoming.

One could easily say that St Bernard is still living among us.
He is not merely the object of learned borrowings, for general
works appear almost every year—biographies, sketches and
summaries of his teaching appear either for the first time, or
in new editions or translations. This sort of book rarely adds
to the knowledge we have already, but it does at least prove
that for an enormous public quite outside monastic circles,
Bernard's character, historical role and spiritual message continue to hold living interest. These same interests are shared
by the specialists, whose works will help, we hope, to form a
richer and subtler picture of Bernard, a picture which one
day will be shared with the reading public. The result of all
their different researches has been to demonstrate the com-
plexity of Bernard's personality, of the times in which he
lived, of the teaching which he formulated, and of the influence which he exercised. Occasionally we find people who

---

2. Eugene Manning, *Bibliographie bernardine (1957-1970), Documentation
cistercienne* 6 (1970) IV+81 pp. In the present notes I shall only mention works
not included in this publication, or those which have come out since 1970.

give vent to their aggressiveness when writing about St Bernard, while others use him to promote their particular religious theory. Objectivity is commoner than it once was, however. No one will revise Bernard's process of canonization, but we are at least more prepared to see things in their true light and to abandon those legends which merely flatter his disciples. The truth, about which Bernard spoke so well, will only gain by this. What he said about "love of the truth," the object of all his striving[3] and the source of all his humility,[4] must be applied to him just as much as to those who attempt to penetrate his mystery.

TEXTS

At the root of all work on St Bernard lies the study of his writings. Some surprises may still be in store for us if new manuscripts are discovered, but they will be the exception rather than the rule. The only real event in the recent history of Bernardine texts has been the discovery by John F. Benton of an important twelfth-century manuscript preserved in the United States. A manuscript is an experience. Like the human being who created it and whose works it transmits, a manuscript has a history and, as it were, a personality. This particular manuscript originated in England, where St Bernard was so much loved—though not by everyone, of course. It so happens that this new document's chief importance stems from what it tells us about the *Letters* which the abbot of Clairvaux launched, with an ardor that must be rare in the history of polemics, in opposition to the election of William Fitzherbert as Archbishop of York. Many of them have only survived from one solitary and late source, so the new manuscript has permitted a fresh edition of these letters which, if they do not add much to the posthumous

---

3. St Bernard, SC 77:5; OB 2:264: "Veritas est quam quaerit et quam vere diligit anima eius. Et revera quis fidus verusque animae amor, nisi utique in quo veritas adamatur. Rationis sum compos, veritatis sum capax; sed utinam non forem, si amor veri defuerit! "

4. Hum 2-3; OB 3:17-8. There are many other texts on truth.

glory of the man who dictated them, at least help us to know him and therefore to understand him better.[5] The same volume contains, among other interesting pieces, a rare copy of a treatise by Isaac of Stella, and two delightful unknown works which have now been edited and which reveal the great psychological finesse which could exist in the medieval cloister.[6]

The problems of authenticity, then, have mostly been solved. It is now mainly the apocryphal writings which need to be catalogued and restored to their rightful authors whenever this is possible. They will then have to be re-edited, studied, and above all explained.[7] One wonders why all these writings were attributed to St Bernard? To what literary genre did they belong? Did they owe much to Bernard's teaching? How were they disseminated? When were they most popular and who read them? The only one of them which has received much attention recently—and even here no definite conlcusions have been reached—is the *Salve Regina*. Clearly there is still work for the rising generation to do. The late Fr Damien van den Eynde showed great tenacity

5. *Lettres de S. Bernard trouvées depuis les Mauristes, II. Les lettres du manuscrit de Claremont,* forthcoming in the *Mélanges* offered to Marcel Richard (Berlin, 1974). Quite recently, fragments of Sermons and Sentences have been found in Norway in a twelfth-century manuscript which has been analysed by L. Gjerlow, "A Twelfth-Century Victorine or Bernardine Manuscript in the Library of Elverum," *R Ben* 82 (1972) 313-38. And the librarian of Keble College, Oxford, Mr M. B. Parkes, kindly allowed me to examine ms. 37 in his library, the analysis of which he is going to publish. This manuscript may contain new sentences of Bernard. In order to verify the authenticity of such texts, H. Rochais has drawn up a method which he has used in his different publications on the *Sententiae*. In particular he has collected a series of reference cards of various "themes" and "expressions" which allow for a comparative study of each sentence and Bernard's works as a whole. Dr R. W. Hunt, keeper of the manuscripts of the Bodleian Library also showed me a manuscript from the Lyell fund similar to that of Elverum.

6. These texts are edited in "Deux témoins de la vie des cloîtres au moyen âge." *Studi medievali* 13 (1972) 1-9; analysis in "Modern Psychology and Interpretation of Mediaeval Texts," *Speculum* 48 (1973) 476-490.

7. For a new series of *Corpus christianorum* devoted to the *opera spuria,* an inventory and an edition of these texts is projected. A letter of a Pseudo-Bernard is published under the title "Un témoin de l'antiféminisme au moyen âge," *R Ben* 80 (1970) 304-9.

in his patient research into the dating of St Bernard's *Letters,* and an equally tenacious effort will be required to continue his work; he dealt with about fifty *Letters,* but over four hundred remain. Only when this task has been completed will it be possible to undertake a critical biography of the abbot of Clairvaux. Meanwhile, the last two volumes of the critical edition of the *Letters*—now in the press—will at least show what is known and what can be conjectured concerning their date, as well as the persons and events mentioned. An essential bibliography relative to the known historical facts will also be presented. Another project (which will take some time to complete, although most of the necessary documentation has already been gathered together) will be the production of a general bibliography of all the *Letters,* treating them not just from the historical, but also from literary and doctrinal points of view. This will pave the way for a complete commentary on these important texts.

Another major tool, as useful for the study of the development of Bernard's thought as for the analysis of his style, will be the word-concordance which has been undertaken by the Cistercian Abbey of Achel in the Netherlands and is now nearly complete.[8] The countless index-cards which have been compiled will enable us to make an exhaustive study of Bernard's vocabulary and, what is more, of the symbols through which he projected his ideas. This in turn will throw light on the way his imagination worked and the way he thought. The patient toil which has been expended in compiling this card library will thus contribute to a deeper understanding of the man Bernard. The concordance has been based on the new critical edition, in the preparation of which it has been so useful, and it will enable us to use the edition more accurately and more profitably. The concordance should not be expected to solve all the problems posed by St Bernard's

8. *Kartoteek Bernard Konkordans,* St Benedictus-Abdij, Borkel en Schaft (N.B.), The Netherlands. This concordance contains the matter for the volume of indexes which will finish the critical edition of the *S. Bernardi opera.* The way in which this material is to be used, the selection and ordering necessary, raises more than one problem. These are being examined and a decision is impending.

works, but it will have achieved its aim if it helps us to define them more exactly.

A critical apparatus is often useful if the editor simply selects the variants, retaining those which have some interest and eliminating the mistakes which would only distract and mislead the reader. The editor offers suggestions which the reader may indeed prefer to those adopted (Fr Denis Farkasfalvy's familiarity with Bernard's doctrine and style allowed him to make a judgement of this sort on an important point.[9]) In the case of the exceptionally rich Bernardine manuscript tradition, however, the critical apparatus serves another purpose: it helps us to see how the author worked on his texts and how he went about revision. We can observe the hesitations of the man of letters and the ways in which he attempted to improve the expression of his thought. The critical apparatus allows us to discover in St Bernard both the writer and the artist. His art of composing, the care he had for the use of the right literary genre, and the musicality of his sentences have already been the subject of one or two studies. But practically everything still remains to be done in this field. Any future studies will be based on the critical edition and carried out with the help of the word-concordance, and perhaps one day, who knows, by means of computors, and in the light of the growing contribution of structuralism to the study of stylistics.

We can already see that the theories about what we might call "the two faces of St Bernard," formulated when the search for manuscripts first began, are now being confirmed. His first face is the one he himself turned both on his contemporaries and on posterity when, during his last years, he carefully revised and corrected his major works, selecting, rearranging and setting in order a large number of his *Sermons* as a sort of commentary on the liturgical year. He also arranged about half his *Letters* according to a strict plan which eventually made this official collection a program of

9. Denis Farkasfalvi, O CIST *L'inspiration de l'Ecriture Sainte dans la théologie de S. Bernard*, Studia Anselmiana 53 (1964) p. 44.

reform for the whole Church.[10] Then, in the *Letters* which did not go through this "personality control" we see another side of Bernard's character: more spontaneous and more attentive to the realities of everyday life; the atmosphere is one of joyfulness, gaiety, even fun.[11] Bernard was both these men. We may ask to what extent he managed to prevent his role from dominating his personality, to realize self-unity and be sincere in spite of his literary art? These are questions which textual criticism can only suggest. There comes a time when the paleographer must give place to the psychologist.

EVENTS

The part Bernard played in the history of his times has been thoroughly studied. The Cistercian Congresses held for some years past in the United States and Canada, besides producing several publications,[12] have helped define more exactly Bernard's position vis-à-vis the Cistercian Order, monasticism as a whole, the Church, society, and tradition. He was conservative, but his mind was too inventive, too accommodating, too filled with the spirit of God to remain attached to the past without trying to recreate it. He did not always succeed, nor did his efforts always have a lasting result. Like every other man he had his cultural limitations to the time and place in which he lived. We may ask to what extent he was aware of this and suffered from it? Did he have an intuition that sociological conditions and the weight of institutions would sooner or later dominate the powerful surge of renewal which he was trying to promote? That is his mystery and God's secret. But a European may legitimately

10. "Lettres de S. Bernard: histoire ou littérature? " *Studi medievali* 12 (1971) 1-74; "Recherches sur la collection des épîtres de S. Bernard," *Cahiers de civilisation médiévale* 1 (1971) 205-19.
11. The sermons of the first genre are in OB 5; those of the second are in OB 6-1 and especially OB 6-2.
12. M. Basil Pennington, OCSO (ed.), *The Cistercian Spirit* (Spencer, 1970); *Rule and Life* (Spencer, 1971); and *Contemplative Community* (Washington, 1972).

think—and this without in any way wishing to flatter his friends—that in the United States today, since the death of Thomas Merton and perhaps on account of his invisible pre-sense, Cistercian life is showing evidence of a lucid fervor and courageous liberty strangely akin to St Bernard's.

Bernard's interventions in the life of the Church are being carefully examined, especially in England,[13] and still more in Italy, with a rigour which puts his character to a daunting test. The patient investigation and identification of persons, dates and localities as they are revealed by charters and other documents has allowed P. Zerbi to present the abbot of Clair-vaux against the background of his human relationships, his friendships, and his animosities. Without these he stands out as a lone figure, like a portrait without a frame, or like a head without a body. If we really want to get to know him, we must study his contemporaries as much as himself. This is to be seen especially in connection with Abelard. Bernard and Abelard came into conflict not only over specific doctrines and theological methods but also over the correct way to reform the Church and to bring to an end the factions which were causing so much trouble at Rome. In the Roman Curia which had to confirm the sentence passed by the Council of Sens, Bernard was not without enemies, and we can only understand the campaign he waged there against the back-ground of the religious and political upheavals then going on around the Pope. It is only in the light of the attitudes of the two opposing parties at Rome, and especially of their leaders, that we can understand the intense activity of Bernard's chancellery in this business. By taking these considerations into account we also learn something about the chronology of Bernard's *Letters*: their destination and the part played by secretaries—especially Nicholas of Clairvaux—in the drafting of them. During the colloquium on mediaeval humanism held

---

13. Albert Stacpoole, "The Monastic and Religious Orders in York, 650-1540," *The Noble City of York* (York, 1971) 620-7. L. G. D. Baker, "The Genesis of English Cistercian Chronicles in England, The Foundation History of Fountains Abbey," ASOC 25 (1969) 14-41; "The Foundation of Fountains Abbey," *Northern History* 4 (1969) 29-43; other works are forthcoming.

at Cluny in July, 1972, and focused on Abelard and Peter the Venerable, many of these problems were touched upon. The proceedings of this Congress and the book being prepared by P. Zerbi are expected to be important and perhaps decisive publications.[14]

Several works in the last few years have advanced our knowledge considerably beyond where things stood in 1953.[15] Twenty years ago we could do no more than sketch a sort of contrast-history, opposing Bernard and Abelard. Today however we have a better knowledge of these two men, their background and their influence, and are thus able to see more clearly all that they had in common and to judge the exact nature of their differences. We shall eventually be in a position to elaborate a history-synthesis on the basis of the models proposed in 1969 by D. E. Luscombe[16] and in 1970 by R. E. Weingart.[17] These two authors were able to deal impartially with two great conflicting minds. The first dealt with Abelard's influence and the second with his sources. Weingart pointed out that generally speaking the Master of Le Pallet was in agreement not only with the Augustinian doctrines which had hitherto held the field, but also with the teaching of contemporary monastic theologians, especially St Anselm, St Bernard, and the "school of the Cistercian mystics."[18] In both cases we notice a dependence

---

14. P. Zerbi has already published "Panem nostrum supersubstantialem. Abelardo polemista ed esegeta nell'Ep. X," *Contributi dell' Instituto di storia mediaevale. II. Raccolta di studi in onore Sergi Mochi Onor* (Milan, 1972) 624-638.

15. "Notes abélardiennes," *Bulletin de Philosophie médiévale* 13 (1971) 68-71.

16. D. E. Luscombe, *The School of Peter Abelard. The Influence of Abelard's Thought in the Early Scholastic Period*, Cambridge Studies in Medieval Life and Thought, Second Series, Vol. 14 (Cambridge, 1969). Reviewed in *The Ampleforth Journal* 74 (1969) 411-2.

17. R. E. Weingart, *The Logic of Divine Love, A Critical Analysis of the Soteriology of Peter Abelard* (Oxford, 1970).

18. Ibid., p. 122, n. 6. In a review in *Medium Aevum* 41 (1972) 59-61, I indicated similar references. Colin Morris, *The Discovery of the Individual, 1050-1200* (London, 1972) p. 73, writes in connexion with Abelard's teaching on penance that he "was expressing, in his usual incisive way, the convictions of most of his contemporaries." Here are other indications of the superficial and over-facile character of contrast-history. First, there was a tendency to oppose Abelard and the liturgy he introduced at the Paraclete to St Bernard and Cistercian

on Platonic thought, a tendency towards interiorization, and an emphasis on love in God and for God. But as far as grace and free will and the soteriological value of Christ's death were concerned, it was sometimes Abelard who did not or would not grasp St Anselm's teaching, and at other times it was Bernard who did not correctly interpret Abelard's thought. The value of these carefully written books lies in the help they give us in understanding how very difficult it was in those times for even the keenest minds to assimilate the contradictory riches inherited from the Church Fathers and the divergent doctrines subsequently derived from them. The time had not yet come for religious thought to repose peacefully on classical scholasticism. Nowadays, when the cleverly structured doctrines which scholasticism elaborated no longer seem to satisfy us, now that men like Lonergan, Rahner, von Balthasar, Küng and others propose new methods and grapple courageously with new problems, sustaining a polemic which is unfortunately not entirely free from bitterness, it is easier

liturgy. Today we are discovering in the *Ordinarium* of the Paraclete many specifically Cistercian elements. For example, the hymns were borrowed directly from the Cistercian hymnal. (I am indebted for this information to Fr Chrysogonus Waddell OCSO). Second, the sort of architecture Bernard liked was said to be opposed to that of Cluny. But a recent careful study has pointed out that the church at Fontenay—the monastery which Bernard liked best and which served as a model for several of his foundations—was, in its conception and construction, influenced by several factors, the most important being Cluny itself. It has, in particular, certain columns and colonnettes which are only there for the sake of art. These observations bring up the problem of the evolution Bernard went through in his relations with Cluny, and that of the apparent or real inconsistencies which might exist between his passionate declaration and his acts. It is easier to hold that he avoided having any clear cut ideas about architecture. He did not want to elaborate a Bernardine esthetic. He thought it more important to promote spiritual attitudes compatible with different esthetic conceptions and realizations. Such is the conclusion arrived at by P. Gilbert, "Un chef d'oeuvre d'art cistercien peut-être influencé par Cluny, l'abbatiale de Fontenay," *Académie royale de Belgique, Bulletin de la Classe des Beaux-Arts,* 3 (1970) 20-45, with illustrations. Concerning the "Bernardine" or "Claravallian" plan, fresh precisions have recently been given by R. Courtois, "La première église cistercienne (XIIe siècle) de l'abbaye de Vauclair (Aisne)," *Archéologie médiévale* 2 (1972) 112-3. The author notes (p. 114) the similarity between the plan of Vauclair and that of Fountains in Great Britain: "the first abbot of Vauclair, the englishman Henry Murdac, who from 1134 onwards presided over the destiny of Vauclair," was to become abbot of Fountains some years later. Cf ibid., pp. 104-5.

to realize something of the keen, albeit slightly confused, battle of wits which went on in the twelfth century over the burning questions of the day. Bernard and Abelard, each in his own way, took part in this conflict, and in it each gave the measure of the keeness of his intellect and of his talent in polemic. Both men entered the fray with an extremely rich personality, but, in spite of the workings of grace, one still tainted with imperfections.

We sometimes read rather summary judgments, not worth quoting, on Bernard's interventions on behalf of the Second Crusade. He is tagged with rather futile names inspired by present-day propaganda: he is reproached for not having been "anti-war," "pacifist," and "non-violent" like certain groups today. We have to see Bernard's activities on behalf of the Crusade in the context of a society whose values were very different from our own. The manuscript tradition, which must always be our starting-point, proves that the *Encyclical* which Bernard sent out all over Europe was far from the result of an uncontrolled impulse. In fact it was a very carefully drafted text, adapted according to its intended destination by Bernard's well-organized chancellery. It was the fruit not only of a great deal of thought, but also of profound contemplation of the mysteries of salvation. The fact that throughout the centuries it has been read by spiritual men and women quite uninvolved in military or political activities indicates the true character of the *Encyclical.* It was regarded as a call to conversion rather than a call to arms.[19]

It was also a call to peace among all peoples. That it went unheard and that the Crusade ended in failure says much about the internal divisions of Christendom and the universal acceptance of the law of violence. The Crusade was not the only war on which Bernard had to take a stand; there were others both before and after. Armed combat was the normal way of resolving disputes in medieval society. The Abbot of Clairvaux was aware of this and he realized that it did not lie

---

19. "L'encyclique de S. Bernard en faveur de la croisade," *R Ben* 81 (1971) 282-308; "A propos de l'encyclique de S. Bernard sur la croisade," *R Ben* 82 (1972) 312.

within his power to change the situation, for this would have presupposed a radical transformation of the structure both of the family and of the economy. Bernard was a man of the spirit, but he had his feet firmly on the ground and so, taking his inspiration from a doctrine elaborated two generations before him by the eminent canonist Anselm of Lucca, he did his utmost to restrain men's combative instincts and to persuade them to be ruled by their consciences rather than by their baser motives. Since this tendency to violence could not entirely be done away with, Bernard tried to make it an occasion for doing penance and returning to God. He could not abolish war just like that. It existed, and the most he could do was to attempt to make it, if not holy, at least sanctifying, which according to him, it certainly could be, whatever the outcome. Success might well prove to be an "unhappy victory" if the war had been motivated by pride, love of power or the abuse of military strength.[20]

Moreover, it had not been Bernard's idea to take part in the campaign for the Crusade. The invitation had come from Pope Eugenius III. But the Pope was only the Sovereign Pontiff. He could do nothing without the Prophet whose voice was sure to gain a hearing. So the Pope called the Prophet to his aid and Bernard, invested with a power he had not wanted, used it according to his personal convictions. He broadened the scope of the campaign, originally intended to be confined to France, and extended it to the whole of Christendom. This idea proved to be the illusions of a monk who thought of the whole church as one religious community. Bernard attempted to direct to the Holy Places idle young men whose martial amusements were the plague of the lowly and poor.

He opposed the massacre of the Jews. Through his spiritual and doctrinal influence he brought about a permanent transformation in the character of the *Encyclicals* which since the time of Gregory VII had been issued concerning the Crusade. Bernard transformed the promise of pardon, indulgences, and

20. "St Bernard's Attitude to War," *Studies in Medieval Cistercian History II,* CS 24 (Washington: Cistercian Publications, forthcoming).

privileges into a declaration of love.[21] There is a story told about Cardinal Suhard, archbishop of Paris, who after World War II had written long pastoral letters which were translated into many languages. The papal nuncio, Angelo Roncalli—the future John XXIII—was instructed to tell him, with a kind of gentle reproof: "Formerly encyclicals went out only from Rome. . . ." But once upon a time one came from Clairvaux. And while many of the encyclicals issued from the papal chancellery have been forgotten and some have not even survived, Bernard's has never even to our own day ceased to be published, translated and meditated upon. Eugenius III did not err when he charged an abbot with reminding the Church what the Spirit had to say.

DOCTRINES

We may now ask whether this Prophet, whose eloquence was matched by his elegant style, was also a thinker and teacher. Whatever else may be said, it is an undeniable fact that in comparison with the Schoolmen, who were the professionals of religious teaching, Bernard's part in the evolution of theology has never ceased to capture the attention of medievalists. About ten recent works have tried to define his method and his contribution to medieval thought about matters of faith. He is acknowledged to hold a place in the history of both theology and philosophy, but to which discipline does his contribution really belong? Are we dealing merely with piety or with a true dialectic? How does he define the relationship between authority and reason? Is it possible to analyse his personal experience? What was his intellectual and cultural milieu? There is still a great deal to be said on all these points, for Bernard's genius defies categorization. The most original contribution to work in this field has been made by John Sommerfeldt, Executive Director of the Institute of Cistercian Studies at Western Michigan University. He is concentrating his research on Ber-

21. "Pour l'histoire de l'encyclique de S. Bernard sur la croisade," forthcoming in the Mélanges offered to E. R. Labande (Poitiers, 1974).

nard's epistemology, for he thinks that Bernard's concept of knowledge should give us the key to his apparent inconsistencies. According to his theory, Bernard has a specific and unique logic arising from his personal spiritual inspiration, difficult to define and impossible to classify in the categories with which we are familiar.

Bernard applies this system to the principal problems of dogmatics and ethics: in Book Five of his treatise, *On Consideration,* he treats of the unity and trinity of God and of the two natures of the Word Incarnate. Elsewhere he mixes elements of speculative Christology with a meditative contemplation of the mysteries celebrated in the liturgical year. More than once his references to the interior experience of Jesus have something about them which we would be tempted to call modern did we not know it to be Biblical. This is true, for example, of the forceful pages where he comments on those passages in the *Letter to the Hebrews* and in Deutero-Isaiah which describe the misery which the Word Incarnate suffered in order to learn mercy through obedience. "In order to be numbered with his brothers," he was willing "to share all our afflictions, save sin itself."[22]

To Mariology Bernard made no new contribution, nor did he set out to do so. He thought it more important to stress Mary's faith, which made the Incarnation possible. Arguing in his usual incomparable style, he encouraged the development of what we might call the "feudalization" of the Mother of God. Like all his contemporaries he gave the "handmaid of the Lord" titles which in politics and law invested her with the power and prerogatives of an empress, a queen, an advocate, the head of an army, and many other persons of rank. In no way, however, did he reduce our relations with Mary to the juridical level, because he constantly reminded us that her power springs from her humility.[23] Bernard is even recognized as having made some contribution to "Josephology."

22. Hum 6-12; OB 3:21-25. The terms which speak of learning something (*didicere*) and of experiencing it (*experimentum, experiri, experientia*), occur some ten times.
23. "Faith and Culture in the Devotion to Mary," forthcoming.

As to the notion of "Sacrament," he gave it a wider meaning than that suggested by the list of the seven sacraments, which was first drawn up in his times. On this point, as also on the the subject of confession, which he saw as the praise of God by the confession of sins, Bernard was nearer to the Fathers than to the Schoolmen—which explains once more why he is so close to modern thought. Bernard's anthropology was certainly based on a particular conception of man's nature and faculties, but it also took into account the workings of grace and the other means of salvation which God offers to a Christian. The presence and activity of God in the world leads man to discover the significance of the concupiscence he feels within him; it means that he is sinful. Man's spiritual growth starts with this self-knowledge, the recognition of his wretchedness. The result of this humiliating discovery should not be to make man hate or feel sorry for himself, but rather to humble him, to fill him with joy and a desire for God, and compel him to develop his capacities to the full. Christian humanism consists in setting free the image of God which is in each one of us. Although this image is found in all men, the full and perfect image of the Father was manifested only in the Incarnate Word. It is the mystery which we celebrate in our liturgy, and it is this holiness of which we must partake when we receive the sacraments, especially the eucharist and penance—symbolized by the washing of the feet— once we have been initiated into Christ's risen life by baptism.[24]

The ascetic strives to make good use of the opportunities for salvation, which are indeed open to every Christian but will not bear fruit without his free collaboration. Chiefly they are mortification, obedience, submission to a spiritual father and willing acceptance in the case of monks of the demands of monastic observance. Just as Bernard elaborated a theology of the Crusades which had existed in practice long

24. "Imitation of Christ and Sacrament in the Theology of St Bernard," forthcoming in *Cistercian Studies* 9 (1974) 36-54 (German version, 1963). On the image of God according to St Bernard—a subject often dealt with—we may expect further light from the thesis nearing completion of B. Piault. The anthropology of St Bernard is also being studied by Hisao Yamasaki who is preparing a doctoral thesis at the University of Tokyo.

beforehand, he also proposed a new doctrinal interpretation of the Cistercian Order. He perceived clearly the intentions of the Founders of the Order, defined the role of contemplative community within the Church, and recognized those elements of the Rule which provide real means of union with God and imitation of Jesus Christ, as distinct from other secondary elements which he never mentioned.[25] This broad yet concise vision, this sure intuition of the spirit of the Gospel helped Bernard to determine the limits of obedience, or more exactly—because the horizon of virtue stretches into infinity and leads to God—the limits of the right to command and the duty to obey: everything is subject to charity, which Bernard calls his lady: *Domina caritas.*[26]

Bernard used this formula when he talked about the Church, and it is probably his ecclesiology which arouses most interest among historians. Bernard's attitude to the mystery of the Church has been much studied, especially the marriage symbolism which he applied to it in commenting on the *Song of Songs,* and the lofty ideal he had of the papacy, of the duties incumbent on bishops, of the virtue of clergy, and of the discipline of the Christian layman. Here as elsewhere, St Bernard did not simply propound a theory based on strict speculative logic. His theology is "committed," and strengthened by a reforming impulse. Doctrine is not lacking, but it can only be understood in the light of particular situations, where any one of several aspects may be stressed at different times. Thus Bernard could talk about the pope's temporal power on one occasion, about the use he may make of the "two swords" on another, or else about the independence from the Roman Curia which the bishops so rightly claimed. We must therefore be careful not to project into his writings such modern concepts and terms as "collegiality" and "subsidiarity". Neither Bernard, the popes, nor the

25. "S. Bernard de Clairvaux et la communauté contemplative," *Collectanea OCR* 34 (1972) 36-84. In English in *Cistercian Studies* 7 (1971) 97-142. "St Bernard and the Rule of St Benedict, *Rule and Life,* CS 12, pp. 151-67. Forthcoming in French in *Collectanea OCR* 35 (1973).

26. The expression is to be found in Ep 14, PL 182:117; commentary in "St Bernard and the Church," *The Downside Review* 85 (1967) p. 293.

circles in which they moved had any precise idea of the implications of papal and episcopal authority. Feeling their way, so to speak, in the darkness of history, they fulfilled their pastoral role. Bernard hoped that in the absence of clear ideas they would at least have a pure heart.

The most recent work to shed light on Bernard's concept of the Church has come from Msgr. B. Jacqueline.[27] During the nineteenth century and the first third of the twentieth, Bernard was considered no more than a pious writer who, though he was certainly gifted and able to stir one's innermost feelings, had no doctrinal depth. In 1934, however, Étienne Gilson published an extremely influential book which made people begin to realize that Bernard was indeed a theologian. But no one ever asked very seriously whether he was also a canonist—and probably if the question is put as badly as that, the answer is, "No." Bernard was far too great to let himself get tangled up in categories, especially a category he was known to treat with gentle irony.[28] However, his writings and methodology show that he had firsthand knowledge of Ivo of Chartres, a good legal education, an astounding facility for wielding the technical terms of canon law, and a real ability to interpret laws and apply them to monastic problems as well as to relations between the Pope, the secular authority, and bishops.

As in other areas of his activity, the best way of understanding St Bernard's legal theories is by identifying his sources. These are gradually being tracked down and Bernard's use of them given careful attention. First among his sources was the Bible, and here Fr Denis Farkasfalvy has done some very important work, particularly on the subject of inspiration. The results of his researches appeared at the very moment when the Second Vatican Council was pre-

27. The title of his thesis is *Episcopat et Papauté chez Bernard de Clairvaux,* (Paris: J. Vrin, 1973). I thank Msgr B. Jacqueline for having shown me the manuscript. A summary has already appeared under the same title in *Collectanea OCR* 34 (1972) 218-229.

28. Pre 57; OB 3:29: "Praetermitto et aliqua de canonibus quae vos requiritis, tum quoniam nostra non refert qui monachi sumus, tum quia in libris eadem ipsi facile reperire potestis, si quaerere non gravemini."

paring a statement on inspiration and attempting to disentan-
gle this mystery from the clear but over-rigid categories
imposed on it by apologetics which have tended to leave no
room for the delicate shades of meaning required when we
talk about this subject. This first general view of St Bernard's
ideas on inspiration was therefore all the more appreciated.
In the words of one scholar well- qualified to judge: "How
much richer is this way of seeing things than that of the
theories in force up to now. We have much to learn from it.
Even if in our modern studies on inspiration we are obliged
to diversify our terms and our concepts, we would do well to
set out from these rich organic views rather than from over
rational pedagogical theories.[29] Other works have dealt with
particular Biblical themes which Bernard interpreted in the
light of the patristic tradition, but he never simply borrowed
from the past; he opened up new vistas and made unex-
pected poetic variations: the return to paradise, sober inebria-
tion, fertile overshadowing, the evangelical beatitudes. His
exegetical methods and the strongly Biblical character of his
thought reveal a psychology, an interior language and a type

29. L. A. Schokel, review (in Spanish) of *L'inspiration de l'Ecriture* (cited
above, note 9), in *Biblica* 46 (1965) 476-7. The reviewer gives a very solid summary of the principal ideas of the book. We may add the judgment of Jacques de
Vitry who said in his *Historia occidentalis* that, like St John, Bernard drew his
interpretation of the Scriptures from the breast of our Lord. The source of his
doctrine is his personal experience: *The Historia Occidentalis of Jacques de Vitry:
A Critical Edition*, ed. J. F. Hinnebusch, (Fribourg, Switzerland, 1972), p. 114.
Concerning the Scriptural sources of St Bernard, E. Gilson pointed out the importance of a "johannine group": Fr Bernard Oliver, a Cistercian of Azul in Argen-
tina, has set out to verify this hypothesis, comparing at the same time St Bernard
and St Anselm. G. P. Violi, in a study entitled *La Bibbia nei Sermones super
Psalmum "Qui habitat" di S. Bernardo,* which, it is to be hoped, will be published,
has discovered in the group of *Sermons* which he has examined a "mathean
group": out of approximately 1400 citations or reminiscences, almost 150 come
from St Matthew. The use of the *Letter to the Romans* in the *De gratia et libero
arbitrio* would also be worth going into. The liturgical background of the citations
should be studied. The approaching edition of the most ancient Cistercian bre-
viary, formerly attributed to Steven Harding, in *The Bibliotheca Cisterciensis*, will
provide elements for such enquiry. A card index of all the quotations of the Bible
which are not those of the Vulgate, with identification of their sources in the
liturgy and the Fathers, is under way. It will have to be completed and then put
to use.

of imagination modeled almost exclusively on Holy Scripture. There are, of course, other sources: historians have more than once pointed out the influence of Origen and the Platonic school as well as that of St Anselm.

POSTHUMOUS REPUTATION

The history of St Bernard and the impact of his thought does not come to an end with his death. His influence has continued down the centuries and scholars are continuously finding traces of it. One of the first writers to be influenced by him was Geoffrey of Auxerre, one of Abelard's students "converted" by Bernard. He became the Abbot of Clairvaux's disciple, secretary, biographer, and ultimately his successor. But he was never simply an imitator of Bernard, as was Nicolas of Montieramey. He did better than that: he retained and handed on in living form the message of the man who had moulded him to the Cistercian spirit. He did this through his activity within the Order (he was abbot of several Cistercian houses) and also through his writings. Some of these are *Sermons* he either delivered or wrote in monasteries, while others are commentaries on the *Song of Songs* and the *Book of Revelation.* Fr F. Gastaldelli is editing the corpus of Geoffrey's works, and intends also to study his teaching and in particular his ecclesiology,[30] comparing it with Bernard's own ideas on the Church. Another way in which Bernard continued to influence his Order after his death was through the foundations which he made in Spain and elsewhere. Not all of these were successful, of course; the direct action of a

---

30. Already Fr F. Gastaldelli has published *Ricerche su Goffredo di Auxerre. Il compendio anonimo del Super Apocalypsim. Introduzione ed editione critica,* Bibliotheca Veterum Sapientia 12 (1970); *Goffredo di Auxerre, Super Apocalypsim, edizione critica a cura di Ferruccio Gastaldelli* (Rome, 1970). In preparation are *Goffedo di Auxerre, Expositio in Cantica Canticorum, edizione critica* (Rome, 1973) *Edizione critica dei Sermones di Goffredo di Auxerre* and research on the sources which should enlighten us on the works of both Geoffrey and St Bernard: *I padri greci nella biblioteca di Clairvaux nel secolo XII; L'ecclesiologia nei commenti biblici di Goffredo di Auxerre.*

powerful personality often meets with resistance from others not so great.

No one, however, could prevent Bernard's ideas and his reputation for holiness from being spread abroad; he soon became the patron of monasteries and parishes in Bavaria and many other countries. In architecture his buildings at Fontenay and elsewhere were taken as models for other foundations, and in course of time a real "Bernardine plan" was created, different from the "Benedictine plan." He played a crucial role in the formation of that Roman Christendom whose imagery and works of art form one of the peaks in human creativity. The anonymous authors of long invocations to St Bernard praise the "true science" in which he excelled and which "merits being called real wisdom." These and many other devotional formulas show that Bernard's spiritual influence did not die.

Bernard's writings were soon translated into French and German, and these texts are now being edited and studied. Those *Letters* which he did not include in the official register were brought together in many minor collections which are going to be analyzed in order to find out where, when and why they were written, and whether they were collected for purposes of reform, propaganda or edification. Through paleography, geography and chronology we shall eventually be able to trace the main channels of Bernard's widespread influence and to draw maps to show where it was most intense. Bernardine themes have already been detected in Latin texts such as the *Meditations on Self-Knowledge* or the *Jesu dulcis memoria,* echoed in Jean de Beaugenais in the second-half of the twelfth century. In vernacular literature, Bernard's influence is more or less explicit in one of the manuscripts of *Chastel perilleux,* in the *Legende du Graal,* in the ¡*Somme e Roy*, and then in Dante, Heinrich Suso and Hus' disciple Nicholas of Dresden,[31] who, according to a Czechoslovak medievalist, gave the reforming ideas of the abbot of Clair-

31. For the Middle Ages, to the witnesses of the influence of St Bernard mentioned in the *Bibliographie,* may be added the text edited by L. Reypens, *Meester Wilhem Jordaens, De Oris Osculo of de Mystieke Mondkus* (Antwerp, 1967).

vaux "an entirely new revolutionary accent."[32] Bernard never lacked opponents either. A. H. Bredero has devoted to his posthumous reputation a provocative book in which he shows him in the midst of the conflicting and contradictory interpretations which history has put on his career.[33] The influence of St Bernard is to be seen in scholasticism, in the political and religious struggles which masked the end of the middle ages, in the works of Luther, Calvin, and Pascal, and even in the statements of John XXIII and Paul VI. His message was so rich and varied, so incisively formulated in such a variety of different causes, that the supporters of opposing theories rivaled each other in invoking his support, never fearing to drag his words out of their context. He had uttered so many wonderful words that people were tempted to attribute to him still more. Paul Valéry, for example, ascribes to Bernard words which he never wrote (but which are not unworthy of him).[34] Blondel, too, was well-acquainted with Bernard's authentic works: it is now known that when he was preparing *Action* he copied more than thirty passages and retained about ten of them for his final draft.[35]

So we see that Bernard left to posterity several differing portraits of himself. In the generation which followed his own, the character trait most often stressed, especially in monastic circles, was his charm, his gaiety, and the joy which mingled both with his gentleness and with his fervor. (After

32. J. Nechutova, "Husovo Kázáni *Dixit Martha* a Mikuláśez Drázdan traktat *De purgatorio*—Kotázce Husovy literárni pirvodnosti," *Listy filologické* 88 (1965) 147-57, according to the review given in German by P. Spunar, *Scriptorium* 22 (1968) p. 359, n. 860.

33. See also chapter entitled "La survie," pp. 109-45 of *S. Bernard et l'esprit cistercien* (Paris, 1966). English and Italian translations are in preparation: CS 16 (1975). For the sixteenth century, to the witnesses of influence we mentioned in the *Bibliographie*, add Chlichtove, according to J. P. Massaut, *Josse Chlichtove: L'humanisme et la réforme du clergé* (Paris, 1968), 2 vols; see the Index, at the name of *S. Bernard*, 2:419.

34. Mrs. Judith MacManus, School of French, Kensington, New South Wales, Australia, has been kind enough to draw my attention to these citations, for which I thank her.

35. C. Mahamé "Les auteurs spirituels dans l'élaboration de la philosophie blondélienne, 1883-1893," *Recherches de science religieuse* 56 (1968) 232-7: "Saint Bernard."

all, he was celebrated as a zitherist, and even described himself as a "juggler."[36]) Later, when the memory of Bernard as a person had faded, he stood out in men's minds more as a master than anything else, and his ideas were made to serve various causes. In the Baroque period and in the nineteenth-century Catholic restoration he served as a model of affective piety (although largely on account of legends and apocryphal texts). Vacandard's scientific biography, published in 1895 and not yet superseded, drew the attention of medievalists to the part played by Bernard. Today people are more interested in his doctrine; in the recent *Bibliographie Bernardine*, the largest section is devoted to his theology.

PERSPECTIVES

Is it possible to predict, on the basis of existing research, what aspects of Bernard will interest future generations? Certainly three. They are connected with the three disciplines in favor today: sociology, psychology, and linguistics. First sociology. This not only analyzes recent or contemporary situations which can be studied statistically, but also the history of societies. John Sommerfeldt in the United States began by trying to locate Bernard precisely in the context of the social, economic, and political structures of his day. In France, G. Duby has begun to study the mass movements which threw up, but also set bounds on, strong personalities like the Abbot of Clairvaux and others. Even while these pages are being written, there are monks in Latin America who are wondering what contribution Bernard can make to the "theology of liberation."

36. "Le thème de la jonglerie chez S. Bernard et ses contemporains, *Revue d'histoire de la spiritualité* 48 (1972) 385-400; "Ioculator et saltator. S. Bernard et l'image du jongleur dans les manuscrits," *Translatio studii; manuscript and library studies honoring Oliver L. Kapsner,* ed. Julian G. Plante (Collegeville, Minnesota, 1973). To the texts already mentioned concerning Bernard's gentleness, in the *Bibliographie* (especially "Temoins de la devotion a S. Bernard," reprinted in *Recueil d'études sur S. Bernard III,* (Rome, 1969) pp. 336-42 may be added the witness of Geoffrey of Auxerre, *Super Apocalypsim,* ed. F. Gastaldelli, p. 116: "Quam dulcissime nobis pater noster sanctus Bernardus dum adviveret. . . . ." (*See* above note 30) The whole context speaks of *iocunditas.*

Already in his recent *Vie et Mort des Instituts Religieux: Approches Psychosociologiques*, Fr Hostie has dealt with St Bernard. Attempting to fathom the significance of religious groups, he observes that St Bernard and the band of companions who entered the Order of Cîteaux found there a goal to whose attainment they could dedicate themselves.[37] In every age it is not so much a glorious past that counts as an aim for the future. The sons of St Bernard are compelled to ask themselves whether they still have one today. Doubtless this sort of standard is to some extent irrelevant to the monastic life. Unlike the adherents of ideologies, monks give themselves to God simply for the sake of him and his kingdom, while ordinary concepts related to the future—progress, evolution, revolution, planning and so forth—need to be complemented by some sort of hope, whether it be based on renewal, re-creation, resurrection, or eschatology. But the greatness of St Bernard lay precisely in the fact that he united so harmoniously desire for God and attention to actuality, or as he himself said, the need of the moment, *quod tempus requirit.*[38]

In sociology, much use is being made of the concept "utopia," which "attempts to change the existing order by inspiring a collectivity, or an important part of a collectivity, with the desire to transcend its situation,"[39] and in this research hypothesis is being applied to monasticism. Between the economic plan of the first Cistercians and the reality which they created,[40] between Bernard's ideal life and the existence which he led, there are contradictions which some people find irritating: how often the Abbot of Clairvaux has been accused of not living up to what he preached! Perhaps it is not sufficiently clear that there is nearly always a gap between the value-system adopted by a group and the behavior

37. R. Hostie, SJ *Vie et mort des ordres religieux. Approches psychosociologiques* (Paris, 1972) p. 88.
38. Csi 2:9; OB 3:417, 2-3.
39. J. Séguy, "Une sociologie des sociétés imaginées: monachisme et utopie," *Annales. E.S.C.* 26 (1971) p. 328.
40. R. Roelb, "Plan and Reality in Medieval Monastic Economy: The Cistercians" *Studies in Medieval and Renaissance History* 49 (1972) 83-114.

of individual members,[41] between the "ideology proclaimed"
and the "life lived"[42] between "charisma" and "social
grace,"[43] between the "writer's utopia" and the "practi-
tioner's utopia"[44] between the "monastic project" and the
"real world."[45] An appreciation of these distinctions would
allow a coherent reading of historical events which are at first
sight contradictory.[46] By applying this method to a consideration of the relationship between town and country,[47] a
sociologist inevitably comes to the same conclusions as a
specialist in the philosophy of medieval language: Abelard
was a professor living in town whereas Bernard belonged by
his convictions to the desert of the rural world.[48] This did
not prevent the Abbot of Clairvaux from intervening in many
towns in France, Italy, Lotharingia, the Rhineland and
Bavaria. He was free with his own mission just as he was
with juridical structures when they were obstacles to his
spiritual intuitions. Maybe J. Séguy is correct when he writes
that: "St Bernard upholds the tendency to give primacy to
the individual conscience over obedience to superiors, in
keeping with Romans 14:3. He repeats the Apostle's words,
Omnino non expedit spiritum velle extinguere. And again,
perfecta obedientia legem nescit."[49]

This leads to the frontiers of another science which will one
day have to be applied to St Bernard: psychology. This will
have to be done respectfully, of course, because grace modi-
fies our spontaneous urges and makes each man not a problem to be solved, but a mystery which only God can understand. The literature which is interposed between the reader
and the writer, especially if he is talented, also has to be
treated with care. Style is both a medium and a defence

41. G. Duby, "L'histoire des systèmes de valeurs," *History and Theory* 11
(1972) 15-25.
42. J. Séguy, p. 345.
43. Ibid., p. 352.
44. Ibid., p. 354.
45. Ibid., p. 338.
46. Ibid., p. 353.
47. Ibid., pp. 342-344.
48. J. Jolivet, *Arts du langage et théologie chez Abélard* (Paris, 1969) 361-362.
49. J. Séguy, pp. 351-352.

mechanism. Any psychological examination must be done with sincerity and objectivity. St Peter Damian lost nothing when, on the occasion of the ninth centenary of his death in 1972, his writings and those of his biographer were examined with a view to discovering the stages of his affective development. It is too late to submit men of the Middle Ages to therapy: some managed to be saints without it. But we must not be afraid of the truth which an enquiry, so far as it is possible to make one, might uncover about the development of these men's minds. Such an examination must be more than a simple study of mentality or the projection of the problems of ideals of the writer, be he medievalist, spiritual author, or novelist, on to a person of the past. A clinical judgment scientifically made is something very difficult to arrive at, but we cannot say that it is impossible until we have tried. Psychological work is already being done on Bernard's writings. It is planned to hold a congress on "Bernard and Aggressiveness," which promises to be a long job, for it will have to examine his behavior in all the different conflict situations in which he found himself. Perhaps in the long run, realizing more clearly the limitations of the man Bernard—and man he never ceased to be—we shall admire all the more the victories of grace within him.

Finally a third discipline which must be applied to Bernard's writings is linguistics, understood as a study of language in its broadest sense. The inquiry will have to cover Bernard's imagination, his use of symbols and the way in which they were expressed, the way in which he arranged words and phrases, and the sonority which they achieved. Every aspect of aesthetics, literary creation, and the mysterious genesis of a poetical work will have to be examined.

More and more, Bernardine studies, like so many others, will become interdisciplinary: we shall be on the frontiers of spirituality, theology, psychology, sociology and linguistics. Whatever cannot be done by a single specialist will be carried

out by groups of research workers. The perspectives are unlimited.

Clervaux Abbey   Jean Leclercq OSB
Luxembourg

Translated by
Garth L. Fowden

ST BERNARD AND THE HISTORIANS

THE COMMEMORATION of the eight-hundredth anniversary of the death of Bernard of Clairvaux took place in the year 1953.[1] Diverse congresses were held on that occasion and reports and discourses were collected and published. Special numbers of many different periodicals appeared and a great number of books were published or reprinted in which attention was drawn in one way or another to the Abbot of Clairvaux. There was even an encyclical letter.[2]

The number and length of these publications form only a relative peak in the continuous stream of publications which repeatedly deal with this saint year in and year out. These writings study the place held by St Bernard in the history of the twelfth century, and reveal his many-sided importance in the eyes of his contemporaries and posterity. These writings deal with him iconographically and call attention to him as monk, mystic, politician, writer, preacher, theologian, and

---

1. This paper was originally presented as a lecture *Bernhard von Clairvaux im Widerstreit der Historie*, on 10 February 1965, in the Auditorium of the Johannes-Gutenberg Universität, Mainz, (Germany) and published by the *Institut für Europäische Geschichte, Mainz, Vorträge Nr. 44* (Wiesbaden: Franz Steiner Verlag, 1966). We wish to thank the Institute and the publisher for allowing the publication of this translation, which has been adapted in view of later publications.

2. See Jean de la Croix Bouton, *Bibliographie Bernardine 1891-1957* (Paris, 1958), pp. 83-131. A translation of the encyclical letter *Doctor Mellifluus* has been edited by Thomas Merton in *The Last of the Fathers* (New York-London, 1954) pp. 93-116.

28 *Bernard of Clairvaux*

moralist. They analyse his use of the Bible and other sources. And there are the bibliographies which offer information about all that has been published concerning St Bernard in the course of the centuries.[3]

Among this literature, the tracts, sermons, and letters of St Bernard himself command the central position.[4] These writings have been handed down, totally or in part, from numerous manuscripts, and in translations and compilations. The many editions which appeared at the advent of the art of printing form a continuation of the tradition handed down in manuscript and by its size demonstrates how much the spiritual legacy of this last of the Fathers of the Church has retained the interest of posterity. The name of St Bernard has also been tied traditionally to many writings of which he was neither the author nor the inspirer.[5] This accretion has led to many legends being built up around him. In addition, his spiritual legacy became the common property of a wider tradition, in which others secretly borrowed from his works: in the twelfth century Hugh of Saint Victor, in the thirteenth Bonaventure, and in the fourteenth Gerhard Groote.[6] In the fifteenth and sixteenth centuries, when interest in the mystic authors of the twelfth century revived, men looked especially

3. L. Janauschek, *Bibliographia Bernardina . . . usque ad finem anni MDCCCXC* (Vienna, 1891; repr. Hildesheim, 1959); J. Bouton, O.C.; Eugene Manning, *Bibliographie Bernardine 1957-1970: Documentation Cistercienne* 6 (Rochefort, Belgium, 1972).

4. In 1947 Jean Leclercq and Henri Rochais, originally with assistance of C. H. Talbot, began to prepare a new critical edition of the *Opera Sancti Bernardi*. Vols. I-II (Rome 1957-8) contain the *Sermones super Cantica canticorum*; vol. III (1963) the *Tractatus et opuscula*; vols. IV, V, VI-1 and VI-2 (1966-1972) give *Sermones per annum*, the *Sermones variae et de diversis*, and the *Sententiae*; vols. VII-VIII, the *Epistolae*; a ninth volume will provide an index.

5. There are also writings in existence, composed under the influence of St Bernard, that is to say, sermons pronounced by the abbot himself, but written up by others. See J. Leclercq, *Etudes sur saint Bernard et le texte de ses écrits*, ASOC 9 (1953). *Recueil d'études sur saint Bernard et ses écrits*, 3 vols. (Rome, 1962-1969). H. M. Rochais, *Enquête sur les sermons divers et les sentences de saint Bernard*, ASOC 18 (1962). For other publications of Leclercq and Rochais on this subject, see Manning, pp. 43-57 and 67-9.

6. See M. Bernards, "Der Stand der Bernhardforschung," *Bernard von Clairvaux, Mönch und Mystiker. Internationaler Bernhardkongress, Mainz, 1953*, Veröffentlichungen des Instituts für europäische Geschichte Mainz, 6., ed. Josef Lortz (Wiesbaden: Franz Steiner Verlag, 1955), pp. 19-20.

to St Bernard.[7] A telling example of this is the story told by the chronicler of St Alban's: In 1423 Abbot John Whetamstede, well-known for his interest in humanism, because ill while on a journey to Rome. He recovered from this illness only after a dream in which St Bernard appeared to him and obtained from him the promise that he would in the future devote himself to reading and disseminating the Saint's writings.[8]

The reputation of his writings led to his being called "*Doctor Mellifluus.*"[9] It also led to his becoming the object of many popular and even spectacular legends. It was said that he demonstrated his power over the devil by making him function as the rim of a broken wagon-wheel.[10] Bernard's mystical piety, which especially directed itself to the Mother of God, led to the persistent legend that Mary had suckled him, the so-called *lactatio.*[11] However, the objections that he

---

7. G. Constable, "The Popularity of Twelfth-Century Spiritual Writers in the Late Middle Ages," *Studies in Honor of Hans Baron* (Florence, 1971) 5-28; "Twelfth-Century Spirituality and the Late Middle Ages," *Medieval and Renaissance Studies* 5 (1971) 27-60.

8. *John Amandesham, Annales monasterii S. Albini,* ed. H. Riley, 2 vols. Rolls Series, vol 28 (London, 1870-71) 1:151. Cf also Constable, "The Popularity," pp. 17-18, and n. 72.

9. J. Leclercq, *Etudes,* pp. 184-191. See similar figures of speech from contemporaries in *Vita prima sancti Bernardi,* II, viii, 51 and III, iv, 17; PL 185:298 and 307 (*Etudes,* p. 185). Also Hugo Metellus: "Sub lingua tua lac et mel, non dolus, non sel;" *Inter ep s. Bernardi* 179; PL 182:687-8; Peter the Venerable in a letter to St Bernard, *The Letters of Peter the Venerable,* ed. G. Constable 2 vols. (Cambridge, Mass., 1967), 1:364-5: Ep 149 (= Ep 6, 3; PL 189:402). The probable origin of this figure of speech is to be found in an Antiphon of Praise for the first Sunday of Advent: "cum in diebus istis montes stillabunt dulcedinem et colles fluent lac et mel;" compare Joel 3:18. See also J. Leclercq "De quelques procédés du style biblique de S. Bernard," *Recueil* 3:250 (=*Cîteaux* 15 [1964] 333). This passage is to be found also in a letter from St Bernard to Aelred of Rievaulx: see A. Wilmart, "L'Instigateur du Speculum Caritatis d'Aelred de Rievaulx," *Revue d'ascétique et de mystique* 14 (1933) 390 and n. 9.

10. See *Vita et miracula D. Bernardi Clarevallensis abbatis, opera et industria regularis observantiae eiusdem Hispaniarum ad alandam pietatem universis ordinis Cisterciensis,* pars prior (Rome, 1587) (Vatican Library R. I. - 103). There is an etching of this legend (reproduction 44) with the annotation: "Ex traditione vocatus ab Innocentio II in fine schismatis rotam curru vectus infregerta eiusdem rotae functioni miraculo substituit."

11. It is an old legend later connected to St Bernard. H. Barrée, "Saint Bernard docteur marial," *Saint Bernard théologien (Actes du congrès de Dijon, Septembre, 1953),* ASOC 9 (1953) p. 94, and n. 41. See *Cîteaux in de Nederlanden* 7 (1956)

had against the introduction of the celebration of the feast of the Immaculate Conception, which he had explained in a letter to the canons of Lyons,[12] caused him to have a stain on his habit when he appeared in a vision after his death.[13] Repeatedly, St Bernard was reputed to be the author of the hymn, *Jesu Dulcis Memoria*;[14] and, just as mistakenly, the closing words of the *Salve Regina* have been attributed to him.[15] The author of the *Divine Comedy* also contributed to his fame. In the thirty-first canto of *Il Paradiso* Dante lets his guide, Beatrice, step aside for the Abbot of Clairvaux because she herself is unable to realize completely the wish of the poet to conclude his journey through heaven by seeing Mary and standing before the face of God.[16] Although in less sublime ways, St Bernard has continually been the object of admiring praise. The panegyrics are numberless in which his blessed memory is brought forward again for each generation.

Where attention remains focused on his writings, the evaluation of St Bernard remains positive. It is difficult to overestimate the profound influence of his writings. In the opinion of Henri Bremont the influence of St Bernard in regard to the theocentrical orientation of the Christian

165-198 and *Le Moyen Age* 70 (1964) p. 333 (The Virgin bares her breast); also J. Canal, "Sanctus Bernardus et Beata Virgo Miraculo Lactationis in textu inaudito," *Ephemerides Mariologicae* 7 (1957) 483-490. The persistency of this legend has inadvertently been demonstrated by G. Chevalier, *Histoire de saint Bernard,* 2 vols. (Lille, 1888) 1:308, n. 1.

12. St Bernard Ep 174; PL 182:332-6. See Leopold Grill, "Die angebliche Gegnerschaft des hl. Bernhards von Clairvaux zum Dogma von der Unbefleckten Empfängnis Marias," ASOC 16 (1960) 60-91.

13. This is recounted by a defender of this feast, which was celebrated earlier in England, Nicholas of St Albans (†after 1176). He was told this story by a Cistercian monk: C. H. Talbot, "Nicolas of St Alban and St Bernard," *R Ben* 64 (1954) p. 57, n. 3. For the origin of this festival see S. P. J. van Dijk, "The Origin of the Latin Feast of the Blessed Virgin," *Dublin Review* 228 (1954) 251-267 and 428-443. H. F. Davis, "The Origins of Devotion to Our Lady's Immaculate Conception," Ibid., 375-404. See also David Knowles, *The Monastic Order in England* (Cambridge, 1963) p. 510, n. 3.

14. A. Wilmart, *Le Jubilus dit de saint Bernard* (Rome, 1944).

15. H. Barrée, p. 94. See J. Canal, *Salve Regina Misericordiae. Historia y Layendes* (Rome, 1963). Idem, "En torno a la antifona Salve Regina Puntualizando," RTAM 133 (1966) 342-255.

16. A. Masseron, *Dante et Saint Bernard* (Paris, 1953) 72-143.

conscience was greater than that of St Augustine.[17] Whether this opinion is correct or not, it is certainly St Bernard's writings which have given him his *Nachleben* in history.

The part that historians have played in perpetuating the memory of this Saint was originally quite small. Certainly St Bernard did not have to be brought back from obscurity; still, the historians discovered quite late just how much the tradition had been distorted and overgrown with legend. Scholars such as Horstius and Mabillon did very meritorious work in the seventeenth century by separating apocryphal writings from the genuine legacy of St Bernard, although historical criticism of the available version of his live-story was still wanting. Several reasons can be pointed out to explain this, the most important being that already during St Bernard's lifetime a beginning had been made on writing his biography. This was done by William of St Thierry, who died himself in 1148, five years earlier than the Abbot of Clairvaux. Almost immediately after the death of St Bernard, the work started by William was taken up by Ernald of Bonneval, a Benedictine abbot, and by Geoffroy of Auxerre. The latter, who from 1140 was St Bernard's principal secretary, had previously gathered biographical information concerning the Abbot which he placed at the disposal of William of St Thierry.[18]

The resulting *Vita prima sancti Bernardi*, consisting of five books, commanded an extraordinary place in medieval hagiography because of its great length and quality.[19] This *Vita* was handed down in many manuscripts, along with the writings of St Bernard, and for centuries it remained the point of departure for any approach to the historical personality of St Bernard,[20] without there ever being an investiga-

17. *Histoire littéraire du sentiment religieux en France* (Paris, 1926) III:26. Bremont remarked that St Bernard's *De diligendo Deo* was placed by Auguste Comte in the catalogue of his *Bibliothèque positive,* which he said was due to the spiritual level of the treatment of this subject.

18. A. H. Bredero, *Etudes sur la "Vita Prima" de saint Bernard* (Rome, 1960) pp. 73-77; also in ASOC 17 (1961) 218-222.

19. R. Agrain, *L'Hagiographie* (Paris, 1953) p. 311. His opinion concerning the historical reliability of this *Vita* has been refuted.

20. Bredero, *Etudes*, pp. 14-22 (ASOC 17:19-27).

tion of its historical validity. Nonetheless, this document presented a very obvious textual problem. When in 1643, the parson of Cologne, Merlo Horstius, added the text of the *Vita* to his edition of the *Opera Bernardi,* he discovered by comparing some manuscripts that two divergent versions existed. The shortened version, which appeared to him to be the one generally accepted, he chose as the basis of his text, to which he added a number of other passages appearing only in the alternate version. This he did rather arbitrarily; and this style of editing was followed by his successor, Jean Mabillon, who, in similar fashion, added variations found elsewhere. Later, Mabillon's text was reprinted without essential changes in the *Acta Sanctorum*[21] and also in the *Patrologia Latina* of J. P. Migne.[22]

For a long time people were satisfied with this edition. In 1886, however, George Hüffer made a further study of the *Vita prima*[23] for which he re-examined the manuscripts.[24] Hüffer was able to conclude that the editions of Horstius and Mabillon were not based on the oldest version of the *Vita,* but rather on a revised text written by Geoffroy of Auxerre around the year 1165. By a comparison of the two texts, Hüffer arrived to the conclusion that Geoffroy had omitted or changed a number of passages to make the story historically more authentic. This mistaken conclusion was later accepted by the authoritive Bernardine scholar, E. Vacandard.[25] For several years, therefore, it remained the generally accepted opinion that this *Vita prima,* which had previously been accepted as an important source, could justifiably be considered a reliable document. This, even though the many accounts of miracles in this *Vita* had to be viewed as demon-

21. AA SS aug IV (Antwerp, 1749) 256-327.

22. PL 185:225-366.

23. G. Hüffer, *Der heilige Bernard von Clairvaux,* I, *Vorstudien* (Münster, 1886).

24. One should bear in mind the research that G. Waitz had done previously for a partial edition of this *Vita*; MGH SS 26:91-120.

25. "L'Histoire de saint Bernard," *Revue des questions historiques* 43 (1888) 337-389. A summary appears in his *Vie de saint Bernard* with new additions: 1:XX-XL.

strating a medieval mentality which no longer suited our time.[26]

Another important reason why the *Vita prima* had so much authority for Bernardine scholars, even before this misleading opinion was adopted, is found in a passage taken from the work itself. In the first book William of St Thierry stated that it is not possible to describe the more special aspects of Bernard's monastic life to those who did not live in the same spirit in which St Bernard himself lived.[27] This statement may generally be correct, but the author had a special intention when writing this. This statement formed the chief argument in the skillful defence of his friend against the criticism of his contemporaries.[28] A negative judgment of St Bernard meant that the critic was below the level of the Abbot of Clairvaux and thus had no right to pass judgment. Considering that St Bernard was primarily judged through the centuries on his writings, the correctness of this statement of William was acknowledged, while the polemical purpose that lay behind it escaped the notice of the historians. Furthermore, as a canonized saint, Bernard was accepted by historians as sacrosanct. They therefore gave preference to the account in the *Vita* rather than to the data and explanations which would lead to an opinion about St Bernard that varied with, or even came into conflict with the account given in the *Vita*.

The more insight one achieves into the history of the twelfth century, the more one discovers the place Bernard

---

26. R. Agrain, *L'Hagiographie,* p. 311. G. Hüffer, "Die Wunder des heiligen Bernard und ihre Kritiker," *Historisches Jahrbuch der Görresgesellschaft* 10 (1889) 23-46 and 748-806, tried to defend the tales of miracles written down during St Bernard's journey to Germany as authentic and reliable. It is however evident that these stories were written within the framework of propaganda for the crusade, and were later partially rewritten. Bredero, *Etudes,* pp. 77-92 (ASOC 17:222-239); "Studien zu den Kreuzzugsbriefen Bernhards . . . ," *Mitteilungen des Instituts für Oesterreichische Geschichtsforschung* 66 (1958): 331-343. See J. Leclercq, "L'Encyclique de Saint Bernard en faveur de la croisade," *R Ben* 81 (1971) 282-308.

27. Vita Bern I, IV, 19; PL 185-237: "Conversationis autem eius insignia, quomodo vitam angelicam gerens in terris vixit, neminem enarrare posse puto, qui [ms Douai 372, cuius vita] non vivat de spiritu, de quo ille vixit."

28. Bredero, *Etudes,* p. 108 (ASOC 17:252).

held in his day. Thus Achilles Luchaire could say without
much exaggeration at the beginning of this century that the
biography of St Bernard is in fact a description of the history
of the religious orders, the religious reforms, the theology,
including the heresies, and the fate of France, Germany and
Italy over a period of forty years.[29] Indeed, if one must
choose among the leading personalities, one may properly
call the twelfth century the age of St Bernard. But this
accepted classification of his personality does not necessarily
rest on his behavior during his lifetime, but upon his fame
and his importance for posterity. Even though historians are
gradually becoming better informed about his behavior
during his lifetime, many of them still have difficulty setting
aside the St Bernard known through the ages in order to see
the historial person who actually lived in the twelfth century.

A third important reason for the timeless, legendary
character of the St Bernard image is the place which was accord-
ed to Bernard by the Reformation. Here again, his promi-
nence can be attributed to his writings. The first Reformers
referred repeatedly to his statements, at least to those they
knew.[30] The criticism expressed in the *Historia Ecclesiastica*
by Flacius Illyricus was not very fundamental: Bernard was
reproached for giving too negative a view of marriage and

29. "Raconter sa vie serait écrire l'histoire des ordres monastiques, de la réforme, de la théologie, orthodoxe, des doctrines hérétiques, de la seconde croisade, des destinées de France, de l'Allemagne et de l'Italie." A. Luchaire, "Les
premiers Capétiens (987-1137)," *Histoire de France*, ed. E. Lavisse, t. II, 2e
partie, p. 266. This judgment was repeated by A. Fliche, *Histoire de l'Eglise*
(Paris, 1948) 9:13-14, and E. Caspar, "Bernhard von Clairvaux," *Meister der
Politik*, 2 vols. (Stuttgart-Berlin, 1923) 9:563. See also H. V. White, "The Gregorian Ideal and Saint Bernhard of Clairvaux," *Journal of the History of Ideas* 21
(1960) 323.
30. See P. Polman, *L'Element historique dans la controverse religieuse du XVIe
siècle* (Louvain, 1932). He mentions the polemical use of excerpts from the
writings of Bernard by J. Crispinus, in his continuation of J. Piscatorius, *Bibliotheca studii theologici*, III, (Geneva, 1565). For remarks of Luther, Calvin,
Neander and Oekolampadius, see PL 185:638. See also Ailbe Luddy, *Life and
Teaching of St Bernard* (Dublin, 1927: repr. 1937, 1950, 1963). See also G.
Constable, "Twelfth Century Spirituality," pp. 38-39; H. Bach, "Bernard of Clairvaux and Martin Luther," *Erbe und Auftrag* 46 (1970) 453-460, and (1971)
36-43, 120-125 and 193-196. C. Volz, "Martin Luther's Attitude Toward Bernard
of Clairvaux," *Studies in Medieval Cistercian History*, CS 13 (1971) 186-204.

having too little care for physical comfort. He was also accused of idolatry in acknowledging a power of healing and conversion to the eucharistic Host and for performing ridiculous and godless miracles. In defending the Pope, especially when defending his tyrannical power against the emperor, he had shown himself to be a determined advocate of the Antichrist, the more so as he unjustly viewed the papacy as a godly institution. The author of the *Centurions of Maagdenburg* added their criticism of St Bernard for his having preached a crusade.

These reproaches were nearly all drawn from material in the *Vita prima*. But the catalogue of his virtues and talents was taken from the same source: his grasp of the Gospels and the Church Fathers, his self-accusations in matters of ignorance, heresy and sacrilege, his love of peace, his fondness of prayer, his modesty concerning the miracles which he had worked and which he attributed solely to the agency of God, his continual refusal of a bishopric because he shunned Church honors and considered himself less than other people. St Bernard was, as the *Vita prima* tells us, beneficent to all, well-meaning, merciful toward friends, patient with enemies and a protector of the oppressed. The *Centurions* tells further, this time based on his writings, especially on *De consideratione,* that St Bernard seriously reproached popes, cardinals, bishops and other clergymen because of their godless behavior, and that he made bold to call them servants of the Antichrist.[31] The only really critical remark that the *Centurions* made about the *Vita prima* calls attention to the fact that St Bernard seemed to have had no enemies, something which had not been the case even with Christ or his apostles.[32]

---

31. Vol. III (Centuries quatuor, nimirum X, XI, XII ac XIII complectens) (Basel, 1624) 804-21.

32. Ibid., p. 814: "Peculiare etiam est, quod in *Vita* ejus indicatur eum non habuisse inimicos, quod nec ipsi Christo, nec sanctis ejus Apostolis accidit." See Vita Bern, I, xiv, 71. William of St Thierry made a closing speech there: "Si tamen ullum aliquando habere inimicum, qui nulli aliquando voluit inimicari. Sicut enim amicitia nonnisi duorum est, nec nisi inter duos amicos habere potest, sic nec inimicitia nisi duorum forsitan inimicorum."

On the basis of legend and the constant relevance of his writings, admiration in Reformation circles thrived. It is likely that St Bernard was considered a forerunner of the Reformation and not a disciple of the Church of Rome. The first explicit polemics between a Catholic and a Protestant over the place of St Bernard in relation of Rome and the Reformation, to my knowledge, dates from the end of the seventeenth century.[33] Also, in the *Unparteyische Kirchen-und Ketzer Historie,* which was published in 1700,[34] positive admiration had the upper hand, although Bernard was criticized for his persecution of Arnold of Brescia and the heretics of southern France as well as for his share in the conviction of Abelard and Gilbert of Poitiers. The affinity which was felt in evangelical circles for St Bernard appears in an article that George Goetz published in 1701, in an attempt to prove how much Lutheranism owed to St Bernard.[35] Wilhelm Tentzel agreed with this work when it was reprinted five years later.[36]

In this period, however, there was scathing criticism of St Bernard from the ranks of the rationalists, who posed ironical questions as to his historical activities. This occured in the *Dictionnaire historique et critique* by Pierre Bayle, the first

33. J. B. Croph, *Der heilige Bernhardus als ein eifriger Verfechter der Römisch-katholischen Religion* (Augsburg, 1696) and J. B. Renz, *Eine Prob, wie der Romisch-Catholischen Kirche angerühmte Mirakel zu untersuchen und zu beurteilen, bei der Untersuchung eines dem Abt Bernardo zugeschriebenen und von Joh. Bapt. Crophio in seiner Christgesinnten Erinnerung vor die Wahrheit der Römisch-Catholischen Kirche und Lehre producirten Mirakels* (Augsburg, 1699).

34. Vol. I, part I, Book XII, chapter III, pp. 353 and 360-361.

35. *De Lutheranismo D. Bernhardi* (Dresden and Leipzig, 1701); see L. Janauschek, *Bibliographia Bernardina* nos. 1374 and 1400.

36. W. E. Tentzel, *Historischer Bericht vom Anfang und ersten Fortgang der Reformation Lutheri* (Leipzig, 1718[3]) 303-311: "Wie der grobe Mensch unsers herren Esel seyn sol, ihn tragen und mit ihm eingeen gen Hierusalem zu beschawen fruchtbarlichen das Leyden Christi. Nach lere des heyligen Bernhardi, gepredigt zu Nürnberg in Augustinercloster Anno 1518." (So the stupid human being must become the donkey of the Lord to carry him and to go with him to Jerusalem, in order fruitfully to consider the sufferings of Christ. This is the teaching of St Bernard used in a sermon given in Nuremberg . . .). This sermon was given by Link and was already printed in the years 1519 and 1521; see Janauschek, *Bibliographia Bernardina,* nos. 414, 439 and 1452. About this subject see below, p. 00, note 123.

edition of which appeared in 1697.[37] Bayle remarked that St Bernard enjoyed such distinction that all Church matters rested on his shoulders and that kings and nobles chose him as general arbiter in their differences of opinion. St Bernard possessed great qualities and a great deal of dedication, but it was maintained, said Bayle, this zeal made him envious of all who made a name for themselves by the practice of the sciences. It was also said, that because of his credulous nature, he listened too readily to malicious gossip about these scholars, and in this way he had acquired a prejudice against Abelard. Bayle could therefore hardly imagine that human passion did not play a role in the continual activity of St Bernard against all those whom he suspected of heresy and therefore hated. Sometimes St Bernard struggled against imaginary enemies, against heresies which did not exist or which were harmless. But whether he was justified or not, he was able to sow panic in a masterful way, and to let the thunderclap of his victories echo. He was much happier with weeding out heretics than with the destruction of unbelievers. He nevertheless attacked the latter with his wonted weapon, oratory, and with the exceptional weapon of prophecy. But when all the generaous promises with which he assembled an unimaginably large army of crusaders went up in smoke, and people attempted to protest that he had brought the army to slaughter without having himself left his country, he put the matter aside by saying that his prophecies had not come about because of the crusaders' sins.

At first the effect this censure had was restricted. It was only after the appearance of the fifth edition of this *Dictionnaire* in 1734 that there was an explicit rebuttal of this disapproving judgment of St Bernard.[38] In the seventeenth century many opinions about St Bernard opposed this bias of Bayle. Aside from lexicons, historical summaries had hagiographic collections, (the last giving primarily the *Vita prima* in condensed

---

37. Vol. I, 559-561. In the fifth edition (Amsterdam, 1734) vol. I, 778-780.
38. C. Merlin, "Apologie de saint Bernard contre les calomnies qui sont répandues dans le Dictionnaire de Bayle," *Mémoires de Trévoux* (1739) 581-764; 1710-1839.

form),[39] the three volumes of the *Annales Cistercienses* by Angelus Manrique, which appeared in the years 1642-1649, had given a great deal of chronological detail. More coherent, and for our exposition more important, was the biography which Antione Le Maistre published in 1647, under the pseudonym, "Lamy."[40] In this work as well, the influence of the *Vita prima* was dominant. "Lamy" certainly showed that he knew a great deal about the controversy between St Bernard and Cluny, which had not been mentioned in the *Vita*, and also about Bernard's opposition to Abelard and Gilbert of Poitiers, but for the rest he did not vary in the least degree from the *Vita*, of which he made a translation. His personal study formed a supplement in which he continually strove to agree with the views expressed in the *Vita*. Nevertheless, the knowledge which Le Maistre exhibited concerning the writings of St Bernard and other twelfth-century documentation was extensive and thorough, and at the same time his accomplishment as an historian can be seen in his instructive exposition of the attitude of Cîteaux, and especially of St Bernard, to the authority of the bishops.[41] In the learned judgment of Le Maistre, St Bernard was a sacrosanct person. This opinion was not primarily based on historical knowledge, but rather on the traditionally weighty fact that Bernard was a canonized saint.

This work by Le Maistre, published at least five times within a period of forty years, had a great influence on the opinions of others in those days. One can trace his influence in Louis de Maimbourg's explanation of the Second Crusade.[42] His influence is present also in the first edition of the

39. For instance P. Ribanereia, *Flos Sanctorum* (Madrid, 1604); C. Grasius, *Vitae Sanctorum* (Cologne, 1616); H. Adriaensen, *Legende oft d'Leven, Wercken, Doot ende Miraculen van . . . alle Godts lieve Heiligen* (Antwerp, 1608). H. Rosweyde, *Levens der heiligen* (Antwerp, 1641). These writings were often translated or reprinted.

40. *La Vie de saint Bernard . . . , divisée en six livres dont les trois premiers sont traduits du latin, par le sieur Lamy* (Paris, 1647 [8?]).

41. Livre V, chap. XXIV (5th edition, 1684, pp. 500-513: "Quel a esté l'esprit des saints Fondateurs de l'Ordre de Citeaux, saint Robert et saint Bernard, touchant la soumission des Religieux aux Evesques."

42. L. de Maimbourg, *Histoire de Croisades*, 2 vols. (Paris, 1682) I:309-19; II:39-43.

extensive *Histoire Ecclesiastique,* written in 1692 by Claude Fleury, then still a layman. Fleury, who occasionally express-ed sympathy for the rationalistic point of view,[43] followed, at any rate, the traditional point of view in regard to St Bernard. In the matter of the condemnation of the writings of Gilbert of Poitiers at the Council of Reims in 1148, Fleury gave preference to the version of Geoffroy of Auxerre over that of Otto of Freising. The latter had not been at the Council and had been too partial to Gilbert's viewpoint.[44] The passage from the *Vita prima* in which Geoffroy relates St Bernard's behavior toward Gilbert is extremely tenden-cious,[45] but was nevertheless regarded as authoritative by Fleury.

Suspicion toward this traditional representation and judg-ment of St Bernard's actions gradually grew in the eighteenth century. Historical studies which explicitly deal with him, such as those by Villefore and Dom Clemencet,[46] reiterated the stereotyped conceptions. Dom Clemencet admitted, how-ever, that St Bernard went too far when he called Louis VI a second Herod for his action against the bishop of Sens.[47] But this criticism could as well have been written in 1673, during the reign of Louis XIV, than one hundred years later, espe-cially since Clemencet had clearly, in 1762, turned his back on rationalistic criticism of St Bernard.[48] This rationalistic criticism had come from Abbé Simon Irailh, who brought up the question of Abelard and the exhortations for the crusade, in his *Querelles littéraires,*[49] a work in which he showed him-self spiritually related to Voltaire. Irailh was certainly not the

43. See C. Dawson, *The Making of Europe* (London, 1932), Introduction.
44. Vol. XIV (Brussels, 1722) p. 626.
45. Bredero, *Etudes,* pp. 133-5 (ASOC 18:19-21).
46. F. J. Bourgon de Villefore, *La Vie de Saint Bernard* (Paris, 1704: Second edition). Dom C. Clémencet, *Histoire littéraire de S. Bernard, abbé de Clairvaux, et de Pierre le Vénérable, abbé de Cluny* (Paris, 1773).
47. St Bernard Ep 51; PL 182:158-9. See *Journal des Scavans,* 74 (1774): 296.
48. Barral, Le Roy and Dom Clémencet, *Lettre à M . . .* (1762). See Janauschek, no. 1699.
49. S. Irailh, *Querelles littéraires ou Mémoires pour servir à l'histoire des revolu-tions de la République des lettres depuis Homere jusqu'à nos jours (Paris, 1761)* I: 1ff.

only one who shared the opinion of the increasingly widely read Pierre Bayle about the crusade-preaching. Marie-Joseph Chenier, at least, declared, probably not without exaggeration, that historians mentioned St Bernard for the purpose of accusing him for the unfortunate course of the crusade.[50]

To what degree the high esteem for St Bernard diminished in the second half of the eighteenth century because of the influence of rationalism can be seen from the *Institutiones Historiae Ecclesiasticae,* by the professor of theology from Göttingen, Johan Lorenz Mosheim. This work, published in the years 1737-1742, was, several years after the death of the author, translated into French, English, German and Dutch.[51] St Bernard is there sometimes referred to as a good man. Mosheim called him furthermore an ambitious abbot who gave exaggerated praise or merciless accusation and punishment. According to this author, his word had become law and his counsel was accepted by nobles and princes as commands to which the most abject obedience had to be given. St Bernard had sound judgment, in the opinion of Mosheim, but he was not experienced in the art of logic and was in no way used to thoughtful examination and abstract reflection. St Bernard was also considered the primary and most terrible opponent of Scholasticism in those days and, as becomes clear from this judgment, Mosheim sympathized with Scholasticism, at least in this section of his work.

This book has been brought to the reader's attention here because the opinion expressed in it, together with that of Pierre Bayle, form the background of Schiller's opinion, expressed so vehemently in 1802 in a letter to Goethe:

I have been absorbed by my study of St Bernard these days, and am quite pleased by this acquaintance. It would be difficult to find another equally clever spiritual rogue in such an excellent position for playing a dignified role. He was the oracle of his time and controlled his time, in spite

---

51. *Institutiones historiae ecclesiasticicae antiquioris et recentioris,* 4 vols. (Helmstadt, 1737-42) 4:2. An extensive English translation was made in 1758 by A. McClaine. This edition was translated into French (1764), Dutch (Amsterdam, 1771) and German (Leipzig, 1772).

of the fact and especially because of the fact that he remained aloof and let others stand in the important positions. Popes were his pupils and kings his creatures. He hated and oppressed as much as he could, and stimulated but the greatest monkish stupidities. He himself was only a monk and possessed nothing but shrewdness and hypocrisy.[52]

This opinion is evidently unjust and one-sided in that it overlooks completely the great good that St Bernard's works possess. It is futhermore a typical display of eighteenth-century rationalism in which there was no place for an understanding of historical relativity. But it is nevertheless an attempt at a psychological approach to St Bernard, at least to the contradictions in his personality, as they were seen by the historians. Rationalism was not able to attempt such an approach as it did not understand the positive religious values for which St Bernard stood nor the place which such values had in the social structure of the twelfth century. The reaction against rationalism which followed in the Romantic period showed itself unable in its turn to understand that Schiller in his remarks had touched upon the psychological conflict that Bernard as a human being had most certainly known. Between the monk who wished to lead a contemplative life away from the world and the politician whose influence was felt in all areas of the culture of his day a duality grew which was obvious to his contemporaries.[53]

St Bernard himself was aware of this duality in his character, as the letter that he wrote in the latter part of his life to the Carthusian prior, Bernard of Portes, shows:

It is time for me to remember myself. May my monstrous life, my bitter conscience, move you to pity. I am a sort of modern chimera, neither cleric nor layman. I have kept the habit of a monk, but I have long ago abandoned the life. I

52. Translated from a quotation in W. von der Steinen, *Vom heiligen Geist des Mittelalters* (Breslau, 1926; rpr. Darmstadt, 1968) p. 245.

53. Hildebert of Lavardin wrote in a letter to St Bernard; "quam iucundas noctes cum Rachel ducas, quae progenies ex Lia exuberet," PL 182:267B. Also Peter of Celles compared St Bernard to the twice-married Jacob. *Sermones* 76 and 77, PL 202:873-878.

do not wish to tell you what I dare say you have heard
from others: what I am doing, what are my purposes,
through what dangers I pass in the world, or rather down
what precipices I am hurled.[54]

This inward contradiction and this ambiguity were not
noticed in the nineteenth century. In the Romantic period,
St Bernard was re-evaluated as saint. This was even the case
with a follower of freemasonry, Alexander Lenoire, who in
1814 wrote an apology for this organization in the guise of a
history. According to him, St Bernard, thanks to his brotherly love and humility, had let himself be initiated into the
deepest secrets of freemasonry. In this spirit, he supposed
the abbot of Clairvaux had composed the rules of the
Templers.[55] The Romantic period gave rise in general to a
more favorable opinion of St Bernard, as we see, for
example, in Friedrich Wilken's work on the cursades.[56] Still,
the scientific interest which the Romantics showed toward
the Middle Ages, was also applied to the personality of St
Bernard, as appears from the remarkably thorough study
which August Neander devoted to Bernard and his time. The
first edition of this work appeared in 1813. Neander, in con-
fining himself to an historical description in which his
admiration for St Bernard clearly had the upperhand, left his
reader to question how the contradictions in St Bernard's
character could be explained.[57] The conclusion of this

54. Ep 250:4; PL 182:451: quoted from B. S. James, *The Letters of St Bernard
of Clairvaux* (London, 1953) no. 326.
55. *La France-Maçonnerie rendue à sa véritable origine ou l'Antiquité de la
Franc-Maçonnerie par l'explication des mystères anciens et modernes* (Paris,
1814), p. 235: "Cet esprit de modestie, d'humilité et de charité si fortement
recommandé par les dogmes de la Franc-Maçonnerie, animait saint Bernard, qui
lui-même s'etait fait initier à ces derniers mystères et qui, en conséquence, dressa
une Règle pour l'organisation des Templiers, qui étaient eux-mêmes Franc-
Maçons."
56. *Geschichte der Kreuzzüge*, vol. 3 (Leipzig, 1817) pp. 1-83; vol. 4 (1826) p.
107.
57. *Der heilige Bernhard und sein Zeitalter*, p. 522: "Eines Urtheils über den
Mann bedarf es nicht mehr, sein Leben und seine Wirksamkeit schildern ihn
genugsam, soweit in dem Räthsel un Spiegel des äussern Lebens, der Sprache und
des Handlens das Innere sich uns offenbaren kann." Quoted according to the 2nd
edition, Hamburg-Gotha, 1848. ("An evaluation of this man is unnecessary. His
life and his work sufficiently portray him, insofar as the riddle and mirror of
external life, language and behavior can reveal the inner life.")

Lutheran author, while praising the saintliness of St Bernard, gave full recognition to his short-comings as an human being.[58]

These human failings were recognized by E. Vacandard, who after many preliminary studies, published in 1895, his exhaustive study, *Vie de saint Bernard.*[59] The purpose of this author, whose work has been superceded only in some details by the biography of St Bernard by Watkin Williams[60] and the collected biographical studies published in 1953 by the Commission d'histoire de l'Ordre de Cîteaux,[61] was to relate the life story of the abbot of Clairvaux within the framework of his time, in political as well as spiritual terms. Furthermore, the author gave special attention to the literary and spiritual aspects of a number of St Bernard's tracts. Vacandard's work encountered the emotional criticism of a number of contemporaries[62] and suspicion in Cistercian circles, where it was thought that the work was too deliberately secular and scientific.[63] While attempting to base his opinion on historical data, Vacandard continued to hold the view that Bernard was a canonized saint. He took the standpoint that saints should be treated with genuine veneration, since they stand above the rest of mankind by virtue of their moral pre-eminence.[64] Vacandard implicitly admitted that the treat-

58. Ibid., pp. 522-3.

59. In the later editions, the appendices giving the chronology of the letters and the itinerary are left out. The 4th edition is somewhat revised, so that the indices are left out and many notes are considerably shortened. The most important biographies which appeared between Neander and Vacandard were undoubtedly: T. Ratisbonne, *Histoire de saint Bernard,* 2 vols. (1841); J. Morrison, *The Life and Times of Saint Bernard,* (Oxford-London, 1863); G. Chevalier, *Histoire de Saint Bernard,* 2 vols. (Lille, 1888); R. S. Storrs, *Bernard of Clairvaux. The Times, the Man and his Work* (New York, 1892).

60. *Saint Bernard of Clairvaux* (Manchester, 1935; 2nd edition 1952 [1953]).

61. CHOC, *Bernard de Clairvaux* (Paris, 1953) preface by Thomas Merton.

62. E. Vacandard, "La vie de saint Bernard et ses critiques," *Revue des questions historiques* 62 (1897) 198-9.

63. *L'Union Cistercienne* 21 (1896?) p. 277: "Le Livre de M. Vacandard pourra plaire et être utile aux érudits, mais nous ne le croyons pas fait pour l'édification des âmes chrétiennes, encore moins des âmes réligieuses, surtout dans l'Ordre de Cîteaux." Quoted from Jean de la Croix Bouton, *Bibliographie bernardine,* p. 10, no. 79.

64. Preface: "Sans oublier qu'on ne doit aux saints que la vérité, nous estimons que par leur élévation morale ils sont au-dessus du reste des hommes et méritent d'être traités avec un souverain respect."

ment given to Abelard by St Bernard showed a deficiency in his saintliness.[65] And in another case, he betrays surprise at St Bernard's support for the bit of disloyal craftiness whereby peace was made between Louis VII and the count of Champagne.[66]

The way in which these reproachful remarks concerning St Bernard's failure in certain matters are stated makes it obvious that this author, in spite of his historical objectivity, wished to retain his view of St Bernard as saint, and considered his saintliness a matter beyond discussion. It was this *a priori* which brought Vacandard to the same mistaken conclusion as Hüffer: he accepted the *Vita prima* as being accurate, even to the point of embroidering it, although he finally came to contradict himself.[67] In any case, this *a priori* explains why the attempt at a psychological explanation of the ambiguous behavior of St Bernard is missing in the work of Vacandard.

A treatment of this aspect is absent as well in the descriptive biographies of Luddy[68] and Williams. The latter, however, has given some attention to critical witness. Luddy collected only those testimonies about St Bernard which affirmed through the ages the accepted opinion of his sainthood. Williams denounced in the preface of his works several disparaging opinions which had been given during the nineteenth century. On the other hand, Williams stated himself that St Bernard, as he is described in a defense written by one of the adherents of Abelard,[69] is completely recognizable as the person described by William of St Thierry and Geoffroy of Auxerre.[70] This statement fails to explain the ambiguity in Bernard's character. In the works of other authors in the course of our century, we were given a more or less vulgarized biography of St Bernard, mainly based on the work of Vacandard; a psychological approach to the contradiction be-

65. Vacandard, *Vie de saint Bernard* (ed. 1920) II:259-60.

66. Ibid., II:188.

67. See Bredero, *Etudes*, p. 14, n. 1 (ASOC 17).

68. A Luddy, *Life and Teaching of St. Bernard* (Dublin, 1927; rpr. 1927, 1950 and 1963).

69. *Berengarius scholasticus, Apologeticus pro Petro Abaelardo*, PL 178:1857-70.

70. Williams, Preface, p. X.

tween the mystic and the politician remained untouched.[71]

71. G. Goyau, *Saint Bernard* (Paris, 1927). His explanation of the ambiguity is that St Bernard was making an analogy between his interior tensions and those of the Church in her confrontation with the world: "le drame intérieur dont toute sa vie son âme avait été comme angoissée n'était autre que le drame de la vie de l'Eglise, conviée par le Christ à la conquête du monde, et tout en même temps avertie par le Christ que son royaume n'est pas de ce monde." (p. 204). R. Dumesnil, *Saint Bernard, homme d'action* (Paris, 1934), explains the contradiction in his character as a consequence of the age. "L'homme ne se sépare point du saint, et l'homme est bien de son temps;... Certains ont parlé de sa dureté. C'est qu'ils ont précisément oublié en quelle époque il vécut; car cette dureté est moins de Bernard que de son témps." (p. 22). For the works of G. Rensonnet, *Saint Bernard* (Verviers, 1928), and of P. Miterre, *Saint Bernard de Clairvaux. Un moine arbitre de l'Europe au XIIe siècle* (Genval, 1929), we quote only Hugo Lang here: "There is no end to the biographies of St Bernard! It is so easy to tap a little Vacandard." SMGBO 47 (1929) 400. From the year 1953, we must mention: Daniel-Rops, *Quand un saint arbitre l'Europe, Saint Bernard* (Paris), A. Fusciardi, *San Bernardo abate di Chiaravalle* (Abbazia di Casamari); H. Hoever, *Der heilige Bernhard*, Religiose Quellenschriften 2 (Düsseldorf); J. Schenk, *Der Adler, der in die Sonne blickt, Bernhard von Clairvaux* (Ratisbon); E. Von Schmidt-Paul, *Bernhard von Clairvaux* (Düsseldorf); J. Calmette and H. David, *Saint Bernard* (Paris). Although these works have not all the same quality, they share the same respect for the canonized St Bernard. The only exception is the study written by Calmette and David. These authors did not supercede Vacandard by a more thorough study of the sources, but rather by returning to St Bernard, the man, and by recognizing the ambiguity in his character: p. 142: "Sa vie de moine avait épousé à la fois Rachel et Lia ... nous y verrons surtout la marque irrécusable de ce qu'on pourrait appeler des deux versants de sa nature: le coté affectif, qui a besoin des épanchements de l'amour, et le coté autoritaire, qui par atavisme féodal, le voue au commandement impératif et exigeant, sur lui-même et les autres;" p. 149-150: "Le grand drame intérieur de Bernard ... vient de tiraillements continuels et parfois tres douloureux entre ses aspirations contemplatives et les impératifs de l'action ... L'antinomie, dont il se plaint ... elle réside au fond de lui-même." See also p. 184, where the activities of St Bernard are interpreted as consistent with his mystical moments. Although the authors of this very positive and historical biography wished to show themselves exponents of the liberal ideas of the university and French humanism and opposed to an exclusively clerical dialog (p. 15), this psychological explanation of St Bernard seems to me still inadequate. Compared with the later work of Bruno Scott James, *Saint Bernard of Clairvaux* (London, 1957), the biography of Calmette and David goes deeper. It is true that James admits: "saints are born like all of us with the stain of original sin and all its consequences" and that "it takes time for them to mature in sanctity." (p. 67), but just like E. G. Coulton, *Five Centuries of Religion* (Cambridge, 1923), which Williams so much admired, James avoids the human ambiguity of St Bernard. Insight into this problem is even more noticably missing in I. Vallery-Radot, *Bernard de Fontaines, abbe de Clairvaux* 2 vols. (Tournai, 1963-1969), although the secondary title of the first volume, which confines itself to the years 1090-1130, reads: "Les noces de la grace et de la nature." The other biographies of Bernard published between 1959 and 1970 are mostly of a popular nature and accept the *vita prima* as a trustworthy historical source. We see in their historical interretation a great respect for the canonized St Bernard. See Manning, nos. 79, 91, 126, 132, 308, 327, 347 and 413.

This question was posed with greater frequency in other places, however. Jacob Burckhardt repeated the opinion of Schiller in a modified form,[72] while A. Hausrath, who devoted himself to the cause of St Bernard's opponents, nevertheless found some positive aspects in his character.[73] The opinion of Erich Caspar was much more objective. In an all-inclusive sketch of the abbot of Clairvaux he wrote: "In the apparently contradictory union of unworldly saint and zealous agitator traveling the whole of Europe, he offers a psychological problem of more than contemporary significance." At the same time he admitted: "The most intimate center of his being from which his personality must be discovered is his religious nature."[74] Wolfram von der Steinen also implicitly dealt with the ambiguity of St Bernard. He examined thoroughly the derogatory remarks of Schiller, Burckhardt and others, and gave whole-hearted recognition to this admission,[75] as did Hilde Fechner, who, in agreement with Max Weber, advocated a sociological explanation for the ambiguity in Bernard's character.[76]

The doubt which continued to cloud this question appeared at last to be cleared up by Friedrich Heer. In his book, *Aufgang Europas*, published in 1949 and dealing with the twelfth century, he gave the title "The Chimera of the Age" to the chapter about St Bernard.[77] Heer treats St Bernard there as an advocate of the old political-religious way of life, yet at the same time his struggles against the abuses of the feudal religious relationships furthered new tendencies which he denied in principle were new. "Thus a

---

72. *Weltgeschichtliche Betrachtungen,* ed. W. Kaegi (Bern, 1947) p. 354.
73. *Weltverbesserer der Mittelalters, vol 2, Arnold von Brescia* (Leipzig, 1891) 40-3.
74. "Bernhard von Clairvaux," in *Meister der Politik,* 3 vols. (Stuttgart-Berlin, 1923) III:63. In H. Heuter, "Bernhard of Clairvaux, Züge zu einer Charakteristik," *Zeitschrift für Kirchengeschichte* 1 (1877) p. 44, I found a first mention of this ambiguity.
75. *Vom heiligen Geist des Mittelalters,* pp. 147-290.
76. *Die politische Tätigkeit des Abtes Bernhard von Clairvaux in seinen Briefen* (Bonn-Cologne, 1933) p. 40 with a reference to M. Weber, "Die Wirtschaftsethik der Weltreligionen (Zwischenbetrachtung: Theorie der Stufen und Richtungen religiöser Weltablehnung," *Gesammelte Aufsätze zur Religionssoziologie* 2 vols. (Tübingen, 1920) I:540.

strange display is enacted," wrote Heer. "St Bernard summoned the modern side of his spirituality against Cluny, while calling upon the old, conservative, sacramental, symbolic, religious-political elements in his personality to respond to Abelard and the heretics. In this two-fronted war waged by St Bernard we are able to see that the ambiguity of his historical position is due to his function as the mean in a century of crisis."[78]

A similar point of view was at the same time brought forth by the Dutch art historian, Frits van der Meer, who pointed out the importance of St Bernard in the evolution from Romanesque to Gothic architecture,[79] but did not present his theory as all-inclusive, as had Heer. Heer's conclusions concerning the ambiguity in Bernard's character are debatable in that he supposes the abbot of Clairvaux to have seen the supporters of the new age as a closed front. This assumption is probably based more on the idea created by Geoffroy of Auxerre's defence of Bernard's behavior than on Bernard's own thinking.[80] Furthermore, Heer did not concern himself with the problem of the double standard which St Bernard as monk and as politician seemed to uphold.

Nevertheless, the development of this point of view remains an important step forward in the historical-psychological approach to the personality of St Bernard. In spite of expert criticism of Heer's book as unfounded and unclear,[81] his chapter on St Bernard met with agreement and emulation. In 1953 it was translated into French,[82] while others carried his

---

77. (Vienna-Zürich, 1949) 182-235.

78. Ibid., p. 197.

79. *Keerpunt der Middeleeuwen* (Utrecht-Brussels, 1950). It seems to me regretable that this notable study about the twelfth century as the turning point of the Middle Ages has never been translated.

80. See Bredero, *Études*, pp. 133-136 (ASOC 18:19-21). Basically St Bernard had little interest in humble heretics; see R. Manselli, *Studi sulle Eresi del secolo XII*, Instituto Storico per il Medio Evo, Studi Storici, fasc. 5 (Rome, 1953) p. 108.

81. F. L. Ganshof, *Mitteilungen des Institutes für Oesterreichische Geschichtsforschung* 61 (1953) 434-440.

82. *Saint Bernard, homme d'Eglise*, Cahiers de la Pierre-qui-vire, vols. 38-39 (Paris, 1953) 15-22.

"Chimera" theme still further in pointed essays.[83] In Cistercian circles, however, there was no enthusiasm for this method of approach. As late as 1954 a luke-warm review of Heer's book appeared in one of their periodicals.[84] In another context it appeared clear that a psychologically-oriented method was not welcome among Cistercians.[85]

This last point is not hard to understand. In these circles where the writings of St Bernard primarily and continually form the subject of meditative study and are the source of contemplative spirituality, the high degree of holiness which St Bernard achieved in his lifetime is stressed even more strongly than in the descriptive biographies. This holiness is considered a visible charismatic blessing given to St Bernard. According to the interpretation which must be considered normative for current Cistercian opinion, and which can be classified as a theological opinion, God in his compassion so blessed St Bernard that his historical importance must finally be sought in the love that God bears for the world. Understanding is shown for the fact that the historians must look at various secondary points, so long as these remain subordinate to the essential point of St Bernard's holiness. This is important because through the histories of the saints men are educated into the mystery of Christ. Thus, the details of such a history are not essential; it is Christ himself who must be sought in their history.[86]

83. *Die Chimäre seines Jahrhunderts, Vier Vorträge über Bernhard von Clairvaux,* ed. J. Spörl (Würzburg, 1953). J. Bernhart, "Chimaera mei saeculi," *Das Hochland* 45 (1953) 521-9. B. S. James, "Man of Contrasts: St Bernard of Clairvaux," *The Listener* 1273 (23 July 1953) 144-46. A. Frachboud, "Le problème Action Contemplation au coeur de saint Bernard: Je suis la chimère de mon siècle," *Collectanea OCR* 16 (1954) 45-52, 128-136 and 183-191.

84. *Cîteaux in de Nederlanden* 4 (1953) 263.

85. *Collectanea OCR* 19 (1957) 331: a review of my article, "The Controversy between Peter the Venerable and Saint Bernard of Clairvaux," *Petrus Venerabilis,* Studies and Texts, Studia Anselmiana 40 (Rome, 1956) 53-71.

86. CHOC, *Bernard de Clairvaux,* Preface by Thomas Merton, p. x. The English version of this essay is published in *The Tablet* (London) 23 May and 30 May, 1953, 201:438-439 and 466-467. See also J. Leclercq, *Saint Bernard mystique* (Paris, 1948) p. 236: "Le cas de saint Bernard pose à l'historien le problème des rapports que Dieu maintient entre la sainteté et le tempérament. Bernard est homme: ses faits et gestes tombent sous les sens. Les savants qui ont pour fonc-

However important a theological approach to saintliness may be, historical research remains an anthropological field of study. Although theology and history have many points of contact, and although historians must bear in mind the importance of theological opinions and convictions in the life of human beings, one cannot curtail historical research into the psychological aspects of the growth of holiness in a one-sided approach which begins with the holiness which the subject finally attained. The process of canonization itself requires research into the heroic exercise of virtue before any proclamation can be made,

In the case of St Bernard, historians are nearly always motivated and controlled by a theological interest, which explains the fierce one-sidedness of the rationalistic reaction against this sort of writing. The reasons why a theologically-founded point of view of Bernard has often colored the relationship between theology and history has been thoroughly discussed above. St Bernard was not primarily the discovery of historians, his fame was not confined to his own time. The Reformation did not reject him, though the most pronounced interest in him naturally came from quarters where he continued to be held in high regard as a spiritual father.[87]

tion de les enregistrer dans les annales et les chroniques s'arrogent parfois le droit de les juger; mais ils oublient souvent cette autre donnée de l'histoire, également contrôlable, égalment incontestable: Bernard est un homme de Dieu;" p. 240: "Il se mêle à l'action, mais il n'abandonne pas sa contemplation; il a reçu le don de les concilier autrement que par l'alternance: par la fusion de l'une et de l'autre; en lui le conflit qui oppose l'action et la contemplation chez tant d'hommes de Dieu est résolu par Dieu sur un plan supérieur à celui de la psychologie humaine. C'est pourquoi, sans doute, Bernard se plaint moins que bien d'autres de ce déchirement qui les partage entre les domaines successifs òu leur activité s'exerce: il n'est pas divisé, il garde l'unité d'esprit."

87. Thomas Merton, *Saint Bernard de Clairvaux, "le dernier des Pères"* (Paris, 1953), p. 63: "Un cistercien d'aujourd'hui ne doit pas vouloir rivaliser avec Bernard prédicateur de la croisade; mais sa vocation l'oblige à posséder quelque chose de l'amour de Bernard pour l'Eglise et son pays. Par-dessus tout, il doit marcher dans la voie que lui a tracée Bernard épris d'amour pour le Christ crucifié. Quand on écrit sur un saint comme Bernard il est presque impossible de ne point adopter dès le debut, un style de panégyrique." This passage is not in the American and English editions of this book (*The Last of the Fathers* [New York, London, 1954]).

Furthermore, his contemporary life story was written in a manner far more agreeable to a theologian than to an historian. This same biography, however, gained the reputation of an interesting and reliable source for historical research.

In recent years, the historical value of the *Vita prima* has at last become the subject of renewed research and little of the opinions of Huffer and Vacandard remain.[88] Even the supposed theological value of this biography has become doubtful. The three authors of the *Vita prima* wrote according to the schematic norms of contemporary hagiography with the unmistakable aim of furthering the canonization of St Bernard.[89] For this, a written *Life* was necessary: to support the request and to promote the pastoral aims which lie behind every canonization, the devotional education of believers through the life history of the saint, by praising his clearly-defined exercise of virtue and by relating stories of miracles and exorcisms performed by him.[90] The pre-arranged plan to which a *Vita* had to conform can plainly be seen in the part written by Geoffroy of Auxerre but is also present in the work of the other authors.[91] William of St Thierry skillfully concealed this plan, while at the same time answering the criticism of St Bernard's contemporaries. He was willing to admit that St Bernard possessed some dubious qualities, yet he saw these as beside the point. He reminded us of St Bernard's visible charismatic holiness—visible to all those who live in his spirit. This aspect makes an extraordinary document of the first book of the *Vita prima*, but as an historical source for the life of St Bernard this book remains nevertheless doubtful, or at least tenuous. At the same time it offers an example of how reality can be biased, as in this case, toward the absolute saintliness of St Bernard.[92]

---

88. Bredero, *Etudes sur la Vita prima de saint Bernard* (Rome, 1950); repr. ASOC 17 (1961) 3-72 and 215-260; 18 (1962) 5-59.

89. Ibid., 117-161 (18:33-46).

90. J. Leclercq, "Saint Bernard docteur," *Recueil d'Etudes sur saint Bernard et ses écrits*, II:388, 8 (*Collectanea OCR* 16 [1954] 258 n. 11).

91. Bredero, *Etudes*, p. 104 (17:248).

92. Ibid., pp. 106-7 (17:250-1).

Concerning the textual revision of the entire *Vita*, it has been undeniably determined that Geoffroy undertook this work in 1163, immediately after Pope Alexander III's refusal of the first request for canonization. Textual changes in the accounts of the miracles omitted witnesses who were mentioned by name and who were still living. It can be determined from manuscripts in which the revisions were only partially carried out that this aspect was more important than the literary improvements which were also carried out.[93] The only story which was added in the second version was that of a vision which occured to William of Montpellier, monk of Grandselve, on the night Bernard died. According to this vision, St Bernard entered into heavenly bliss immediately.[94] This addition can be explained in the same way, since it can be deduced from a cartulary of the abbey of Grandselve that William of Montpellier died in 1161,[95] in the period between the appearance of the first and second versions.

The recent research into the historical value of the *Vita prima* has thrown doubt on this important source in the biographical literature on St Bernard, and has brought previous historical research, including the psychological method, to an impasse. There are indeed increasingly more details coming to light about St Bernard's life, thanks mostly to local studies. But it is imperative to follow a new method to study his life in its totality; his ambiguity must not only be illustrated but must be psychologically explained. These explanations have primarily been sought in the history of his youth and in his relationship to his mother who died prematurely,[96] but the passages from the *Vita prima* upon which

93. Ibid., p. 146, and n. 9 (18:32 and n. 3). See also "The Canonization of Saint Bernard and the Rewriting of his Life," *Citeaux* 25 (1974) p. 3.

94. Vita Bern, V, III, 22; PL 185:363C-364C. See Bredero, *Études,* p. 55 (17:58).

95. Ms. Paris B. N. lat. 11008, fol. 7^r, 8^r and 9^r. In three charters of endowment from 1161, William is named as witness; in later acts, his name does not appear.

96. L. Bouyer, *La spiritualité de Cîteaux* (Paris, 1955) p. 45. [The Cistercian Heritage (London: A. R. Mowbray, 1958) p. 30]. J. Leclercq, *Saint Bernard mystique,* pp. 18-9. See J. Calmette and H. David, *Saint Bernard,* p. 352.

these explanations are based can no longer enjoy the respect that they met with in past expositions.[97] The possibilities of a new system of research are at any rate available if one begins a minutely thorough study of the one most important aspect in St Bernard's life. In the many biographies dealing with him, this aspect is dealt with only generally and in passing. Williams alone gave increased, though still insufficient, stress to it.[98] When St Bernard entered Cîteaux in 1113, this monastery had just one other affiliation, La Ferté-sur-Grosne, founded in 1112.[99] In 1114, Pontigny was founded, and in 1115, Clairvaux and Morimond were founded simultaneously. By 1153, when St Bernard died, the order had 344 monasteries spread over all Europe. Of these, sixty-nine were direct affiliations of Clairvaux, and they in their turn had founded seventy-five houses, from which had sprung another twenty-two monasteries. Clairvaux then possessed *in toto* an affiliation of 166 monasteries.[100]

This large expansion of the Cistercian order, for which St Bernard is generally considered primarily responsible, can hardly be exclusively attributed to his great power of enlisting men of which the *Vita prima* speaks. In our times this is being studied in greater detail.[101] The founding of monasteries was a material concern as well. This care was often

97. Bredero, *Études*, pp. 130, n. 3; 142, n. 2 and 144, n. 3 (18:16, n. 2; 27, n. 5 and 29, n. 10).

98. William, pp. 26-95.

99. Bredero, *Études*, p. 59, and n. 1 (17:62, and n. 1). A charter of endowment probably exists from the year 1111. In any case, the foundation of La Ferté took place before the entrance of St Bernard in Cîteaux. The refusal of La Ferté to accept a tutelage from Clairvaux in the Cistercian order, which can be presumed from the manuscript tradition of the *Vita prima* in this abbey, is supported by the absence of affiliations of La Ferté after 1132. Furthermore, La Ferté founded only three monasteries during St Bernard's lifetime, although this abbey was in a good economic state. Compare *Recueil des pancartes de l'abbaye de la Ferté-sur-Grosne*, ed. G. Duby (Paris, 1953).

100. L. Janauschek, *Originum Cisterciensium* (Vienna, 1877). F. van der Meer, *Atlas de l'ordre* (Amsterdam-Brussels, 1965) pp. 22-8 (Arbre généalogique).

101. Vita Bern, I, III, 15; PL 185:235: "Iamque eo publice et privatim praedicante, matres filios abscondebant, uxores detinebant maritos, amici amicos avertebant, quia voci eius Spiritus sanctus tantae dabat vocem virtutis, ut vix aliquis aliquem teneret affectu." See A. Dimier, *Saint Bernard "pêcheur de Dieu"* (Paris, 1953).

alleviated, certainly, by unsolicited gifts from land-owners, who then profited from the agricultural work of the Cistercians.[102] And one must not forget the spontaneous help received from bishops who wished to have one or more Cistercian monasteries in their dioceses, all the more so in that these monasteries did not wish to be exempted from episcopal authority of the bishops.[103] But even considering all this, the great expansion of the Cistercian order is not explained in full. On further examination we see that many existing monasteries passed into the hands of Cistercians because the already existing community was replaced or because this community joined itself to Cîteaux, often with a number of affiliations. This was the case with the abbey of Obazine in the bishopric of Limoges, and with the congregation of Savigny. In such cases there was even the possibility of compensation being given, as was probably true in the case of the abbey of Cheminon.[104]

Up till now, no attention has been given to the role played by St Bernard in such material matters, with the exception of studies of a local nature such as those dealing with the found-

102. This matter is not yet wholly clear. See G. Duby, *Rural Economy and Country Life in the Medieval West* (London, 1968) 70-72. B. Bligny, *L'Eglise et les ordres religieux dans le royaume de Bourgogne au XI et XII siècles* (Paris, 1960) 334-9. Bennett D. Hill, *English Cistercian Monasteries and their Patrons in the Twelfth Century* (Chicago, 1968).

103. J. B. Mahn, *L'Ordre cistercien et son gouvernement* (Paris, 1951) 135-7. V. Tirelli, "Di un privilegio dell'abbazia di Chiaravalle della Colomba nel Piacentino: una nota sulla exemptio dell'Ordre cisterciense," *Bulletino dell' Instituto Storico Italiano per il Medio Evo* 72 (1960) 191-217. J. de la Croix Bouton, *Histoire de l'Ordre de Cîteaux* (Westmalle, 1959) 181-2. The authority of the bishops over Cistercian abbeys, however, was restrained by the direct influence which the general chapter of the Cistercian Order exercised on their monasteries, and also by the rights of the abbots of Cîteaux and her four elder daughters to supervise their affiliations.

104. Cheminon, which was founded in 1102, belonged to the Order of the Canons of Arrouaise, and was acquired as an affiliated abbey of Trois-Fontaines in 1138. In 1135 St Bernard reformed the collegial chapter of Châtillon-sur-Seine (Saint Vorles) and give this to the "monks" of Ruisseauville who belonged to the Order of Arrouaise; this was officially accepted about 1142. E. Barthélemy, *Recueil des chartes de Cheminon* (Paris, 1883) pp. 50-1. DHGE 12:588-90. E. Petit, *Histoire des ducs de Bourgogne de la race capétienne*, 2 vols. (Paris, 1888) II:22-3, pièce 256. L. Milis, *L'Ordre de Chanoines réguliers d'Arrouaise*, 2 vols. (Bruges, 1969) I:162, n. 6, and 168-9.

ing and development of a given monastery.[105] In the numerous biographies of the abbot of Clairvaux, the example of
the *Vita prima* is followed, the authors of which avoided this
subject for reasons of tact rather than ignorance. This shows
Bernard in a role which justly calls for criticism. The details
which exist concerning St Bernard's relations with the affiliations of Clairvaux and other Cistercian monasteries are not
plentiful.[106] With the few published details concerning these
establishments[107] and with what we know about the journeys
of St Bernard the historian does not get far. However for
Watkin Williams, who examined this material, it was not difficult to connect the founding of Chiaravalle in 1135 with
the visit of St Bernard to Milan. The founding of La Grâce-
Dieu and Buzay in the same year are clearly connected with
the action of St Bernard against William of Aquitaine, whom
he persuaded to disavow the antipope Anacletus, and with his
subsequent journey to Brittany. Also, the taking over of the
abbey at Aulne and the founding of Cambron and Loos in
1147 have to do with the journey of St Bernard to Belgium
when he returned from his second campaign in Germany on
behalf of the crusade.[108]

Still, the question which is posed here has a deeper significance and has to do with Bernard's wordly activities for the
promotion of Cistercian expansion. First-hand information
about this is scarce, but not so scarce that one should let
himself be misled by the information offered in the *Vita
prima*. There it is stated that St Bernard disregarded the
material side of the matter completely, and that the people
with whom he dealt never troubled him about this.[109] The

105. The majority of these studies are unpublished dissertations or articles in
regional periodicals. An exception is the publication of the Société de l'Histoire
du Droit et des Institutions des anciens Pays Bourguignons, Comtois et Romands,
*Les débuts des abbayes cisterciennes dans les anciens Pays Bourguignons, Comtois
et Romands* (Dijon, 1953).

106. CHOC, *Bernard de Clairvaux,* pp. 166-82.

107. *Gallia Christiana, Instrumenta,* and the published *Cistercian Cartularia.*

108. Williams, pp. 50-51, 80 and 82, Cf A. Lebigre, "Les débuts de l'abbaye
Cistercienne de Buzay en pays de Rais, 1144-1250," *Revue historique de droit
francais et etranger* 45 (1967) 451-82.

109. Vita Bern, I, vi, 27; PL 185:242.

fragmentary monastery *cartularia* offer little or no information about this matter, and the documents which have not been lost by carelessness, religious wars, and the French Revolution, give no direct or sufficient answer to this question. Therefore indirect sources must be used for this investigation, often supplemented by comparisons and hypotheses. After these sources and documents have been gathered from almost all the Cistercian monasteries which were founded in Bernard's time, one can draw conclusions and reconstruct the missing data in individual cases. Only then can one form a reliable picture of the activities of St Bernard regarding the promotion and expansion of his Order.

How these activities sometimes were viewed by his contemporaries becomes clearer from the rebuff offered by the Abbot of Dalon (which remained outside the Cistercian order until 1162) to the Abbot of Clairvaux upon the occasion of St Bernard's acquiring le Bueil, an affiliation of Dalon, for his order. He compared St Bernard to the man who owns ninety-nine sheep, and who secretly takes away the lamb of a poor man in order later to receive him with great show as a friend.[110]

In these activities political calculation had its place. For example, St Bernard benefited from the penitence of highly placed gentlemen who had lived as public sinners and who preferred the gift of a monastery to a penitential pilgrimage.[111] Boxley Abbey in Kent was founded because of the temporary penitence of the notorious William of Yperen.[112] The abbey of Longpont received gifts from Raoul de Vermandois in 1144, when he was excommunicated because

---

110. *Gallia Christiana* 2:632. See J. Leclercq, "Lettres de Saint Bernard: histoire ou littérature," *Studi Medievali* 12 (1971) p. 2, n. 2; L. Janauschek, *Originum*, p. 148.

111. After his conversion, William of Aquitaine died on pilgrimage to Compostella. Suger, *Vie de Louis le Gros*, ed. H. Waquet (Paris, 1964²) p. 280, n. 3. Compare A. Richard, *Histoire des Comtes de Poitou*, 2 vols. (Paris, 1903) II:50-2.

112. *The Victoria History of the County of Kent*, 2 vols. (London, 1926) II:153-5. The motives of William, however, were not only penance and piety; see Hill, *English Cistercian Monasteries*, p. 54.

of his concubinage with Adelaide of Aquitaine.[113] It must be noted that in 1148, the council of Reims, where St Bernard had a powerful influence, recognized this union as a legal marriage.[114] Last of all, there is the acquisition of the abbey of Moureilles in 1152, in the territory of Bishop Gilbert of Poitiers. He certainly would not have given his help. This acquisition, about which all details are lacking, was possibly arranged through the agency of Eleanor of Poitou, who at that time was divorced and remarried and who in these circumstances also made a rather demonstrative donation to the abbey of Fontevrault.[115]

Aside from this, there remain questions of another sort: the share which St Bernard had in the appointment of bishops and his interference in arguments concerning their elections. In the cases where he failed, as in 1138 in Limoges, the door of the respective diocese remained closed to the Cistercian Order.[116] In the archbishopric of Bourges, where he installed

113. *Gallia Christ.*, X, Instrumenta ecclesiae Suessionensis, XXX, col. 117-8. Raoul calls himself one of the founders of this abbey in this charter of endowment: "Dignum est ut ecclesiam vestram quam a fundamentis aedificavimus, de beneficiis nostris augeamus." But in the charter of foundation (Ms. Paris B. N., coll. Picardie, vol. 289, no. 1) Raoul is not mentioned. Ibid., col. 111-2.

114. Williams, II: pp. 209 and 215. *The Historia Pontificalis of John of Salisbury*, Nelson's Medieval Classics, ed. M. Chibnall, (London, 1956) p. 14.

115. E. Huber, "Notice sur deux cartes de Louis VII et d'Aliénor d'Aquitaine en faveur de l'abbaye de Fontevraud," *Revue des sociétes savantes des départements,* 5e serie, T. III (1872): ". . . ego Alienordis . . . postquam a domino meo Ludovico . . . causa parentele, disiuncta fui, et domino meo Henrico . . . matrimonio copulata, divina illustratione tacta, sanctarum virginum fontis Ebraudi congretionem visitare concupivi, et quod mente habui, opitulante gratia Dei, opere complevi." Furthermore, the good relationship between Gilbert and the monastery of Fontevrault was completely spoiled; see N. M. Häring, "Bischof Gilbert von Poitiers und seine Erzdiakone," *Deutsches Archiv für Erforschung des Mittelalters* (1965) 160-1.

116. In 1137, Pope Innocent II had the intention of giving the Abbot of Vézelay, Alberic, a friend of St Bernard's, the office of Bishop of Limoges. Although Vézelay belonged to the congregation of Cluny, Peter the Venerable prevented his appointment because he was irreplaceable as abbot of the difficult abbey, where his election as abbot had been forced by Cluny in 1129; see G. de Valous, *Le monachisme clunisien des origines au XVe siècle,* 2 vols. (Ligugé and Paris, 1935, repr. Paris 1970) 2:59. It seems, however, that Peter made no objections, when the Pope named Alberic as Cardinal-bishop of Ostia in 1138; see R. Manselli, "Alberico, cardinale vescovo d'Ostia e la sua attivita di legato pontifico," *Archivio della Società romana di Storia patria* 78 (1955) 28-9. In 1142, after a long struggle for election, Geraud-Hector d'Escorailles, a nephew of the late

Pierre de la Châtre as bishop despite the resistance of Louis VII,[117] the number of direct affiliations of Clairvaux grew remarkably and at the same time other Cistercian monasteries were founded there as well.[118] Attention deserves also to be given to the archbishopric of Rouen, where in 1130 the conservative Cluniac Hugh of Amiens was elected. The Cistercians entered there in 1145 with the support of Geoffroy, the bishop of Chartres, and founded at the border of Rouen and Chartres (which was itself a suffragan bishopric of the archbishopric of Sens) the abbey of Estrée.[119]

The tentative impression that I have acquired from this incomplete research, from which I have given only a few results and deductions, is that the political activity of St Bernard in his day, insofar as he was not motivated by papal

---

bishop of Limoges, Eustoge, who had died in 1137 (1138?), was chosen; see M. Pacaut, *Louis VII et les élections épiscopales dans le royaume de France* (Paris, 1957) p. 87. During the administration of these two bishops there were no affiliations founded or obtained in the diocese of Limoges. The abbey of Cîteaux was able though, in 1147, to acquire the monastery Obazine, together with two affiliations in this bishopric, Bonaigue and La Valette. Furthermore, in the bishopric of Bourges, on the border of Limoges, the abbeys La Colombe (affil. of Preuilly-Cîteaux) and Aube-Pierres (affil. of Clairvaux) were founded in 1146 and 1149. See below note 118.

117. M. Pacaut, pp. 92-100.

118. In 1129 Loroy, (Affil. La Cour Dieu-Cîteaux) and le Landais (Affil. l'Aumône-Cîteaux); in 1135 Les Pierres (Affil. Clairvaux); in 1136 Noirlac (Affil. Clairvaux). In 1138 Barzelle (Affil. le Landais) and Chalivoy (Affil. Pontigny—this abbey was founded on the border of the bishopric of Nevers, just as in the bishopric of Auxerre the abbey les Roches, [Affil. Pontigny] was founded on the border of the bishopric of Nevers: In Nevers itself no Cistercian monastery existed). In 1145 La Prée (Affil. Clairvaux) and Olivet (Affil. la Cour Dieu). In 1146 la Colombe (Affil. Pontigny; see n. 116); In 1148 Varennes (Affil. Vaului-sant-Preuilly): In 1149 Fontmorigny (Affil. Clairvaux) and Aube-Pierres (Affil. Clairvaux; see n. 116). Bishop Pierre de la Châtre, who was finally recognized by Louis VII in 1144, was a nephew of Haimeric, the papal chancellor. Haimeric was a friend of St Bernard and counselled the abbot in his political activities during the schism of Anacletus.

119. Archives départementales de l'Eure (Ebreux) H 319 fol 4r - 5v. Geoffroy, bishop of Chartres, collaborated in that period closely with St Bernard, who is not mentioned in this charter. Hugh of Amiens has been supposed to be the author of a Cluniac defence against the Apology of St Bernard: C. H. Talbot, "The Date and Author of the 'Riposte'," *Petrus Venerabilis*, Studia Anselmiana 40 (Rome, 1956) 72-80. The acquisition of the Congregation of Savigny in 1147 procured for Clairvaux in the archbishopric of Rouen the abbeys of Beaubec and Foucarmont.

request, can be attributed to his continual striving for the promotion and expansion of the Cistercian Order. Even when the initiative for his mingling in politics originated elswhere, he never let a chance escape for founding or acquiring new monasteries, as for example in Italy at the close of the schism with Anacletus,[120] when he may have played Roger of Sicily and Pope Innocent II off against each other.

120. After the conclusion of the schism of Anacletus, Pope Innocent at the Second Council of the Lateran, dismissed the former adherents of the antipope. J-L 1:885, sub 30. *Chronicon Mauriacense* III, MGH SS 26:44-5. St Bernard, who had reconciled those adherents with the pope, was outraged at this dismissal: "Quis mihi faciet iustitiam de vobis?" Ep 213, PL 182:378. It seems, though, that St Bernard found a way to take satisfaction from the pope for the fact that he had not kept his promise. In 1130, Anacletus gave the Crown of the Kingdom of Southern Calabria and Apulia to Roger and his heirs. Thus he had a firm supporter in Roger. At the close of the schism in 1139, Pope Innocent ventured to wage a campaign against Roger, together with Robert of Capua. The papal army suffered a heavy defeat. The Pope himself was captured (22 July 1139). According to the peace treaty made three days later at Mignano, the Pope was forced to recognize, though he obtained some restrictions, the royal title bestowed upon Roger by Anacletus; see H. Wieruszowski, "Roger II of Sicily, 'Rex-Tyrannus' in Twelfth-Century Political Thought," *Politics and Culture in Medieval Spain and Italy* (Rome, 1971) pp. 55-6 (= *Speculum* 38 (1963) 48-9). Roger, indeed, brought about a unified state in Southern Italy, something which the papal politics had formerly tried to prevent. In 1140, during a new period of strife between Innocent and Roger, Roger's son married a daughter of the mighty count Thibaut of Champagne, a close friend of St Bernard. The bride was accompanied by Cistercian monks on her journey to Southern Italy, where the monks took over the monastery of Sambucina in Calabria. Although St Bernard had earlier called Roger "Tyrannus Siculus" and "Dux Apuliae, quem sibi Anacletus papae usurpatae coronae ridicula mercede comparavit" (Ep 130 and 127; PL 182:285 and 282) he quickly reconciled himself with Roger after Mignano and thus made a new affiliation for Clairvaux. See H. W. Klewitz, "Die Anfänge des Cistercienserordens im normannisch-sizilischen Königreich," SMGBO 52 (1934) 236. At the same time, St Bernard acquired the abbey of Tre Fontane in the immediate surroundings of Rome. The monks whom St Bernard wished to send out to establish a new monastery with the help offered by the abbot of Farfa established themselves through the personal intervention of the Pope in Tre Fontane, which belonged earlier to Benedictines who had taken the side of Anacletus. See *Ep Anacleti*, IV, PL 179:692-6. Vita Bern, II, vii, 48 and III, vii, 24; PL 185:296 and 317. It seems quite possible to me that there is a connection between St Bernard's reconciliation with Roger (by which he acquired Sambucina) and the conciliatory attitude of the Pope (who had the ruined monastery of Tre Fontane rebuilt for the Cistercians), and that St Bernard exploited the awkward position of the Pope, who certainly disliked the reconciliation of St Bernard with Roger. This assertion, however, requires further research into the many parallel references which can be found concerning relationships between St Bernard and other Benedictine monasteries. See Bouton, in CHOC, *Bernard de Clairvaux*, p. 219, n. 2.

If our opinions, which are posited with reservations, are borne out by further research into the founding of the Cistercian monasteries of those days, they will lead not only to a clearer reconstruction of the political behavior of St Bernard. They will help as well to explain his historical performance by bringing us to the core of his political activity and of his spiritual, mystical exhaltation. Both these contradictory sides of St Bernard's character appear to spring from his monastic ideals, which were strongly directed towards the Cistercian way of life. His monasticism also explains his struggle with Scholasticism.[121]

The realization of these ideals was sought by St Bernard not only in the material expansion for which he mingled in politics at many different levels. This material goal was the result of his spiritual and monastic exaltation, for which the Cistercian way of life offered him unique opportunities. Concerning this, the theologians have always been correct. This evaluation is evident in his conflict with Cluny, which he viewed—at least after the forced abdication of abbot Pons of Melgueil and before his quasi-successor Peter the Venerable entered into monastic reforms—as an integral part of the world he wished to escape.[122] His struggle to achieve blessedness for himself and others was anchored in his monastic way of life and in his own monastery, Clairvaux. He compared the contemplative monk, in one of his sermons, to those who accompanied the Lord close by at his entry into Jerusalem.[123] Jerusalem was for him, as for his contemporaries, the equivalent of Eternal Life.[124] In one of his letters he referred to Clairvaux as "the heavenly Jerusalem" and he said

---

121. See below, n. 132.
122. Bredero, "Cluny et Cîteaux au XIIe siècle: les origines de la controverse," *Studi medievali* 12 (1971) 149-52. "Pierre le Venerable: les commencements de son abbatiat," *Actes du colloque l'humanisme andounième siècle: Pierre le Vénérable et Pierre Abelard*, Paris 1974.
123. Palm 2:7; OB 5:50: "Porro qui adhaerent ei, contemplativi sunt."
124. Sept 1:3; OB 4:347: "O Jerusalem, civitas Regis magni, qui ex adipe frumenti satiat te, et quam fluminis impetus laetificat, in te nec pondus utique, nec mensura, sed satietas est et affluentia summa! Sed nec habes numerum, quippe *cuius participatio eius in idipsum.*" (Ps 121:3).

that entering Clairvaux was better than pilgrimage to the real Jerusalem for the procurement of eternal life.[125] Elsewhere, St Bernard called the monastery "the mighty fortress of Christ, from which he yearly drew his best and most precious income. He brings there the enormous treasure which he has won from his enemies, for he has great confidence in the power of this fortress."[126]

It is difficult to imagine that St Bernard is referring only to Clairvaux here, and not to all the other monasteries and affiliations of his Order as well. Because of the rigid central leadership of the Order, in which he had a part, if not the most important place,[127] all the abbeys demonstrated great uniformity, and St Bernard counted them as fortresses of God and dwelling places of all those called to the holy life. In his writings, Clairvaux was the obvious symbol of the Cistercian way of life. It embodied the monastic ideal which had a central place in the whole of his theological thought.[128] To what extent Clairvaux as symbol was integrated into his mystic reflections is clearly seen in a cryptogram that he secretly worked into one of his sermons on the *Song of Songs* and which only rather recently has been discovered.[129] This cryptogram was based on a certain number of syllables, to be

---

125. Ep 64; PL 182:169-70: "Et, si vultis scire, Clara-Vallis est. Ipse est Jerusalem, ei quae in coelis est, tota mentis devotione, et conversationis imitatione, cognatione quadam spiritus sociata." See Bredero, "Jérusalem dans l'Occident médiéval," *Mélanges R. Crozet*, 2 vols. (Poitiers, 1966) 1:271.

126. Ded 3:3; OB 5:381: "Optimos inde singulis annis et pretiosos in oculis suis redditus accipit, et praedam multam, quam hostibus eripit, in hunc munitionis suae locum solet inducere, et habet fiduciam in multa fortitudine eius." See also Ep 112; PL 182:255-6, directed to Geoffrey of Lisieux, who returned to the world: "Revertere, quaeso, revertere priusquam te absorbeat profundum, et urgeat super te puteus os suum; priusquam, unde ulterius non emergas; priusquan ligatis manibus et pedibus proiiciaris in tenebras exteriores, ubi est fletus et stridor dentium; priusquam detrudaris in locum tenebrosum, et opertum mortis caligine."

127. CHOC, *Bernard de Clairvaux*, pp. 147-182; Bouton, *Histoire de l'Ordre de Cîteaux*, p. 125.

128. P. Desseille, "Théologie de la vie monastique selon saint Bernard," *Théologie de la vie monastique*, Etudes publiées sous la direction de la faculté de Théologié SJ de Lyon-Fourvière, 49 (Paris, 1961) pp. 503-525.

129. SC 74:5; OB 2:242. See T. Deroy, *Bernardus en Origenes* (Haarlem, 1963) p. 151.

exact, one hundred fifty-nine, which make up the passage dealing with surrender to God, undoubtedly one of the most mystical passages in his writings. When one writes 159 in Roman letters, the letters CLIX are obtained. Since the letter X is equal to the letter "s,"[130] these letters form a contraction of the word *Claravallis,* that is to say, *Clairvaux.* The game is then not yet at an end. Directly following the passage about surrender to God, of,which surrender Clairvaux formed the hidden symbol, a quotation follows from the *Acts of the Apostles* (17:28): "Because in God, we live, we move, we are."[131] Clairvaux and the Cistercian way of life was literally interwoven with his most exalted mystical thought.

The historical personality of St Bernard must be seen through the spiritual and material effect he had upon the monastic ideal. However much the behavior of St Bernard in the world was affected by his spiritual exaltation, there were also human failings, which is not strange even in the saint. However, one finds such failure, strangely enough, where one finds his human capability: in his versatile activities for the material promotion of the Cistercian Order. An investigation into these activities must be more fully based on the direct and indirect data concerning the growth of his Order in those days. The point of departure for this investigation is the exclusive monastic ideal of St Bernard, which offers, because of its equivocal nature, the possibility of seeing the human failings of St Bernard that seem to negate his saintliness as clearly positive values which he represented and strove for continually in an heroic manner.[132]

---

130. Ibid., p. 153.

131. After "et ipsum interius erat" St Bernard added: "Et cognovi verum quidem esse quod legeram: quia *in ipso vivimus, movemur et sumus.*" (Act 17:28). OB 2:243.

132. Within the framework of this explanation, the behavior of St Bernard toward Abelard and Gilbert of Poitiers, which was so difficult for contemporaries and posterity to interpret or to accept, becomes clear. Although the abbot of Clairvaux understood little of the exact teaching of this philosopher, according to the contemporary opinion of John of Salisbury: "Seculares vero litteras minus noverat;" (*Historica Pontificalis,* ed. M. Chibnall, Nelson Medieval Texts [London, 1956] p. 27), it must have been obvious to him that the scholastic methods which they followed stood out in sharp contrast to traditional, monastic thought, and

To support this conclusion I would like to return finally to the remark which William of St Thierry made concerning the manner in which the life of St Bernard must be understood; that is, according to his own mentality. When one, in an historical approach to his personality, takes into consideration the overweening power of his monastic convictions and the form which these took in his contemplation and behavior, it can finally be seen that this statement, in spite of its relationship to the polemics of its own day, can stand up to historic criticism. The quotation from William which is given above, continues thus:

> Only he who gives and receives can understand how greatly the Lord lavished blessings on him [St Bernard] from the very beginning of his monastic life, how he filled him with the grace of election, how he inebriated him with the abundance of his house.[133]

The historian must take into account this blessing of God before giving his judgment upon the man, Bernard of Clairvaux. Many historians have objected to this task, more so while others, stressing his saintliness, too often forgot the man. May the method of research advocated here finally be able to give a satisfactory answer to the controversy about St Bernard in the opinion of the historians.

Adriaan H. Bredero

The University of Tilburg
Tilburg, The Netherlands

---

formed a great threat to the way of thinking in which St Bernard himself had been schooled. The abbot of Clairvaux reacted to this threat in a manner difficult to reconcile with his canonized saintliness. This way of acting becomes more understandable when brought into the context of his unwavering vigilance in matters which he considered essential to the monastic way of life. This vigilance drove him sometimes to fanatical behavior which embarrassed his defenders and deprived others of the possibility of giving a positive evaluation of this Saint in retrospect.

133. Vita Bern, I, IV, 19; PL 185:237D-238A.

THE CANONIZATION OF BERNARD
OF CLAIRVAUX

THE CANONIZATION OF ST BERNARD took place on the eighteenth of January, 1174.[1] Pope Alexander III ordered that the first abbot of Clairvaux be included in the catalogue of acknowledged saints and that his commemoration be celebrated publicly.[2] We know of the Pope's decision from some four letters of that date which the Pope had sent to the Church of France, to Louis VII King of France, to the Cistercian Order, and to Gerard, abbot of Clairvaux.[3] These notices of the canonization of St Bernard are supplemented by a letter from Tromund, abbot of Chiaravalle near Milan,[4] to Gerard, abbot of Clairvaux.[5] From this last letter it is clear that Abbot Tromund was one of the advocates in the process that led to the canonization at Rome.

1. PL 185:619-21; and A. Dimier, "C'est en 1174 et non en 1175 que saint Bernard fut canonisé," *Cîteaux, Commentarii Cistercienses* 12 (1961) 80-85.
2. PL 185:622-3: "Eum apostolicae sedis auctoritate catalogo sanctorum adscribi mandavimus et comemorationis suae festum decrevimus,"
3. J. Fontanini, *Codex constitutionum quas summi pontifices ediderunt in solemni canonizatione* (Rome, 1729) pp. 20-24. *Acta Sanctorum*, augusti IV (ed. 1867) pp. 244-5. PL 185:622-5. Jaffé-Loewenfeld, *Regesta Pontificum Romanorum* II (Leipzig, 1888; repr. Graz, 1956), no. 12330 (*Contigit olim*), no. 12331 (*Novit, ut credimus*), no. 12329 (*Quoties honesta*) and no. 12328 (*Sicut de religione*). See Appendix. On the manuscript tradition of these letters, see Bredero, *Etudes sur la Vita prima de saint Bernard* (Rome, 1960) 154, no. 2 and 6 (repr. ASOC 18 [1962] p. 39, n. 4 and p. 40, n. 4).
4. This Abbot Tromund must not be confused with Master Tromundus, papal notarius, 1185-6, who afterwards became a monk of Clairvaux. S. J. Heathcote, "The Letter Collection attribued to Master Transmundus," ASOC 21 (1965) 86-9.
5. PL 185:626-7. J-L 7742. See below n. 68; also the Appendix to this volume.

Relatively speaking the information about the canonization of St Bernard is fairly extensive. Yet this information
does not go far enough to make clear to us how the process
was conducted, how the supplication was prepared, which
were personal motives for the request of canonization, and
which considerations made the Pope decide to canonize Bernard. On the other hand, two of the letters mention that the
Pope had rejected a first request for canonization in 1163, at
least for the moment;[6] but this gives little answer to the
questions put here.

All the same, it is possible to find out more about these
various aspects of St Bernard's canonization if we supplement
these documents with other data relative to this canonization
and with what is generally known about the processes of
canonization in those days. Till now, however, little attention
has been paid to the actual canonization of St Bernard.

This is remarkable in that this canonization was clearly
significant for the *Nachleben* of St Bernard.[7] For, judging by
the data concerning other canonizations, one can see that the
continuance of a saint's commemoration was one of the aims
of a canonization.[8] Yet it appears that none of the many
commemorations of St Bernard paid any attention to the
actual fact of his canonization, not even in the years suitable
for such a commemoration.[9] Even the *Acta Sanctorum* paid
little attention to it. The Bollandists of those days limited
themselves to the publication of the four letters by Alexander III with a very general commentary.[10]

Anyone who knows anything about canonization processes
of those days or about papal letters regarding canonizations

---

6. The letters addressed to the Church of France and to the Cistercian Order.

7. See my other contribution to this volume (Chapter Two).

8. In granting the canonization of Hugh of Grenoble, about 1133-6, Pope Innocent II ordered that the Life of the new Saint be written and be handed down
to posterity. PL 179:256.

9. From the years 1724 and 1874 two published commemorations do exist but
these took place on the liturgical feast of St Bernard and not on the date of his
canonization. See L. Janauschek, *Bibliographia Bernardina . . . usque ad finem
anni MDCCXC* (Vienna, 1891, repr. Hildesheim, 1959), nos. 1491 and 2521.

10. AA SS, augusti IV, 243-245.

knows that the *Lives* of the Saints concerned were of primary importance in them. Yet there is no apparent connection between the extensive life story of the abbot of Clairvaux, the *Vita Prima Sancti Bernardi*, which was 'published' in its first version in 1155 or in the beginning of 1156, and his canonization. At least no positive connection was supposed to exist until this *Life* was analysed more closely as an historical source.[11] Actually, there is a clear indication that they are connected. For when the first request for canonization was rejected in 1163, a revision of the first version of this *Vita Prima* was undertaken.[12] On the other hand, a negative connection between this work and the canonization was indeed supposed. The postponement of St Bernard's canonization was ascribed to a lack of reverence which, according to this *Life*, St Bernard was said to have shown for some kings and prelates.[13]

At the root of this supposition was a statement by Alan of Auxerre, author of a *Vita Secunda* written between 1167 and 1171.[14] In the prologue of his work Alan mentioned a criticism to this effect, expressed at the time by Geoffrey of Langres, regarding the *Vita Prima*.[15] This supposed negative connection was obviously an obstacle to finding out more about the request for canonization. On the other hand, Vacandard, the most outstanding biographer of St Bernard, at the end of the nineteenth century did suppose a positive connection between the *Vita Secunda* and the canonization in 1174, although it is only a vague indication which he used to depreciate further the value of this hardly impressive writ-

11. The first to note that this Life was written with a view to canonization was J. Leclercq, "Saint Bernard Docteur," *Collectanea OCR* 16 (1954) p. 285.

12. Bredero, *Etudes,* 138-141 (18:24-6).

13. G. Chevallier, *Histoire de Saint Bernard,* 2 vols. (Lille, 1888) 2:413.

14. Bredero, 139, n. 9 (ASOC 18:25, n. 4) gives 1167-1170. The terminus *antequem,* being determined by the election of Abbot of Clairvaux as bishop of Clermont, is probably 1171. Compare M. Preiss, *Die politische Tätigkeit und Stellung der Cisterzienser im Schisma von 1159-1177,* Historische Studien Heft 248 (Berlin, 1934) p. 126.

15. PL 185:469.

ing.[16] In this way the actual connections were reversed by these suppositions. For the connection of the *Vita Secunda* with the canonization was only negative; at least it offers an explanation why a second application for canonization came only ten years after the first, although the revision of the *Vita Prima* had been already completed in 1165.

These purported connections between both *Vitae* and the request for St Bernard's canonizations can easily be understood. The *Vita Prima* enjoyed great reputation with Vacandard. The revision, done in 1163-1165 by an only then-living author, Geoffrey of Auxerre, was considered by Vancandard as a proof that this author had developed an increasingly critical attitude.[17] This opinion found general acceptance, and even up to 1953 it was believed that this writing possessed a much greater historical reliability than other hagiographical writings of the Middle Ages.[18] Therefore no connection was seen between the *Vita Prima* and St Bernard's canonization. Moreover a more systematic study of the canonizations of those days started only a few decades ago and only then was the connection between canonization and hagiography noted,[19] a connection, which was simply noted, however, and not analysed.[20]

16. E. Vacandard, "L'Histoire de Saint Bernard," *Revue des Questions historiques* 43 (1888) p. 376. Idem, *Vie de saint Bernard*, 2 vols. (Paris, 1920⁴) 1:XLIII: "... on y aperçoit l'intention de canoniser le fondateur de Clairvaux: dessein bien légitime sans doute, mais peu favorable à l'impartialité de l'historien." About the value of this *Life*, see S. St Clair Morrison, "An Amorphous Amalgam: the Vita Secunda by Alan of Flandres," *Collectanae OCR* 18 (1957) 21-26.

17. *L'Histoire de Saint Bernard*, p. 364. Compare Bredero, *Études*, p. 9 (17: 13).

18. R. Aigrain, *L'Hagiographie, ses sources, ses méthodes, son histoire* (Paris, 1953) p. 311.

19. S. Kuttner, "La réserve papale des droits de canonisation," *Revue historique de droit français et étranger*, 4th series, 17 (1938) 172-228. E. Kemp, "Pope Alexander and the Canonization of Saints," *Transactions of the Royal Historical Society*, 27 (1945) 13-28. Idem, *Canonization and Authority in the Western Church* (Oxford, 1948). About more specialized aspects of canonization, see Bredero, *Études*, p. 13, n. 1 (17:16, n. 1) More recently A. Garcia, "A propos de la canonisation des saints au XIIe siècle," *Revue de Droit canonique* 18 (1968) 3-15.

20. Bredero, *Études*, pp. 147-9 (18:33-5).

An analysis of the documents in which St Bernard's canonization was explicitly mentioned was not made, as I have stated before. Its results might have been dubious. There are textual difficulties in such an analysis. For example, to what extent should one take literally the rather general phrasing in which these letters mention the merits and sanctity of St Bernard? Should they not be considered a more or less standardized manner of speaking, current in this kind of correspondence and derived from liturgical texts, as is clearly the case elsewhere? [21] Textual interpretation must therefore make reservations. The examination of St Bernard's canonization will profit more by a comparison with analogous situations in other canonizations. Thus, for example, from the correspondence for the canonization of St Edward the Confessor which was at last finalized in 1162, [22] one can conclude that Pope Alexander III announced St Bernard's canonization to the Church of France, to King Louis VII, and to the Cistercian Order, because they had supported the request for canonization which had been submitted by Clairvaux. [23] As appears from the correspondence connected with the earlier request for canonization for Edward the Confessor, the Pope wanted extensive support for the request; and this was afterwards obtained. [24]

It is therefore obvious that an explanation of St Bernard's canonization should commence with a general account of

21. See C. A. Bouman, *Sacring and Crowning* (Groningen, 1957) pp. 55-58, who notes the misunderstanding of medieval charters containing liturgical texts. In the hagiographic description of Saints we suppose an analogous misunderstanding about their virtues, enumerated in their *Lives*. Those enumerations, as indicated by H. Delehaye, *Les Légendes hagiographiques* (Brussels, 1927[3]) p. 24 (See also *Vita Bern*, III, I, 1; PL 185:303B-C) must be related to prayers as *Clementissime Deus* and *Omnipotens et misericors Deus*, (PL 138:1107), which belong to the monastic profession-ordinances. About those profession-ordinances see P. Hofmeister, "Benediktinische Professriten," *Studien und Mitteilungen zur Geschichte des Benedictinerordens* 74 (1963) 246-50.

22. B. W. Scholz, "The Canonization of Edward the Confessor," *Speculum* 36 (1961) 38-60.

23. *Ep. Alexandri pontificis ad Clarevallenses* "Placuit ergo nobis quod . . . canonizationem ipsius voto laudabili postulastis." (PL 185:624D).

24. Scholz, "The Canonization . . . ," p. 47. At the request of 1161 the Pope received thirteen petitions; ibid. 50.

canonizations of those days. In the light of this, familiar data
can be interpreted or new data can be found. One must also
bear in mind, however, that there were repeatedly special
reasons why a particular canonization was requested or granted. This fact has already been examined for the twelfth
century.[25] At that time, however, it was thought that it
might be misleading to look for motives for St Bernard's
canonization that were alien to his sanctity in the ecclesiastical sense.[26] Insofar as in this examination of motives for
cannonization attention was paid to the political backgrounds of those intentions, this supposition is correct. But
in canonizations where no princely interests were involved
and which clearly had a meaning within the Church (a concept that used to be rather popular), one need not exclude in
advance the notion that interest of a more profane nature
also played a role. The veneration of a saint honored God and
at the same time emphasized the value of the saint's example
for the faithful of later generations. It could however also
include profane interests by which some would profit more
than others. For this reason some attention must also be paid
to this aspect.

Canonization, at least formal canonization,[27] came about as
a means to check the veneration of saints which developed
from the cult of the martyrs of the early Church.[28] The term
canonizare in the sense of officially recognizing someone as a
saint dates only from the beginning of the eleventh centu-

25. M. Schwarz, "Heiligsprechungen im 12. Jahrhundert und die Beweggründe
ihrer Urheber," *Archiv für Kulturgeschichte* 39 (1957) 43-62.

26. Ibid., p. 58.

27. Next to the formal canonization, the official recognition of a saint after a
canonization process, there existed also the *canonizatio aequipollens*. This canonization certified an already longlasting cult of a saint, whose reputation of sanctity
had been commonly accepted. *Dictionnaire de droit canonique*, vol. 3 (Paris,
1942) p. 10. The canonization of Pope Gregory VII was an *aequipollens. Dictionnaire de Théologie catholique*, 21 (Paris, 1950) 1636-7. AA SS maii VI (ed. 1866)
p. 103. Compare J. N. A. M. Huijbregts, *Frankrijk en het officie van Gregorius VII*
(Tilbourg, 1968) pp. 24-28.

28. E. Kemp, *Canonization and Authority*, pp. 3-23. H. Delehaye, *Sanctus, essai
sur le culte des saints dans l'antiquité* (Brussels, 1927) 122-161.

ry.[29] The need for checking the cult of the saints was already felt in the early Church[30] but became more pressing in the Frankish Kingdom when the founding of new sanctuaries caused a great demand for relics. Meeting this demand sometimes led even to the veneration of entirely unknown saints whose life-stories were conjured up to give an appearance of authenticity to the proffered relics.[31] Formal canonization—entering a saint's name in a liturgical calender—counted then as a *nihil obstat* with regard to the liturgical action which recognized the sanctity of the person one wished to venerate. This involved the elevation or translation of the relics, i.e., the exhumation of a saint's body and its interment in an altar at his grave or its transfer to a sanctuary elsewhere. In those days permission for elevation or translation was given by a local bishop or a provincial council.[32]

The Pope's part in these episcopal canonizations was presumably limited to taking note of them, at least insofar as the bishops kept to this earlier usage.[33] Of a canonization in the eighth century it is known that the bishop concerned asked the Pope's opinion beforehand.[34] The first canonization to be initiated by the Pope himself, at least the first one for which a papal bull of canonization is known, took place

29. Kemp, *Canonization*, p. 58. J. F. Niermeyer, *Mediae Latinitatis Lexicon minus* (Leyde, 1960) p. 128; *Mittellateinisches Wörterbuch* 2 (Munich, 1969) p. 184.
30. Mansi, *Concilia* III, 145.
31. Kemp, *Canonization*, p. 23-39. Compare K. Schreiner, "Zum Wahrheitsverständnis im Heiligen-und Reliquienwesen des Mittelalters," *Saeculum* 17 (1966) p. 163 and n. 167.
32. R. Klauser, "Zur Entwicklung des Heiligsprechungsverfahrens bis zum 13. Jahrhundert," *Zeitschrift der Savignysiftung für Rechtsgeschichte,* (1954) p. 89.
33. The Acts of Saint Vigilis, a bishop of Trent who died about 405, mention: "Conscripta sunt autem gesta beati viri ab his, qui Martyrio ejus interfuerunt, gratiaque roborationis (ut mos erat) Papae Romano transmiserunt, ut sacris Martyrium memorialibus inserentur." AA SS junii VII, 147. It is, however, not certain that this text, at least in this version, dates from the fifth century. See *Dictionnaire de Spiritualité,* 2:77.
34. The *Passio Kilani,* written about 840, mentions that the relics of St Kilian and his fellow martyrs were translated in 752 by Burchard, bishop of Würzburg "cum consilio et praecepto Zachariae papae mediante Bonifatio archiepiscopo...." MGH SS *rerum merovingicarum* V, 728.

in 993 during a Lateran Council.[35] A large number of papal
canonizations are known to have taken place in the eleventh
and twelfth centuries.[36] This development can be ascribed to
the greater authority that the Popes acquired in the Latin
Church. This was reason enough for the Popes themselves to
exercise control over this important part of the devotional
practices of those days. The increase of the Pope's prestige,
on the other hand, led to the wish to have the veneration of a
saint recognized by the Pope, just as in other affairs people
liked to obtain ratification of their rights from him. A papal
canonization enhanced a saint's prestige.[37]

The exact moment of time at which canonization began to
belong to the Pope by right is not clear. Officially this right
was established in 1200 by Pope Innocent III,[38] but in fact
this was only a confirmation of an already existing right. In
the announcement of the translation of Godehard of
Hildesheim, whose canonization was requested of Pope Innocent II in 1131, a papal canonization was put as a con-
dition.[39] Whether this statement is correct may be doubted.
The local bishop withheld his own decision to canonize because of the Pope's presence in Liège at the time. This
circumstance offered the opportunity of obtaining a papal
canonization.[40] The motivation for the previous decision
mentioned in the prologue of this announcement also raises
doubts: "on account of the deceptiveness on the part of
demons, which do occur repeatedly in the church in such
matters."[41] The needed control over elevation or translation

35. PL 137:845. J-L 3848. This letter of Pope John XV, concerned the canonization of Ulrich of Augsburg, who died in 973.

36. Kemp, *Canonization*, pp. 56-81. Compare T. Klauser, "Die Liturgie der
Heiligsprechung," in O. Casel, *Heilige Ueberlieferung, Ausschnitte aus der
Geschichte des Mönchtums und des heiligen Kultus*, Beiträge zur Geschichte des
alten Mönchtums und des Benediktinerordens, Supplementband (Münster, 1938)
pp. 229-231.

37. Kemp, *Canonization*, p. 62.

38. Klauser, *Die Liturgie*, pp. 100-101.

39. MGH SS XII, 641.

40. Kemp, *Canonization*, pp. 74-5. The Pope, however, postponed the canonization until the great council at Reims in 1131 (J-L 7496).

41. MGH SS XII, 641. "Propter illusiones daemoniorum, quae frequenter in
aecclesia Dei in talibus contingerunt, statutum est. . . ."

of relics there mentioned was already entirely replaced by the requirement of preceding permission,[42] one moreover which no bishop wished to give merely on his own authority. The last episcopal canonization, the solemn translation of Walter of Pointoise in 1153, was so much a collegial event that one gets the impression that taking a decision to canonize became too much for an individual bishop.[43] This also explains why Pope Alexander III, who assumed great reserve towards requests for canonization that came to him,[44] had already reserved to himself, according to some, the right of canonization.[45]

In the course of this development of papal reservation, the process of canonization also took on a more precise form. Already at the first papal canonization, that of Ulrich of

42. The only known exception concerns the intention of Waldemar of Denmark in 1147 to translate the relics of his murdered father. This translation, however, was averted by the papal legate in Denmark, Eskil, the archbishop of Lund. Eskil not only opposed the institution of a cult which was not preceded by ecclesiastical approbation, but he even required authorization by the Pope. Kemp, *Canonization*, pp. 79.

43. This translation was performed by Hugh of Amiens, the archbishop of Rouen, and by the Bishops of Paris and Sens, while the Archbishop of Reims and many other bishops were present, as has been recorded by Hugh of Amiens in a letter to Pope Eugenius III. AA SS aprilis I, 763. The growing scruple of the bishops to proclaim a canonization on their own authority appears also from the canonization process of Arnulf of Soissons in 1120. *Vita S. Arnulphi*, III, 15, PL 174:1433-4. See Kemp, *Canonization*, pp. 71-4.

44. The many requests Alexander III received in 1162-3, when he visited France and took part in the council of Tours, were refused or postponed by him. Kemp, *Canonization*, p. 83.

45. This conclusion has been based on a passage in a letter by the Pope from 1171 or 1172 to the King of Sweden, which appears in the Decretals of Pope Gregory IX (*Audivimus*). The Pope asked that he not venerate as a saint a man who has been killed in drunkenness, giving as an argument: "Non liceret vobis pro sancto absque auctoritate Romanae Ecclesiae eum publice venerari." Kuttner, "La réserve papale . . . " (n. 19), pp. 215-9, refuted this conclusion and has been followed by Klauser, "Die Liturgie . . . ," pp. 99-100. But Kemp, *Canonization*, pp. 99-104, maintains "that Alexander's words . . . were an expression of what he believed was the law, possibly unwritten and customary, but still the law, about the papacy and canonization." Kemp may be right, but on the other hand he did not consider the growing tendency of the bishops themselves to avoid the responsibility for canonization. For the letter itself (PL 200:1261; J-L 13546) compare Sven Tunberg, "Erik den helige, Sveriges helgenkonung," *Fornvännen, Meddelanden fran K. Vittershets Historie och Antikvitets Akademien* (Stockholm) 36 (1941) 257-78.

Augsburg, one can distinguish the three parts that have remained essential in papal canonization: *petitio, informatio* and *publicatio*.[46] With time more and more was required in the *informatio,* and consequently also in the *petitio.* The change also led to a greater personal role for the Pope in the canonization. At first he decided on canonizations during councils, as appears from the canonization texts.[47] This remained the practice until Pope Innocent II's pontificate. Pope Eugene III dropped this custom at the canonization of Emperor Henry II in 1146, the only canonization promulgated by this Pope.[48] Officially Eugene wanted to keep to the democratic consultation of a council but in this case he deviated—according to his own words—from the custom because he wanted to be informed more extensively about the candidate.[49]

At first the information remained limited to an account of the candidate's life and miracles, which was presented to the council where, it was hoped, the request for canonization would be considered. The account was submitted mostly in writing, but also recounted by word of mouth. Petition was followed by deliberation and decision.[50] But already with Innocent II's last canonization the information process had developed. There was a request for the canonization of Sturmius, abbot of Fulda, who died in 779. It was dealt with at the Second Lateran Council in 1139. The *Vita* of Sturmius was read out, but separate testimony was given concerning the miracles that God had wrought after his death on account of this sanctity.[51]

Remarkable, too, is the reason given by Innocent on that occasion for his rejection of the request for canonization of

46. Klauser, "Die Liturgie . . . ," p. 91.

47. J-L 3848, 4112, 4219, 5677, 5762, 6239, *inter* 6797 et 6798, 7028, 7496, 7742, 8007.

48. Kemp, *Canonization,* p. 79.

49. PL 180:1118. J-L 8882. Kemp, *Canonization,* p. 81.

50. Bredero, *Etudes,* pp. 149-50 (18:34-6).

51. J-L 8007; PL 179:450: "attestatione fratrum nostrorum qui de partibus Teutonicis advenerant." Pope Urban II previously refused to grant a canonization, pointing out the difficulty to do so: "nisi et testes adsint qui ejus visa miracula suis oculis attestentur." Kemp, *Canonization,* p. 67.

Edward the Confessor. The translation of the King's body to Westminster had taken place in 1102, presumably with previous episcopal approval.[52] The request for canonization which reached Innocent II concerned, therefore, a papal confirmation after the fact of an episcopal canonization. Innocent did not grant it and his refusal was undoubtedly connected with the political complications of that moment over the dynasty in England.[53] The reason given by the Pope, however, was the lack of support from outside Westminster circles. An application in which more persons and groups were involved might have offered greater possibilities for information.[54]

Pope Eugene III also wanted wider information for the canonization he pronounced. Perhaps for that reason no further canonizations were held during his pontificate. Did this Pope forego canonizations during councils because the information remained too limited in such a procedure? Alexander III did not canonize during councils either. This has been explained as a consequence of the growth of papal authority, which sought greater independence in these matters.[55] But it is also possible that this was only an additional reason. That the Pope wanted wider information seems to me to be the kernel of this change of attitude regarding canonizations. The canonization of Edward the Confessor in 1161 and of Anselm of Canterbury in 1163 do not seem to confirm this supposition. Both canonizations had political meaning. Edward the Confessor's canonization in 1161 was partly a sign of Alexander III's gratitude to King Henry II for not

52. Ibid., pp. 76-7. Scholz, "The Canonization of Edward . . . ," (n. 22), p. 38, with n. 3. Osbert of Clare, the abbot of Westminster, asked the Pope for a solemn canonization; ibid., p. 40. The edition of *The Letters of Osbert of Clare,* by E. W. Williamson (London, 1929) was not available.

53. Kemp, *Canonization,* p. 78; Scholz, "The Canonization of Edward . . . ," pp. 47-8.

54. J-L 8182; PL 179, 568: " . . . quia, cum tanta festivitas debeat fieri ad honorem et profectum totius regni, ab omni regno pariter debet postulari." Kemp, 77, no. 6.

55. Kemp, *Canonization,* pp. 79-101.

siding with the antipope.[56] Anselm of Canterbury's canonization took place at the very moment when archbishop, Thomas à Becket, found himself up against Henry II, and so it allows the explanation that it was to support Becket in this conflict.[57]

However, at the canonization of Edward the Confessor the process of information was not neglected. Apart from the *liber miraculorum,* wrote Alexander III, he had also taken note of the letters by witnesses, which Innocent II had received at the time.[58] Thomas à Becket had requested the canonization of Anselm on the occasion of the Council of Tours. For this purpose a *Life* was submitted.[59] The Pope did not deal with the request there. But he did not delay it as he did other requests. Political expediency did not permit any postponement, and he decided to give Thomas à Becket freedom to act, albeit not unconditional freedom. The Archbishop of Canterbury had to take his decision in consultation with the bishops and abbots of England, whom he must convoke for this purpose.[60] In this case Alexander desisted from a canonization that allowed only limited information. He must also have wanted to avoid creating a new precedent for canonization during a council. But the alternative he chose and the conditions he attached show also that Alexander placed more importance on having wider information than on having a direct hand in forming the decision.

The canonization of Thomas à Becket in February, 1173, more than two years after he had been murdered, also points to the importance Alexander attached to information at the

---

56. Ibid., p. 82. Compare the letter of Gilbert Foliot, bishop of London, to Alexander III supporting the request of this canonization, especially the passage beginning with "apostolatum vestrum piissimus rex noster humili devotione suscipiat . . . "; PL 190:854.

57. Schwarz, *Heiligsprechungen im 12. Jahrhundert,* pp. 55-6.

58. J-L 10653; PL 200:107: "visis etiam litteris antecessoris nostri piae memoriae Innocentii papae, vestris quoque testimoniis inde receptis. . . ."

59. Kemp, *Canonization,* p. 83.

60. J-L 10886; PL 200:235-6. The letter dates from 9 June, 1163, when the council of Tours was nearly finished.

process. No written *Life* was available yet, but this did not seem to be an impediment.[61] It does not, however, imply that Alexander lacked information in this case. While after Thomas à Becket's murder there was an immediate outburst of popular devotion to his memory and stories of miracles at his tomb and by his intercession soon circulated, Alexander was reserved at first. In the letters in which he mentioned Becket previous to his canonization, he generally considered the murder an ordinary piece of violence.[62] The exception he made to this point of view[63] may indicate that in Alexander's personal opinion Thomas died a martyr, but that he waited for an official recognition of this until an examination of the recounted miracles had been set up; an examination delayed by King Henry II's attitude.[64]

This change in the role of information in the canonization process, which is important for our considerations, raises questions about the function of the written *Vita*. The only clear point about this is that, as a rule, a *Life* was available at canonizations. This was already the case at the first papal canonization in 993, and this is known also of other canonizations, including those of Nicolaus Peregrinus and Empress Adelaide by Pope Urban II at the end of the eleventh century. At the canonization of Peter Anagni by Paschal II a written *Life* was available, as also at the canonization by Pope Calixtus of Hugh of Cluny in 1120 and of Conrad of Constance and Gerard of Potenza in 1123.[65] We know too

---

61. There exist some early *Lives* of St Thomas à Becket, written shortly after his death, but the *terminus antequem* given for all those *Lives* has been placed after his canonization. E. Walberg, *La tradition hagiographique de Thomas Becket avant la fin du XIIe siècle,* (Paris, 1929). See also D. Knowles, *Thomas Becket* (Stanford, 1971) p. 172.

62. Kemp, *Canonization,* p. 87.

63. J-L 11891; PL 200:727. This letter of 14 May, 1171 was addressed to the archbishop of Tours.

64. For this reason John of Salisbury asked the archbishop of Sens to give witness at Rome: PL 199:359-61.

65. It was asked for instance in connection with the canonization of Conrad of Constance (1123) and of Peter of Tarentaise (1191); Kemp, *Canonization,* pp. 71 and 94.

that at these canonizations it was insisted that a written *Life* be submitted.[66]

At the canonization of Hugh of Grenoble by Pope Innocent II in 1134, however, no written *Life* was available, as was the case with Becket. A written *Life* was apparently not entirely indispensible for the informative process. At the canonization of Hugh of Grenoble, who had died only in 1132, the Pope and the attending archbishops, bishops and cardinals were satisfied with an oral account. The Pope did request from Guigo, prior of the Grand Chartreuse, who had applied for this canonization, that a *Life* be written.[67] The argument for this obligation imposed on Guigo tells a little more about the function of a written *Life* in a canonization process. At least in this case it served to bring out in greater relief the purpose of a canonization, i.e. granting permission to venerate someone as a saint. The *Life* of Hugh of Grenoble had to be written, so that God might be honored in this saint, and the clergy when reading it and the people when hearing it would give thanks to God and obtain forgiveness of sins through the intercession of the saint.[68] Therefore there was a demand for a *Life* at the canonization not only to give the reasons why someone ought to be canonized, but also to show the significance of that person regarding his veneration as a saint. Could this veneration be effected by a written *Life*? [69]

Already long before control over the veneration of saints had become a matter reserved to the Pope, the *Life* of a saint

66. See Kemp, *Canonization,* pp. 56-71. Bredero, *Etudes,* p. 149, n. 5 (18:35, n. 1). T. Klauser, "Die Liturgie . . . ," pp. 229-31.

67. Kemp, p. 67.

68. J-L 7742; PL 179:256: "Quia igitur ipsius vita, quam pie duxit in corpore, et miraculorum coruscatio, qua Deus eum facit apud homines praefulgere, tuae maxime dilectioni non exstant incognita, auctoritate B. Petri et nostra tibi mandamus, quatenus ea quae tibi super hoc nota fuerint, diligenter describendo posterum memoriae tradas: ut et Deus honoretur in sancto, et clerus legens, ac populus audiens, gratias agant Domino, atque ipsius intercessione peccatorum veniam percipere mereantur."

69. This intention was demonstrated by Marbod of Rennes, who composed the *Life* of Robert, the first abbot of Chaise-Dieu († 1067). In his prologue Marbod remarks: "cum gesta sanctorum ob hoc litteris mandentur, ut omnium legentium, vel audentium ad imitandum accendatur intentio. . . ." PL 171:1506.

had had a part to play in his veneration. Was it not above all an edifying text that contributed to the veneration of a saint by recounting his way of life and the miracles wrought at his grave or through his intercession? Already in the eleventh century the *Life* functioned in this way.[70]

For this task hagiography developed a literary genre of its own, partly biographical, partly panegyrical and partly moralizing.[71] Therefore a *Life* was written according to a fixed form, and treated of the saint before he was born, his country, parents and the prodigious announcement of his future greatness. Then it told of his birth, youth, deeds, virtues and miracles, and finally it mentioned the miracles after his death and the veneration he received. This pattern did have variations according to whether the saint were a bishop, an abbot, a monk, or a nun,[72] but underlying each separate model was the *commune hagiographicum*, adapted to the concrete situation.[73]

When the *Life* was submitted together with the request for canonization, this character was maintained, and even demanded. This is clear from the canonization of Ulrich of Augsburg in 993. The *Life* written by his friend Gerard appeared not to comply with this pattern and therefore an entirely newly *Life*, which satisfied the conventional norms,

70. B. De Gaiffier (d'Hestroy), "L'hagiographie et son public au XIe siècle," *Miscellanea van der Essen*, 2 vols. (Brussels-Paris, 1947), 1:138 (repr. in B. De Gaiffier, *Etudes critiques d'Hagiographie et d'Iconologie* [Brussels, 1967] pp. 477-8), concerning the growing need to have a written *Life* of those who were venerated as saints: "Ce n'est pas le lieu d'insister sur la pieuse avidité avec laquelle les fidèles d'alors recherchaient les souvenirs matériels de leurs patrons célestes. Mais il fallait pourtant la mentionner ici, parce qu'elle est l'un des facteurs qui ont le plus contribué au développement de l'hagiographie proprement dite. Tout se tient, en effect, dans la psychologie de ces âmes saintes. La foi en la vertu surnaturelle des reliques fait naître le désir d'en posséder. Ce désir exaucé tôt ou tard amenait, en se réalisant, l'institution d'une fête, et celle-ci, pour être célébrée selon tous les rites, rendait nécessaire la rédaction d'une vie out tout au moins d'une légende à lire à l'office."

71. L. Delehaye, *Les Légendes hagiographiques*, p. 64.

72. Ibid., p. 92.

73. Ibid., pp. 94-96. See Bredero, *Etudes*, pp. 130, n. 3 and 144 with n. 3 (18:16, n. 2 and 29, with n. 10).

had to be submitted.[74] Insofar as the judgment on a *Life* in a process of canonization was aimed at its fostering veneration of the saint, this judgment still emphasized the accepted hagiographical form. The heroic character of the virtue practised, which counted as a criterion of true sanctity,[75] was perhaps more emphasized, the enumeration of virtues and miracles became more systematized and the latter were, at times, even subdivided according to kinds.

The authenticity of what was told did not take first place in this judgment. That was settled by appealing to *viros auctoritabiles,* so strong in the Middle Ages. In a prologue, or sometimes an epilogue, the greater trustworthiness of oral tradition and of the testimony which had been given to the author was pointed out.[76] In this regard there is a statement by Pope Calixtus II made at the canonization of Conrad of Constance concerning the tradition of miracles wrought by this saint.[77] Yet the change which the informative process

74. H. M. Mikoletsky, "Sinn und Art der Heiligung im fruhen Mittelalter," *Mitteilungen des Instituts für Oesterreichtsforschung* 57 (1949) p. 119. The *Life* of Gerard was published in MGH SS IV, 384-425. See Bredero, p. 151, n. 1. (18:37, n. 1).

75. R. Hofmann, *Die heroische Tugend, Geschichte und Inhalt eines theologischen Begriffes* (Munich, 1933), pp. 133-54: "Die Bedeutung der heroischen Tugend in der kirchlichen Kanonisation."

76. L. Delehaye, *Les Légendes hagiographiques,* p. 69. An appeal to oral tradition as testimony of the holiness of their heroes is given by many authors of hagiographic Lives. Of saints canonized in the eleventh and twelfth centuries we found such an appeal in the Lives of Simeon Padolirono (canonized in 1016: AA SS julii VI, 324), of Bononius, abbot of Lucedio (canonized about 1026: AA SS aug. IV, 630), of Romuald (canonized 1032: AA SS febr. II, 106; this *Life* was written by Peter Damian), of Simeon, a recluse near Trier (canonized 1042; MGH SS VII, 209), of Wiborada, a recluse near St Gallen (canonized 1047: MGH SS IV, 446), of Deodat of Nevers (canonized 1049: *Analecta Bollandiana* 16 [1887]: 160), of Gerard of Toul (canonized 1050: MGH SS IV, 490), of Wolfgang of Regensburg (cnzd 1052: MGH SS IV, 525), of Godelava, martyr of Ghistelles (cnzd 1084: AA SS julii II, 404), of Arnulf of Soissons (cnzd 1120; AA SS aug. III, 230), of Godehard of Hildesheim (cnzd 1131: MGH SS XI, 169 and 197), and of Sturmius, abbot of Fulda (cnzd 1139: MGH SS II, 366). In the prologue to the *Life* of Edward the Confessor, written about 1160 by Aelred of Rievaulx on the occasion of the second request for canonization when the informative process had already changed, the author made an appeal to written evidence: PL 195:740.

77. J-L 7028; PL 163:1274: "miracula quae per eum a Deo facta dicuntur, si vera sunt, scripturis et lectionibus memoriter deinceps teneantur."

underwent in the process of canonization in the twelfth century, especially during the reigns of Eugene III and Alexander III, influenced the manner in which *Lives* were written. As long as the information process was of short duration and took place at a council, whether it was preceded by a hearing of witnesses or not, a *Life* was judged on its ability to edify. This judgment was maintained, but with more lengthy informative process made possible if canonization were held outside a council, it was also possible to judge the authenticity of what was recounted in the *Life*. Such a change of mentality is typical of the period in which the change in the informative process occurred.

The result of this new consideration of the information in the process of canonization was that a *Life* was judged by two possibly contradictory norms: its ability to edify and the correctness of what it told. The second norm, however, caused the omission of possible reference by which miracle stories could be checked. Considering the relationship between the *Vita prima sancti Bernardi* and his canonization, this work appears in its textual development as a rather accurate reflection of the consequences which the change in the informative process had on a *Life* written for the process of canonization. This reflection is particularly related to the fact that those requesting the canonization realized the changing circumstances only after they had sent in a first request for canonization.

The initiative for a canonization came from the applicants who prepared the *petitio* by writing a *Life*. Then they put together a dossier which was presented when they submitted the request. The dossier submitted when St Bernard's canonization was requested consisted of the *Vita prima* and perhaps also his writings. The revision of the text which these writings underwent after his death at Clairvaux contains some indications for this.[78] The *Vita prima* was written during the same

---

78. J. Leclercq, *Recueil d'études sur saint Bernard et ses écrits* I (Rome, 1962) pp. 245-251: "Recherches sur les sermons sur les cantiques V, La recension de Clairvaux." In this recension of Clairvaux there has, for instance, been omitted a passage of a letter, which could be interpreted as disgraceful. Idem, *Etudes sur S. Bernard et le texte de ses écrits*, ASOC (1953) p. 90.

time and its first aim was the preparation of a *petitio,* with which the process of canonization could commence. As a matter of fact, the writing of this *Vita* had already been started during the lifetime of St Bernard. The first book was written by William of St Thierry, who had died in 1148. In this book he had inserted biographical fragments collected for the purpose by Geoffrey of Auxerre,[79] Bernard's secretary at that time. William had used these fragments in such a way that St Bernard's sanctity stood out clearly.[80] At the same time this writing was an apology. William had defended St Bernard against criticism from contemporaries; whoever condemned him, fell short of sanctity, because the life and deeds of this abbot could not be understood except by those who lived up to the norms of his sanctity.[81] Between the lines William made it clear that St Bernard's way of acting had sometimes aroused opposition,[82] but at the same time he denied that the abbot had had enemies.[83] The expertise with which William wrote his share of the *Life* is especially clear from the fact that the schematic character becomes visible only by comparing his text to the third book of the *Vita prima.* The author of that book, Geoffrey of Auxerre, resumed St Bernard's biography in such manner that the obligatory character of the underlying scheme remains clearly visible. This is notably the case in his illustrations of Bernard's virtue.[84]

The other books of the *Vita Prima* were written after St Bernard's death. The Benedictine Abbot, Ernauld of Bonneval, wrote the second book and Geoffrey of Auxerre wrote the last three. They divided the task and were probably writing at the same time.[85] Ernauld of Bonneval dealt with St Bernard's political activities, particularly during the papal

79. R. Lechat, "Les Fragmenta de Vita et miraculis S. Bernardi par Geoffroy d'Auxerre," *Anal. Boll.* 50 (1932) 89-122.
80. Bredero, *Etudes,* pp. 104-7 (17:249-251).
81. *Vita Bern,* I, IV, 19; PL 185:237.
82. Bredero, *Etudes,* pp. 107-8 (17:251-2).
83. *Vita Bern,* I, XIV, 71; PL 185:266. See above, p. 000, n. 32.
84. Bredero, *Etudes,* p. 136 (18:22).
85. Ibid., p. 112 (17:256).

schism of 1130-1138. His stories of miracles were limited to the exorcisms which St Bernard performed during that time.[86] Geoffrey started with the last book, an account of St Bernard's last years and death. He sent its first version for criticism to Eskil, archbishop of Lund and a great admirer of St Bernard.[87] As papal delegate in Denmark, Eskil had already been involved in efforts for canonization[88] and perhaps the text was also sent to him to judge its value in connection with a request for canonization. This supposition is based on the circumstance that this first version of the final book of the *Vita* already contained the letter St Bernard was to have sent from his deathbed to Ernauld of Bonneval. One may assume that this letter is not really one of St Bernard's but that it was composed after his death to give the impression that there had been such a close relationship between the Abbots of Clairvaux and Bonneval, that Ernauld's cooperation with the *Vita prima* was implicitly justified.[89]

To what extent the intention of having St Bernard canonized was present already at the composition of the first book cannot be determined exactly. This book did clearly have the intention of venerating Bernard as a saint, a matter implicitly demanded for a canonization. Such an intention is clear from the division of tasks made by the authors in the other books. This was true from the time of the first version of the fifth book, because it already contained the letter to Ernauld of Bonneval. The final editing of the last three books also indicates such an intention. A manuscript from the scriptorium of Anchin, a Benedictine abbey that had close contact with Clairvaux, has a preface for the last three books.[90] In it a number of bishops and abbots present themselves gathered at

86. Ibid., pp. 114-5 (17:258-9).

87. Bredero, "Un brouillon du XIIe siècle, l'autographe de Geoffroy d'Auxerre," *Scriptorium* 13 (1959) 32-3.

88. Kemp, *Canonization*, p. 79.

89. This opinion, given hypothetically in my *Etudes*, pp. 109-11 (17:254-6), has been confirmed by the manuscript tradition of this letter. See J. Leclercq, "Lettres de S. Bernard: histoire ou littérature? " *Studi Medievali*, 3rd séries 12 (1971).

90. Douai, Bibliothèque municipal ms 372. See Bredero, *Etudes*, pp. 40 and 118 with n. 2 (17:43 and 18:4, with n. 5).

Clairvaux shortly after St Bernard's death to prepare this text.[91] As there can be no doubt that Geoffrey of Auxerre was that actual author of these books, this preface must be considered a special form of the usual appeal to persons of authority, whose authority had to guarantee the credibility of what was said. The preface says these bishops and abbots who presented themselves as the authors had kept close contact with St Bernard during his last years. Thus this preface gives a clear indication of the aim with which this *Life* was written; it sought to bring about St Bernard's canonization.

One of the bishops who took part in this meeting was the Eskil mentioned above. A textual analysis of the fourth book makes it evident that during this meeting additions were made to the account of the miracles wrought by St Bernard during his life, by the archbishop of Lund.[92] Therefore Eskil appears to have been closely connected with the preparation for canonization. This clarifies the reason why the first version of the fifth book was sent to him, although according to Geoffrey's introductory letter it was sent to Eskil to inform him about St Bernard's death.[93] When Geoffrey wrote this text, the arrangement for a division of tasks between him and Ernald of Bonneval had already been made, for the report to Eskil contained the letter that St Bernard was said to have written on his deathbed to Ernauld.[94] This fact and

---

91. Ibid., p. 40 (17:43): "Post beati patris nostri Bernardi Clarevallensis abbatis excessum ad ipsius memoriam filiali devotione convenimus nos episcopi et abbates, qui in horam usque novissimam, indigni licet, sacris eius vestigiis adherentes, quod de illo homine Dei hominibus innotescere potuit plenius et perfectius tam nostra ipsorum experientia diuturna, quam illius erga nos speciale dignatione cognovimus. Unde etiam visus est nobis oportere ex hiis aliqua posteris servanda litteris commendari, et ex tanto convivio, quo nimirum ad Domini benedictionem omnis nostra generatio sit refecta, modica saltem fragmenta colligi, ne perirent. . . ."

92. Vita Bern, IV, 24-25; PL 185:334-5. Bredero, *Études,* p. 120, n. 3 (18:6, n. 6).

93. From this introductory letter it also appears that Eskil had already been informed about the death of St Bernard before he received this report from Geoffroy: "Scio, scio iam pervenit ad aures vestras, iam pervenit ad cor, et vestram ipsius animam gladius iste pertransiit, eo siquidem atrocius quo firmius adheserat sancte illi anime que migravit." Bredero, "Un brouillon du XIIe siècle . . . ," *Scriptorium* 13, p. 32.

94. Ibid., p. 39 Ep 310; PL 182:514.

Eskil's share in the final editing of the first version of the *Vita prima* explain why the account of the end of St Bernard's life was sent to Eskil. Not only need Eskil be informed about it, but he must be involved in the canonization which he indeed proved willing to be, considering his share in the final editing of the first version.

Between the completion of the canonization dossier in 1155-1156[95] and the submission of the first request in 1163 lies a lapse of at least seven years. Before 1163 no opportune moment apparently offered itself for the submission of the request. No canonizations took place during the pontificate of Hadrian IV (1154-1159). From the calendar of this Pope's documents it is not apparent that he convoked or visited any council on the occasion of which a request could have been dealt with, if he wanted to continue the old procedure of canonization left by Eugene III. Moreover his pontificate was very much occupied with political difficulties in Italy, with the city of Rome (Arnold of Brescia), with Frederick Barbarossa, and with Roger of Sicily.[96] Neither are there any indications that Hadrian IV had close relations with the Cistercian Order. Papal documents for Cistercian abbeys, which at that time did not as yet enjoy the papal privilege of exemption, were hardly numerous in that period. Neither Cîteaux nor Clairvaux received a papal confirmation of their possessions or their rights.[97]

At first Alexander III's pontificate offered no opportunity of submiting a request for canonization. The beginning of this pontificate was difficult, because Alexander had been elected and recognized only by the cardinals opposed to the

---

95. Bredero, *Etudes,* pp. 120-1 (18:6-8).

96. R. Foreville, "Le pontificat d'Adrien IV," in A. Fliche et V. Martin, *Histoire de l'Eglise,* IX 2 (Paris, 1948) pp. 5-49.

97. The charters of this Pope on behalf of Cistercian monasteries are: J-L 9962 and 9991 (Savigny, 1154-5), 10189 (exemption of tithes in the bishopric Halberstadt, 1156), 10212 (Fountains, 1156), 10252 (Zwett, 1157), 10260 (confirmation of Cistercian institutions), 10275, 10374, 10379, (Pontigny, 1157-8), 10529 (Igny, 1157-9), 10550 (Buillon, 1159) and *Chartes et documents de l'abbaye cistercienne de Preuilly,* ed. A. Cavel and M. Lecomte (Montereau, 1927) pp. 42-3:XLVI (confirmation of possessions and privileges, granting of papal protection).

Emperor. He was the leader of this group. The pro-Emperor group—actually a majority—had chosen its own leader beforehand in order to avoid having to join a minority decision. Especially during the first years it was necessary for Alexander to prevent the Antipope Victor IV from being recognized outside the German Empire.[98] Choosing between either of the candidates was onerous for several religious orders which had monasteries inside and outside the German Empire. Thus Hugh of Montlhéry as abbot of Cluny chose Victor IV—which led to his forced resignation in 1163.[99] The Cistercians, who had many monasteries within the territory of the German Empire, nevertheless chose sides with Alexander III from the very start.[100] Their attitude during the schism recalled for their contemporaries memories of St Bernard's attitude during the years 1130-1138, during the schism of Anacletus II.[101]

This good relationship between Alexander III and the Cistercians opened up opportunities for a canonization request. The opportune moment came when Alexander wanted to have his election as Pope confirmed at the Council of Tours in 1163. Another important fact is that in 1162, the year in which Alexander went to France, Geoffrey of Auxerre returned as abbot to Clairvaux, which he had left in 1159 to become abbot of Igny. The initiative for a request had to come from those who possessed his mortal remains. It is not known whether Geoffrey was appointed abbot for this reason. This is not improbable, for his appointment was made possible by the appointment of the then abbot of Clairvaux, Fastred, to Citeaux.[102]

98. See Fliche - Martin, IX, 2, pp. 50-62.

99. *Bibliotheca Cluniacensis,* ed. M. Marrier (Paris, 1614; repr. Macon, 1815) p. 1660. G. De Valous, *Le monachisme clunisien* 2 vols. (Paris, 1935; repr. Paris, 1970) 1:94, n. 1.

100. M. Preiss, *Die politische Tätigkeit und Stellung der Cisterzienser im Schisma von 1159-1177,* Historische Studien 248 (Berlin, 1934) p. 27 ff.

101. Walter Map, *De nugis curialium* II, 3, ed. M. R. James (Oxford, 1914), p. 65. Pope Alexander himself praised the attitude of the Cistercians in a letter of 1169; J-L 11633, PL 200:594-5.

102. *Chronicon Clarevallense,* PL 185:1247.

The request was submitted to the Pope during his stay in Paris, where he had come from Tours in the beginning of 1163. His stay there lasted till the opening of the council at the end of April. The identity of the applicants can not be discovered from the later announcement of this first request.[103] One may suppose that among them were Cistercian bishops, like Louis VII's younger brother, Henry of France, who had been elected archbishop of Rheims in 1162, and Peter, bishop of Tarentaise.[104] Also Henri Moricotti, who had become a cardinal in 1153 and acted as papal delegate under Alexander in France and Germany.[105] Possibly also other bishops were present such as Geoffrey of Langres and Alan of Auxerre. In addition, a number of Cistercian abbots were among the applicants, including Fastred of Cîteaux, who died in Paris on 21 April, 1163[106] and of course Geoffrey of Auxerre who also took part in the council.[107] The presence of other Cistercian abbots at this request for the canonization, especially those of Savigny, Merci-Dieu, Beaupré, Mortemer, Châtillon near Verdun, and Vaux-de-Cernay can be deduced from the privileges which Alexander III granted to these abbeys during his stay in Paris. The abbot of Haute-Combe may have been present, because he was the liaison between the Pope and Henry of France.[108]

The applicants, conscious of the significance of their Order

103. Pope Alexander indicated them as "magni quidam ac venerabiles viri"; PL 185:622.

104. Henry, who was in 1159 still bishop of Beauvais, became archbishop of Reims in 1162. His election reinforced of the position of Alexander III in France. Preiss, *Die politische,* p. 48. Evidence for the presence of Peter of Tarentaise, who supported Alexander especially at the outbreak of the schism, is only given in a general record about the participation of bishops at the council of Tours in the *Historica Vizeliacensis monasterii,* PL 194:1636.

105. During the period 1162-1167 he signed as a witness the letters of Alexander III; J-L II, p. 145. But his name is lacking in the privileges granted to Cistercians abbeys.

106. He received Extreme Unction from the Pope himself. *Chronicon Clarevallense,* PL 185:1248.

107. At least he gave a sermon there to the assembled prelates. J. Leclercq, "Les écrits de Geoffroy d'Auxerre," in *Recueil d'études sur S. Bernard et ses écrits* 1:41.

108. Preiss, *Die politische,* pp. 56-7.

at that time for Pope Alexander III, must have expected that
the canonization would come up at the Council of Tours. At
first the Pope was said to be willing to grant their request.
But the large quantity of requests for canonizations he received *in diversis provinciis* made him decide to delay.[109] The
way in which the Pope settled the request for the canonization of St Anselm of Canterbury raises some doubt, however,
about the rightness or at least the completeness of the reason
Alexander III gave for delaying the canonization of St Bernard. The large number of requests was presumably a welcome excuse to decide against dealing with requests for
canonization at this council, but the actual reason was rather
the unsatisfactory way in which such processes of canonization had to be conducted. The informative process could not
have that extensiveness that it had acquired during the reign
of Eugene III.

This cause for delay in the case of St Bernard was not missed
by the applicants. The close connection of several applicants
with the Pope make this probable. Geoffrey of Auxerre, who
also attended the council, must surely have noticed it.
After this rejection, he began to revise the text of the *Vita
prima*. There may have been other reasons for this revision,
such as the objections of some of his Order against the
arrogance shown in this *Life* toward some people of standing.
But as the revision of the text took place in connection with
the refusal to deal with the canonization request at a council,
he had to adapt the *Vita* to a different sort of informative
process. At the new request the examination would be
directed not only at the ability of this text to foster veneration of St Bernard, or in other words, to what extent this
Life might bring about the purpose of the canonization. The
informative process would now also consider the correctness
of the contents, which nonetheless had to be written according to fixed forms and norms.

Geoffrey's changes in the text, mentioned before, have

109. PL 185:622. "Cumque nos eidem negotio favorabili satis intenderemus
affectu, supervenit multitudo et frequentia petitorum, qui in diversis provinciis
rem similem postulabant."

been understood by many as expressions of a more critical attitude on his part. These changes are twofold in their nature: partly literary and partly in contents. Of the manuscripts that have handed down of the text of the *Vita prima* some give the old version, *recensio A,* and some give the new version, *recensio B.* In some manuscripts, however, neither the old nor the new version appears to have been followed completely, so that one may here speak of an inter-recension, in which the revision of the text has been taken over only partly.[110] An inter-recension is also found in the manuscript that originates from Anchin. As this manuscript was produced in the scriptorium of Anchin when the revision of the text was still being made at Clairvaux,[111] this inter-recension offers a picture of what was considered of primary and what of secondary importance in the revision of the text. Thus it appears that the literary changes were incidental.[112]

The changes of the contents of the text do indeed show that in *recensio B* of the *Vita prima* more prudence was observed in regard to the great of this world and persons of repute.[113] But not all the textual changes referring to these persons have been made solely out of respect for them. The omission of mention of the prophecies by St Bernard regarding some of them can not be explained by prudence, but rather by Geoffrey's preoccupation with making the contests of the text less verifiable in concrete details. Prominent persons who were mentioned by name could be heard as witnesses if they were still living.[114] The same attitude determined which stories of cures were omitted in

110. See above n. 90 for the Anchin ms. The other mss, following a partial revision of the first recension of the *Vita prima,* are Lincoln, Cathedral Chapter library, 222 (fol. 11-72[r]), London, Lambeth Library 163 (fol. 6-71[r]), Paris Bibl. Nat., fonds latin, 2042 (fol. 103[r]-126[r]) and Vatican, Regina latina 145 (25[r]-89[v]). See Bredero, *Etudes,* pp. 19 et 26 (17:23 and 29-30).

111. Ibid., p. 118, n. 2 (17:4, n. 5).

112. Ibid., p. 146 with n. 9 (18:32 with n. 3). The stylistic corrections, belonging to this revision and enumerated *ibidem,* 142, n. 3 (18:28, n. 1), were not yet included in the Anchin manuscript.

113. Ibid., p. 146 (18:31).

114. Ibid., p. 145 (18:30).

recensio B. In some instances only the name of the witness was withheld, while the story was retained.[115]

In other respects *recensio B* showed greater discretion, too. The exact location where a cure happened was sometimes omitted. Mention of the basilica where the head of the martyr Ceasarius was kept as a relic or where St Germaine lay buried could carry with it the risk that the related miracle might be ascribed to the power of these saints.[116] Thus data which might minimize St Bernard's sanctity were removed from *recensio B.* For that reason also the account of some cures were changed in such a way that they no longer had a gradual effect, but an immediate one.[117] Besides it is also remarkable that a newly added passage, the vision of William of Montpellier in which St Bernard's heavenly bliss was made known to this Grandselve monk during the night of Bernard's death, agreed with the aim of this revision. For it may be assumed that William of Montpellier died about 1162.[118] Another proof of prudence in *recensio B* was the omission of the story of how on his own initiative St Bernard venerated a deceased bishop as a saint.[119]

Geoffroy did not seem quite consistent in this respect. For with regard to Malachy, bishop of Armagh, who died and was buried at Clairvaux, Geoffrey did not mention how St Bernard was premature in venerating this bishop as a saint.[120] But here other motives played a role. St Bernard himself had written the *Vita Malachiae,*[121] which implied that he desired his canonization. When revising the text Geoffrey realized

115. E. g., Vita Bern, III, VI, 19 and IV, VIII, 48; See Bredero, *Etudes,* pp. 43 and 50 (17:46 and 53).

116. Vita Bern, IV, I, 3 and VII, 43; See Bredero, *Etudes,* pp. 44 and 50 (17:47 and 53) and also, ibid., p. 146 with n. 7 (18:32, with n. 1).

117. E.g., Vita Bern, I, XI, 54 and IV, VII, 40; Bredero, *Etudes,* pp. 33 and 49-50 (17:36 and 52).

118. Vita Bern, V, III, 22; Bredero, *Etudes,* p. 55 (17:58).

119. Ibid., IV, III, 21; Bredero, p. 47 (17:50).

120. Bredero, *Etudes,* p. 159 with n. 2 (18:44, with n. 4). There I still supposed that at the first request for the canonization of St Bernard in 1163 a request for St Malachi was added. But the way St Malachi was mentioned in the first recension is too dispersed to justify such a supposition.

121. OB 3:307-378.

that the relationship between St Bernard and St Malachy opened up new perspectives. If St Bernard were canonized, it meant that St Malachy should also be canonized, because St Bernard acknowledged him as a saint. At the request for canonization in 1173, the canonization of St Malachy was also requested, as appears from Tromund's letter to Abbot Gerard. But Pope Alexander III was apparently not prepared to follow this line of thought so the request for Malachy had to be dropped.[122]

In *recensio B,* other passages were also omitted which support the supposition of a more critical attitude on the part of Geoffrey of Auxerre. Among these were the rather extreme temptation against St Bernard's chastity, told by William of Thierry,[123] and an exorcism recounted by Ernauld of Bonneval.[124] In omitting these passages, Geoffrey did indeed display a critical attitude regarding some stock stories from the *commune hagiographicum.*[125] These stories were too common knowledge, and mentioning them might have detracted from the credibility of the *Vita prima.*[126] For the same reason the description of the modesty with which St Bernard as a babe had sucked at his mother's breast[127] was omitted from Burchard of Balerne's epilogue to the first book of the *Vita.*

Thus a seemingly critical attitude displayed by Geoffrey in *recensio B* may be explained also from the development of the informative process. To presuppose in him a desire for historical reliability for the sake of later generations and to propose this to explain the changes in the text, is to attribute qualities to him which are not proper to his times. There were various reasons for the changes in the text of the *Vita*

122. *Epistola Tromundi:* "Quod autem de sancto Malachia opus simile aggredi praetermissimus, consilio factum est principis sacerdotum, qui praemonuit nos in ipsa sermonis origine fieri posse de pluralitate fastidium, quod etiam in uno intentionis nostrae frustraret effectum." PL 185:626.
123. Vita Bern, I, III, 6; Bredero, *Etudes,* pp. 28-9 (17:31-32).
124. Ibid., II, VI, 34; Bredero, p. 38 (17:41).
125. Bredero, *Etudes,* p. 143 (18:29).
126. Ibid., p. 144 (18:30).
127. Ibid., p. 35 (17:38).

prima, such as the need for literary corrections and a greater
prudence toward people of authority, but these qualities are
secondary compared to the necessity for Geoffrey to take
into account the changed information required in the process
of canonization. Had Geoffrey really aimed at greater
historical reliability, he should have removed many other
passages derived from the *commune hagiographicum.*[128]
    There might be an indication that Geoffrey would have
gone further in revising the text if he had not been forced to
resign as abbot of Clairvaux in 1165.[129] However, the textual
change concerned, occuring in a manuscript from Cîteaux
where Geoffrey lived until 1171, is too incidental and is too
much concerned with the glory that befell St Bernard after
his death, for this conclusion to be drawn.[130] In any case,
Geoffrey had no opportunity to make further revisions in the
way he had made them at Clairvaux. For this he depended on
a scriptorium which worked along his lines and where the
assistants were attuned to what he desired. He himself had
built up such a stable working force at Clairvaux before going
to Igny that on his return in 1162 he apparently found it still
intact.[131] Supposing he had found a scriptorium so equipped
at Cîteaux, it would still be doubtful whether he would have
been given the opportunity to make further changes in the
text. For the forced abdication of Geoffroy was not uncon-
nected with the objections which this work had evoked on
the part of some of his Order.
    This question concerns our subject too much for us to pass
by without noticing the reasons for Geoffroy's resignation.
His forced retirement was followed by an attempt to push
aside the *Vita prima* and to have it replaced by a new text,

---

128. Ibid., p. 144, n. 3 (18:29, n. 7). See above, n. 21.
    129. About this abdication, see M. Preiss, *Die politische Tätigkeit und Stellung
der Cistercienser im Schisma von 1159-1177,* pp. 84-92. S. Lenssen, "L'Abdication
du bienheureux Geoffroy comme abbé de Clairvaux," *Collectanea OCR* 17 (1955)
98-110.
    130. Vita Bern, V, III, 23; Bredero, *Etudes,* p. 56 (17:59). See ibid., p. 141, n. 1
(18:26, n. 7).
    131. Bredero, *Etudes,* pp. 26, n. 4 and 140 with n. 5 (17:29, n. 5 and 18:26,
with n. 3).

the *Vita secunda.* Although Alan of Auxerre, the author of this new text, played a considerable part in bringing about Geoffrey's abdication, it has never previously been connected with the opposition existing in the Order to the *Vita prima* and its author. It was usually supposed that Pope Alexander III wished this resignation for the benefit of the English Cistercian monasteries[132] because of Geoffrey's dealings in the conflict between Becket and Henry II.

After leaving England at the end of 1164 the Archbishop of Canterbury clearly had the support of Alexander III. He also had followers within the Cistercian Order, at least he stayed at Pontigny until November, 1166.[133] On the other hand, Geoffrey is supposed to have dissociated himself from Becket's point of view because the then abbot of Cîteaux, Gilbert, an Englishman, had promised King Henry that the Order would keep aloof from the conflict.[134] When the conflict came to a head, Geoffrey's action was apparently not appreciated. Attesting to this is a remark made by Alexander III in a letter to the Abbot of Citeaux to the effect that, according to reliable information received by the Pope from many people, Geoffrey had caused great damage to his abbey because, as a restul of his behavior, he no longer had the same confidence of kings and rulers which his predecessors had had.[135] Concrete data which would make this interpretation acceptable are lacking.[136] Moreover, it is supposed also that the initiative for this forced resignation came from Alexander III because the Abbot of Cîteaux was apparently simply not inclined to bring about the resignation desired by the

---

132. Preiss, *Die politische,* p. 88; S. Lenssen, "L'Abdication," p. 103, has some doubts.

133. R. Foreville, *L'Eglise et la Royauté en Angleterre sous Henri II Plantagenet,* (Paris, 1943) p. 175.

134. Ibid., Preiss, p. 87; Lenssen, p. 106.

135. J-L, 11169; PL 200:349. The explications of Preiss and Lenssen fail to explain why the Pope took action against Geoffrey and not against Gilbert, the abbot of Cîteaux, who instigated this concessive policy.

136. This interpretation is based upon the part that Geoffrey played in 1169 as intermediary to reconcile the Archbishop and the King. Preiss, pp. 106-111; Lenssen, pp. 106-7.

Pope.[137] But the Pope stated explicitly in his letter that
many complaints about Geoffrey's conduct had reached him,
and he mentioned as his advisors in this matter the archbishop of Rheims, Henry of France, and Alan, bishop of
Auxerre.[138]

We know the last as the author of the *Vita secunda*. In
the preface to his text Alan remarked that a lack of reverence
had been shown toward ecclesiastical and secular authorities
in what earlier had been written about St Bernard.[139] Actually we see here an objection to Geoffrey of Auxerre similar to
that in Alexander III's letter to Gilbert, abbot of Cîteaux. As
the Pope stated that he acted on complaints from others, it is
natural to suppose that the initiative to make Geoffrey resign
originated from Cistercian circles. There is also reason to
suppose that objections to the *Vita prima* were at the bottom
of this. In any case it appears that after the revision of the
text of the *Vita prima* a new request for canonization failed
to materialize, but then after Geoffrey's resignation a new
Life was written.

In this complicated affair we cannot preclude the possibility
that a difference of opinion in the Order over its stand in the
conflict between Becket and Henry II played a significant part
in Geoffrey's resignation. But the complaint against Geoffrey
makes one suppose, by its general wording, that his conduct
during his visit to England in 1164 provided a suitable occasion to lodge complaints about him with Alexander III.
The real reason of his forced resignation must be sought more
in the Cistercian Order itself. As abbot of Clairvaux, Geoffrey
was a very influential man, especially after the death of
Fastred of Cîteaux whom Gilbert succeeded only in 1163.

137. Preiss, *Die politische*, pp. 85-6.
138. J-L 11169 and 11171; PL 200:349 and 350. In the second letter, directed
to Henry, the archbishop of Reims, the Pope mentioned he discussed the abdication of Geoffrey with two other former Cistercians, Henri Moricotti, cardinal-
priest of St Nereus and Achilleus, and with Geoffrey, bishop of Langres.
139. Alan quoted Geoffrey of Langres as a witness for this opinion: "Si quis
diligenter advertat, ibidem quaedem aspera inserta reperiuntur, verbi gratia contra
ecclesiasticae et saecularis potestatis authenticas sublimesque personas." PL
185:469.

The more so, because he fostered and interpreted the way St Bernard was remembered in the Order. Opposition against his interpretation had arisen, especially among older Cistercians, who were also followers of St Bernard and had their own memories. Some of them had accepted ecclesiastical office which had put them outside policy-making in the Order. In their uneasiness about his policy, about which there was certainly no unanimity (just as there was none about the conflict between Becket and Henry II), they turned against Geoffrey and against his interpretation. Precisely because he owed his authority in the Order largely to his companionship with St Bernard during many years and then to his share in keeping alive Bernard's memory, the older monks opposing him appealed to their own memories of St Bernard. Thus one can understand why Alexander had received complaints against Geoffrey from many, or at least on behalf of many.

The picture can not become wholly clear owing to a lack of data. But the clearer figures in this opposition group were those mentioned by Alexander in his letters regarding Geoffrey of Auxerre's resignation: Alan, bishop of Auxerre, who returned in 1167 to Clairvaux where he had first entered in 1131; Geoffrey, bishop of Langres, who returned to Clairvaux in 1163, where he had been prior under St Bernard; Henry of France, who entered Clairvaux in 1146, became bishop of Beauvais in 1149 and archbishop of Rheims in 1162; and Henry Moricotti, an Italian who entered Clairvaux in 1148, became abbot of Tre-Fontaine in 1150 and cardinal-priest of St Nereus and Achilles in 1153.[140] Also to be included in this group are Pons, abbot of Clairvaux after the abdication of Geoffrey, and Alexander, a famous canon from Cologne who had followed St Bernard to Clairvaux in 1147. Alexander had become abbot in Grandselve in 1149 but resigned in 1158. In 1168, after the death of Gilbert, he became abbot of Cîteaux.[141] Pons probably influenced his

---

140. A. Dimier, *S. Bernard, "Pêcheur de Dieu"* (Paris, 1953) pp. 174, 184 (Godefroid de la Roche) and 186.

141. J. Marilier, *Chartes et documents concernant l'abbaye de Cîteaux, 1098-1182.* Bibliotheca Cisterciensis 1 (Rome, 1961) p. 27.

election, for Pons himself had been chosen abbot of Clairvaux as the opponent of Geoffrey and was as such interested in the choice of an abbot of Cîteaux with whom he could get on well.

Arguments pointing to Pons as the opponent of Geoffrey are found not only in the obvious fact that Geoffrey's opponents, who brought about his resignation, would see to it that his successor shared their opinions. The main argument is that Pons himself showed that he shared these opinions. Alan of Auxerre, who had returned to Clairvaux, wrote the *Vita secunda* during his abbacy. In its prologue he addressed Pons,[142] which implied that Pons was the one who had ordered this writing. As they were closely in touch about this text, it also follows that Pons agreed to the further objections expressed in this prologue against the *Vita prima*: it was too verbose and contained passages contrary to the truth.[143] Alan would not have written all this if Pons had not agreed about the *Vita prima*. As abbot of Clairvaux he had to take the initiative for a new request for canonization, but as he rejected the *Vita prima*, he needed a new *Life*. Alan produced this for him.

Why a new request failed to be made during Pons' reign of office is not clear, especially since he acted as a negotiator for Alexander III.[144] Perhaps the *Vita secunda,* the work of an old man who can hardly be called an author,[145] was not impressive; this seems to be indicated by the fact that only a few manuscripts of it were distributed.[146] But it may also be

142. PL 185:469: "Venerando Patri Pontio, Dei providentia Clarae Vallis abbati, frater Alanus Autissiodorensis ecclesiae humilis quondam sacerdos, aeternam in Christo salutem."

143. PL 185:469: " . . . breviori perstringimus schedula . . . primo quod scriptorum, tam etsi vera sint, prolixitas onerosa solet esse legentibus. Deinde quod Godefridus, venerabili Lingonicae sedis antistes . . . quaedam in pagina quam breviandam sucepimus minus veritati consona denotabat."

144. Preiss, *Die politische,* pp. 118-123.

145. Besides this *Vita secunda* there exists only some letters Alan addressed to Louis VII, a few charters and his last will and testament. PL 201:1383-92.

146. Only twelve manuscripts of this text are known. G. Hüffer, *Der heilige Bernard von Clairvaux,* 2 vols. (Münster, 1886), 1:148-9, and Bredero, *Etudes,* p. 139, n. 9 (18:24f, n. 4).

that the text was ready too late for Pons to make use of it. Besides, during his abbacy which ended in 1171, Geoffrey of Auxerre regained prestige. In 1169 the general chapter of the Cistercians instructed him to negotiate with Henry II for the sake of the Order's best interests.[147] Actually this was a change of policy. In the Order earlier in that year, the irreconcilable attitude of Thomas Becket still met with clear approval; at least, on April thirteenth the archbishop of Canterbury had repeated his interdict on the followers of Henry II during a stay at Clairvaux, after which Pope Alexander III had requested him to postpone this decision.[148] Geoffrey's mediation led to a peace settlement, to which also the archbishop had to agree, but he did so only with doubts.[149]

The increased prestige of Geoffrey, however, did not yet mean a decrease of Pions' influence. In March, 1169, prior to the publication of Becket's interdict, Pons had left Clairvaux and together with Alexander, abbot of Cîteaux, had gone to Beneventum on an invitation from Frederick Barbarossa. Frederick had asked for these abbots to mediate his still continuing conflict with Alexander III.[150] At first this mediation seemed to open up some possibilities. The Pope excused Pons from the general chapter of the Cistercians, to entrust him with further tasks in this attempt at mediation.[151] Afterwards, however, Pons made the mistake of keeping too little contact with the curia, which later discovered that his mediation resulted in closer contact between the Emperor and the King of France. Thus, the curia stated worriedly, Barbarossa's position against the Pope had grown stronger. This is said to have led to the end of Pons' abbacy. In 1171 he was elected to the see of Clermont—Ferrand, which had long been

---

147. Preiss, *Die politische*, pp. 106-111; Lenssen, "L'Abdication," pp. 106-7.

148. J-L 11626; PL 200:590. Preiss, *Die politische*, pp. 105-6. D. Knowles, *Thomas Becket*, pp. 121-4.

149. *Materials for the History of Thomas Becket*, ed. J. C. Robertson and J. Brigstocke Shephard, 8 vols. (London, 1885), 7:225-6. (The editors call Geoffrey erroneously bishop of Langres): "Secutus fidem vestram potius quam rationem meam, non sine labore mei et meorum quos de diversis locis evocaveram. . . ."

150. Preiss, *Die politische*, p. 118.

151. J-L 11633; PL 200:594.

vacant.[152] Pons' retirement as abbot of Clairvaux meant the end of the rejection of the *Vita prima* in connection with a canonization request. The new abbot was Gerard, the former abbot at Fossanova, where he had been followed in office by Geoffrey of Auxerre.[153] There were regular contacts between the two abbots and these led to a new request for the canonization. This is clear from a letter by Tromund of Chiaravalle. In the process of canonization Geoffrey acted as the advisor of the advocates.[154] So Abbot Gerard pushed the *Vita secunda* aside. Gerard let himself be guided by Geoffrey in another aspect of the canonization. In agreement with the manner in which St Malachy was indicated in *recensio B* of the *Vita* the relationship between St Bernard and the request for Malachy's canonization was joined to that of Bernard's. This, too, is clear from Tromund's letter, along with the note that Alexander III would be more inclined to reject the request for the canonization of St Bernard than agree to this joint request.[155]

As a matter of fact, this joining together of the two requests raises some questions as to its purpose. Did it concern only the official recognition of the sanctity of St Bernard and St Malachy in order to perpetuate in this way the veneration and remembrance of them by later generations? These canonizations could have still other points of importance for Clairvaux. Both St Bernard and St Malachy were buried there, and if they could obtain the honor of the altars Clairvaux would possess an important treasure, the relics of their

152. Preiss, *Die politische*, pp. 125f. Cf. A. H. Bredero, "Thomas Becket et la canonization de Saint Bernard," *Actes du colloque Thomas Becket et la France*, which will appear in 1975. At this Colloquium, held at Tulle in August, 1973, it was pointed out that the veneration of Becket as a saint in the bishopric Clermont-Ferrand dates directly his canonization.

153. Ibidem, p. 128. Afterwards the Pope may have appointed Geoffrey as apostolic legate for the East, but this is not proved. See Gofredo di Auxerre, *Super Apocalypsim,* ed. F. Gastaldelli, p. 15, n. 2.

154. PL 185:626: "Domnus abbas Fossae-novae et episcopus Verulanus, cum requisiti fuerunt, favoris et consilii subsidia ministrarunt." The bishop of Veroli was also a former Cistercian, Fromundus. P. B. Gams, *Series episcoporum,* (Regensburg, 1873-1886; repr. Graz: Akademische Druck-und Verlagsanstalt, 1957) p. 738.

155. See above, n. 122.

own saints. This could strengthen the significance of the monastery, already established by the special role it had played in the Order during St Bernard's life. St Bernard's canonization would effect the social position of Clairvaux, as is clear from a message from Alexander III to Louis VII. The Pope wanted to entrust this monastery to the king out of reverence for him who lay buried there, so that the king might be ever worthy of his protection.[156] From this perspective a double canonization would have provided still greater opportunities, especially in relation to the bishops. But it must not be forgotten that Geoffroy, who supported double canonization, had witnessed how venerated Malachy had been by St Bernard. In any case, the request for the canonization of Malachy was more an affair of Clairvaux alone than of the Cistercian Order. This is also clear from the somewhat phlegmatic answer with which Tromund concluded his, for Clairvaux, disappointing announcement.[157]

There is no direct data about the beginning and duration of the process. The moment of publication, which ended the process, makes one suppose that the request was submitted in the course of 1173; at least that it was being discussed. In Tromund's letter there was mention of bribes (*stipendia*), which he, as a Roman, used more economically than his French principals had allowed.[158] It is difficult to assume that bribes determined or influenced the result of the process. But it is conceivable that they were meant to speed up the finalizing of this case which had been held up so long. The canonization of Thomas à Becket, which was promulgated on

---

156. PL 185:623: "Clarevallense vero monasterium quod fundavit, in quo etiam corpus ejus venerabile requiescit, ita te ob reverentiam ejus habere volumus commendatum, ut eum semper merearis habere patromun."

157. PL 185:626: "Vestrum est igitur gratanter amplecti quod in diebus vestris est collatum in uno, et patienter ferre quod differtur in altero; gratias agendo ei qui coelestibus luminaribus tempora vicesque constituit, ut non idem sit ortus matutini et vespertini sideris, quamvis in utroque par eluceat gloria claritatis."

158. PL 185:627: "Ego, quia ex tenore litterarum vestrarum vestris sum praemonitus stipendiis militare, ita in omnibus Romanam moderatus sum parcitatem, ut prodigalitates Gallicas non sectarer."

21 February 1173,[159] may have been a stimulus to resume the case. We have no actual facts about the course of the process. Tromund mentioned the names of a number of Cistercian abbots who assisted him in various ways. Geoffrey of Auxerre has already been mentioned as an advisor. But others, whose origin cannot be determined, took part in the actual discussions. All the information about this is rather cryptic, although it is clear from what is said about *frater Guido*'s contribution, that the process, and in particular the gathering of information, was not just a formality, and that some arguments were indeed brought forward against the recognition of St Bernard's sanctity. "That the malignity of the opponents waylaid the straight path with greater cleverness than usual" is a significant statement in this context.[160]

Tromund ended his letter by mentioning the final stage of the process, its publication. There was more to it than the dispatch of the message to those who had made the request or supported it. The Pope sang a mass in honor of the new saint. For the mass new prayers had been composed. Tromund sent these along with his letter and advised the recipients not to change them. But the text of these prayers has not been handed down to us.[161] To this publication also belong the letters in which Alexander announced the conclusion of the process: i.e., the institution of a liturgical feast in honor of St Bernard. Although the contents of these letters are hard to understand, on account of the formal word-

---

159. R. Foreville, *L'Eglise et la rogante en angleterre sous Henri II Plantagenet (1154-1189)*, (Paris, 1943) p. 364. In his letter from 10 March 1173, addressed to his legates in England, Alexander III wrote:" . . . in capite jejunii . . . illum sanctum canonizevimus." J. L. 12199; Robertson, *Materials* 7:544; PL200:900. Ash Wednesday of that year was 21 February. *In capite jejunii* could have been also 25 February, the first Sunday of Lent. But at that moment it was probably not yet a custom to celebrate the publication of a canonization only on Sunday. The canonization of St Bernard, on 18 January 1174, took place on a Friday.

160. PL 185:626-7: "Frater Guido per multos labores suos et suorum et per non modicas fratris expensas viam nos fecit habere per devia, eo quod rectum iter curiosius solito insidiantium malignitas obsidebat."

161. The oldest prayers which are known the community of Clairvaux received from Pope Innocent III. PL 185:625.

ing, it is nevertheless clear that for the Pope the importance of this canonization lay in the actual veneration of St Bernard for which he had thus provided the official opportunity.

Thus he summed up in his letter to the Church of France the merits of St Bernard and pointed out the heroic character of his practice of virtue and mortification, which equalled the merits of the martyrs. At the same time the Pope urged his veneration, so that through his intercession and merits the faithful might obtain a lasting reward in heaven.[162] Louis VII in particular was exhorted by Alexander III to receive this gift of divine grace in joyful piety.[163] For the Cistercians the Pope expressed the hope that enrollment of the saint's name in the catalogue of saints and the celebration of his feast might bring, besides honor to God, edification and consolation to the Order.[164] Finally, the community at Clairvaux was praised for the manner in which they had requested St Bernard's canonization. Above all, the Pope exhorted them to follow their Fathers' footsteps in everything and to celebrate the feast of his sanctity so that after deserving a part in his conversion, they would be found worthy of sharing in his beatitude.[165]

To what extent St Bernard's followers did achieve this share no historian can tell. But he can say that the veneration of St Bernard was a joy for the community. This is clear from the letter of Henry, the abbot of Clairvaux, written to King Henry II on the occasion of the second translation of St Bernard's relics in 1178, and which made King Henry a participant in their joy.[166] I take it that this joy has been preserved all through the ages by those who have had or have

---

162. PL 185:622-3.
163. Ibid., p. 623.
164. Ibid., 624: "Unde quoniam hoc ita in gloriam et honorem summi Conditoris exuberat, ut in vestram quoque aedificationem consolationem redundet."
165. Ibid., 625: "Unde, quia vestra potissimum interest, et ejus imitari vitam, et gloriam venerari, satagite in omnibus et studete ipsius sancti Patris et inhaerere vestigiis, et festum excolere sanctitatis, ut cujus conversationis meruistis esse participes, digni habeamini ejusdem beatitudinis fore consortes."
166. PL 185:627. A better text of this letter is given by S. J. Heathcote, *The Letter Collections attributed to Master Transmundus* II, ASOC 21 (1965) p. 219.

some share in the spiritual aims which were pursued by St Bernard in his days upon this earth.

Adriaan H. Bredero

The University of Tilburg
Tilburg, The Netherlands

VIRTUE IN ST BERNARD'S *SERMONS ON THE SONG OF SONGS*

T HE EIGHTY-SIX SERMONS of Bernard of Clairvaux on the *Song of Songs* constitute one of the great classics of Christian spirituality. Here the Abbot of Clairvaux outlined for his monks a methodology of spiritual development. He saw a direct relationship between our virtue or lack of it and our spiritual progress. In the first *Sermon* of the series he insisted that there could be no spiritual progress apart from a life of virtue:

> Before the flesh has been tamed and the spirit set free by zeal for truth, before the world's glamour and entanglements have been firmly repudiated, it is a rash enterprise on any man's part to presume to study spiritual doctrines.[1]

In describing our spiritual development, Bernard allegorized the image of the kiss. We must move toward mystical union with God by gradual steps and not rush in unprepared for the deepest religious experience. First, we must kiss the feet of Christ, by which Bernard meant "a genuine conversion of life."[2] At this point our sins are forgiven. But, having been

---

1. *Sermon* 1:3, *On the Song of Songs I*, tr. Kilian Walsh, *The Works of Bernard of Clairvaux*, Vol. II, Cistercian Fathers Series 4 (Spencer, Mass.: Cistercian Publications, 1971) p. 2. This volume contains a translation of the first twenty *Sermons* of the series and will be referred to as CF4. The translation used for *Sermons* 21 through 86 is Samuel J. Eales, *Cantica Canticorum: Eighty-Six sermons on the Song of Solomon by St. Bernard*. (London: Elliot Stock, 1895), referred to as Eales. The critical Latin text is J. Leclercq et al., *Santi Bernardi Opera*, Vols. 1 and 2. (Rome: Editiones Cistercienses, 1957).

2. *Sermon* 4:1; CF4, p. 21.

forgiven we must not continue sinning. "If I soil my feet again after washing them, is the washing of any benefit? "[3]

The second step, then, is to kiss the hands of Christ, that he may raise us up and adorn us with virtues:

> ... his hand must be your guide to that end. First it must cleanse your stains, then it must raise you up. How raise you? By giving you the grace to dare to aspire. You wonder what this may be. I see it as the grace of the beauty of temperance and the fruits that befit repentance, the works of the religious man. These are the instruments that will lift you from the dunghill and cause your hopes to soar.[4]

The third kiss is the most intimate, the kiss of the mouth. This is what the *Song of Songs* refers to in the first verse, "Let him kiss me with the kiss of his mouth."[5] The kiss of the mouth is that "contemplative gift by which a kind and beneficent Lord shows himself to the soul with as much clarity as bodily frailty can endure."[6] This is mystical union, the highest goal of the spiritual life.

We must avoid, however, the desire for this kiss before we are ready for it:

> I do not wish to be suddenly on the heights, my desire is to advance by degrees. The impudence of the sinner displeases God as much as the modesty of the penitent gives him pleasure. You will please him more readily if you live within the limits proper to you, and do not set your sights at things beyond you.[7]

A life of virtue, then, is the necessary preparation for mystical union. In view of this it might be profitable to examine Bernard's understanding of the virtuous life and its characteristics.

These sermons are full of lists of virtues. *Sermon* 22 is on the four cardinal virtues: wisdom, righteousness, sanctification, and redemption.[8] In *Sermon* 27, Bernard described the

---

3. *Sermon* 3:3; CF4, 18.
4. *Sermon* 3:4; CF4, 19.
5. *Sermon* 4:1; CF4, 21.
6. *Sermon* 4:1; CF4, 22.
7. *Sermon* 3:4; CF4, 18-19.
8. *Sermon* 22:5; Eales, 125.

adornments of the bride: charity, righteousness, patience, poverty, humility, the fear of the Lord, prudence, temperance, and fortitude.[9] In *Sermon* 46 he listed piety, peace, gentleness, justice, obedience, cheerfulness, and humility.[10] *Sermon* 47 is on the threefold flower of holiness which is composed of virginity, martyrdom, and a holy life.[11] It is impossible to discuss all of these in a brief article. Several of the virtues most frequently mentioned will be explained.

Bernard began with the assumption that Christ is the source of all virtue:

> Just as the sea is the ultimate source of wells and rivers, so Christ the Lord is the ultimate source of all virtue and knowledge. For who has the power to endow us with virtues if not he who is the King of Glory? Chaste thoughts, just judgments, holy desires—are they not all streams from that one spring?[12]

By the same token, if we cut ourselves off from Christ we have no hope of developing real virtue. Unfortunately, too many men desire a virtuous life but are not willing to pay the price necessary to achieve it.

> How few there are, O Lord Jesus, who are willing to follow after Thee! and yet there is no one who does not wish to reach Thy Presence, for it is known to all that *at Thy Right Hand there are pleasures for evermore* (Ps 16, 11). On that account, all desire to obtain happiness from Thee, but they have not a similar desire to imitate Thee; they wish to reign with Thee, but not to suffer with Thee. . . . Even carnal men desire for themselves the death of men who are spiritual, and yet shudder at the idea of leading their life. . . . They do not care to seek Him, whom they yet desire to find; they wish to reach Him, but to do so without following Him.[13]

There are two ways in which Christ gives us virtue. The first is by grace; the second is by example and instruction. With-

---

9. *Sermon* 27:3; Eales, 168.
10. *Sermon* 46:7; Eales, 285.
11. *Sermon* 47:4; Eales, 288.

12. *Sermon* 13:1; CF4, 87.
13. *Sermon* 21:2; Eales, 117-118.

out grace, said Bernard, we cannot think good thoughts. Such thoughts are the result of the visit of the Word to us.[14] All of our goodness is of divine origin and to attribute it to our own effort is to defraud God.

> Will you dare to glory in holiness of life? But it is the Spirit who makes holy, that Spirit who is God's, not yours. Even if you are resplendent with prodigies and miracles it is still God's power working through your hands.[15]

As an example Jesus reminds us of all the virtues we ought to have. He is "meek and humble of heart, kind, prudent, chaste, merciful, flawlessly upright and holy in the eyes of all."[16] In his humanity we try to imitate him, in his divinity we go to him as a source of strength:

> Where, I ask you, is true prudence, if not in the teaching of Christ? or true righteousness, if not in His mercy? Where is true temperance, if not in the Life of Christ? or true fortitude, if not in the Passion of Christ? Those only, therefore, who are imbued with His teaching are to be called prudent; those alone to be regarded as righteous who from His mercy have attained the pardon of their sins; those alone as temperate who study to imitate His life: and those alone as courageous who in adversities follow with constancy the example of His patience.[17]

The ability to live a life of virtue is a gift of grace, according to Bernard. The world is full of dangerous temptations and distractions. "To live among the thorns and not to be torn by them, is the effect of Divine power, not of any efforts of your own."[18] We can take no pride in our moral superiority; if we are men of virtue let us give thanks to God that He has made it possible.

In preaching on the relationship between faith and works Bernard used the images of flowers and fruit. Flowers represent faith; fruit represents good works. As there must be a

14. *Sermon* 32:7; Eales, 211-212.
15. *Sermon* 13:7; CF4, 94.
16. *Sermon* 15:6; CF4, 111.

17. *Sermon* 22:11; Eales, 130.
18. *Sermon* 48:2; Eales, 292-293.

flower before the fruit appears, so must there be faith before good works which please God can occur. However, "it is useless for the flower to appear, if it be not followed by fruit."[19] The virtuous soul, when not in contemplation, draws consolation from good works. Mary and Martha are sisters; they are related just as faith and works, contemplation and action, are related.

But as I have said, as often as he falls from the state of contemplation, he resorts to that of action, as to a convenient refuge, from where he may be able more easily to return to his former state. For these two things are intimately related; they are chamber companions and dwell together.[20]

Basic to any virtuous action, for Bernard, is the intention which produces it. Virtue done in order to gain the praises of men gains us no credit before God. "Consequently," said Bernard, "there is the greatest need too for that uprightness of intention by which you will both strive to please God alone and find the strength to adhere to him."[21] He warned his auditors:

You deprive yourself of the life and salvation which you impart to another if, lacking right intention and inspired by self-conceit, you become infected with the poison of worldly ambition that swells into a deadly ulcer and destroys you.[22]

It is the intention of the heart that gives a particular action its color. The quality of the intention will be seen in the quality of the action just as "the fault of the root reappears in the branches."[23]

The virtue which is most frequently and most thoroughly discussed by Bernard is charity. *Sermon* 50 contains the fullest explanation in the series, but mention of charity is made in many others. Bernard said that there are two kinds of charity: charity in action and charity in feeling. The first is

19. *Sermon* 51:2; Eales, 309.
20. *Sermon* 51:2; Eales, 309.
21. *Sermon* 7:7; CF4, 43.
22. *Sermon* 18:2; CF4, 134.
23. *Sermon* 71:2; Eales, 433.

commanded; the second is a gift of grace. We can never fully experience charity of feeling in this life although we can, by grace, make some progress in it. Nevertheless, "the consumation of it is reserved for the happiness to come."[24]

That charity of action is commanded is seen in such scriptural admonitions as: "love your enemies, do good to them which hate you; if thine enemy hunger, feed him; if ye love me, keep my commandments; love thy neighbour as thyself; all things whatsoever ye would that men should do to you, do ye even so to them."[25] But this kind of charity operates on what Bernard called "the lower sphere of life." Charity of feeling operates at a higher level.

Men seem to be most occupied with charity of action. We are busy looking after the temporal good of others, the care of the weak, the maintenance of peace, and those who are in need of our assistance and advice. We are frequently torn away from prayer because of temporal necessity and dictates of charity:

> Charity in act follows its own order, and commences by the last things, according to the bidding of the Father of all. At least it is a charity kindly and just, not an acceptor of persons; nor does it consider the relative value of things, but the necessities of men.[26]

Charity of feeling, however, focuses on "first things." It discerns what is really most important, and it is this kind of charity that brings true knowledge of God and self:

> For true charity consists in this, that those whose needs are greatest receive first; and, again, charitable truth is manifest, in preserving in our affections that order which is founded in the reason. If, then, you love the Lord thy God with all thy heart, with all thy soul, and with all thy strength, rising in the earnestness of that affection above that love of love, with which actual charity is content, and receiving in all its fulness the Divine love (to which that other love serves only as a step), are wholly fired and

24. *Sermon* 50:2; Eales, 303.   26. *Sermon* 50:5; Eales, 306.
25. As quoted in Eales.

pervaded by it, assuredly you have a knowledge of God, although you cannot know Him adequately or as He is (which is a thing impossible to any creature), but at least such a knowledge of Him as you are capable of receiving here below. Then you shall have a true knowledge of yourself also, when you attain a perception of the fact that you have nothing whatever in yourself to deserve love, except in so far as you belong to God, and because you have poured out upon Him all the affection you can command.[27]

We must love our neighbor as ourselves because he is just like us; he is a man. And since we can love ourselves only because we love God, we love all who love God as we love Him. We cannot love an enemy in the same way because he does not love God, but we will love him in the hope that he will learn to love God. We love him not for what he is, but for what he may become. "Charity . . . does not allow that you should refuse to any man, even to your most bitter enemy, some small measure of affection."[28]

Bernard discussed several manifestations of charity. One of these was loving kindness. This virtue is evident whenever charity is shown toward the poor, the oppressed, the sad, and the afflicted. Loving kindness is an ointment that bears healing power. The man who exhibits this is

the good man who takes pity and lends, who is disposed to be compassionate, quick to render assistance, who believes that there is more happiness in giving than in receiving, who easily forgives but is not easily angered, who will never seek to be avenged, and will in all things take thought for his neighbor's needs as if they were his own.[29]

This kind of virtue produces great humility and "you will find men everywhere bearing witness to the perfumed influence you radiate."[30]

In discussing how offenders in monasteries ought to be corrected, Bernard counseled gentleness and compassion wherever possible in view of the Gospel command that we

27. *Sermon* 50:6; Eales, 306.
28. *Sermon* 50:7; Eales, 307.
29. *Sermon* 12:1; CF4, 78.
30. *Sermon* 12:5; CF4, 81.

love our neighbors as ourselves. The love of neighbor combined with grace produces the fruit of charity.

> For it has been said that everyone, from consideration of himself, should be gentle to all others; and following the wise counsel of St. Paul, should know how to make kindly allowance for such as have been overtaken in a fault, considering himself lest he also be tempted.[31]

In an earlier *Sermon* Bernard had discussed a related problem, the charity one who rules over others should have. We should not want to rule over others unless we desire to be of service to them and forward their salvation. We can do this with humility and to their advantage if we have drunk the wine of charity so that we condemn our own glory, forget ourselves, and seek not our own interest. All this must take place under the guidance of the Holy Spirit.[32]

Another manifestation of true charity is seen in the ability to love our enemies:

> It is no small proof of virtue to live a good life among the depraved, to preserve the pureness of innocence, and gentleness of character, among the evil disposed; it is a still greater one to be peaceful with those who are hostile to peace, and to show yourself a friend to your enemies themselves.[33]

Non-Christians deal kindly with those who love them, but we must do good to all men and must "never refuse to do an act of charity, whether spiritual or corporal, to an enemy, or withdraw it once offered."[34]

Near the end of the series of sermons Bernard talked of charity on a higher level. Here he spoke not about charity toward other men, but our love for God. In conversion, in the return of the soul to the Word, the one point at which we are "conformable to him" is in charity:

> It is that conformity which makes, as it were, a marriage between the soul and the Word, when, being already like

31. *Sermon* 44:4; Eales, 273.
32. *Sermon* 23:8; Eales, 135-136.
33. *Sermon* 48:2; Eales, 293.
34. *Sermon* 12:7; CF4, 82-83.

unto Him by its nature, it endeavours to show itself like unto Him by its will, and loves Him as it is loved by Him. And if this love is perfected, the soul is wedded to the Word.[35]

The Bridegroom, Christ, is himself Love. As Lord, God requires that we fear him; as Father, he should be honored; but as Bridegroom, he should be loved. Love is the highest of these three attitudes and is the highest response we can make to God:

Of all the feelings, affections, and movements of the soul, love is the only one by which the reasonable creature is able to respond to its Creator, and even in some sort to repay, though not upon equal terms, the goodness which it has received from Him. . . . For when God loves us, He desires nothing else than to be loved, because He loves us that He may be loved by us, knowing that those who love Him become blessed by their love itself.[36]

Charity is essential to faith, said Bernard, "Separation from charity is the death of faith."[37] Love animates our faith by works of charity. Furthermore, it is love that makes up for our imperfections. Speaking of a man who does many acts of charity, Bernard said, ". . . if his life and behavior are less than regular, remember that love covers a multitude of sins."[38]

Another virtue which received a good bit of attention from Bernard was humility. In *Sermon* 42 he described two types of humility: one born of truth, the other produced by charity. In the first a man is humble because he simply faces the truth about himself and recognizes his obvious short-comings. This is an enforced humility which comes from a realistic evaluation of one's situation. The higher form of humility is voluntary. It comes from the heart and is created by an inpouring of charity. The example of this is Jesus Christ who emptied himself and took the form of a servant. This is a humility freely chosen, not imposed by necessity. In

35. *Sermon* 83:3; Eales, 508.
36. *Sermon* 83:4; Eales, 509-510.
37. *Sermon* 24:8; Eales, 148.
38. *Sermon* 12:9; CF4, 85.

order to attain this level of humility we must willingly submit
ourselves to other people, not because we ought to but because we want to do it:

> It is not enough to be subject to God, unless you are
> subject also to every human creature for the sake of God;
> whether to the Abbot, as to the superior of all, or to the
> Priors, as authorities constituted by him. I say even more
> than this: I say, subject to your equals, and even those who
> are inferior to you. For *thus it becometh us,* says the Lord
> himself, *to fulfill all righteousness.* If, then, you wish to be
> perfect in righteousness, make the first step towards him
> who is less than you; defer to your inferior, show respect to
> your junior.[39]

Bernard warned against the danger of a false humility when
making confession. There is a temptation to reveal immoral
behavior, not because we are humble, but because we want to
appear humble. We destroy the virtue in humility when we
seek to be praised for our humility. A genuinely humble man
will prefer obscurity. He will not seek to have his humility
acclaimed in public. He is happiest if no one notices him.
Bernard warned, "But a confession that makes humility a
sham not only fails to merit pardon, it provokes God's
anger."[40]

The highest graces cannot be obtained without humility,
said Bernard. Many men sought higher graces before they
were ready for them. Moses asked to see God's glory (Exodus
33:13-23) but God would not show his face. James and John
wanted to sit at Jesus' left and right in the Kingdom, but
were refused (Matthew 20:20-23). We must not seek the
higher graces without humility:

> For it behooves one who aspires to things lofty to have
> lowly thoughts of himself, lest while he exalts himself
> above his measure he fall below himself, not being steadied
> and rendered firm by sincere humility. And because very
> great graces are not to be obtained except with the merit of
> humility, it is essential that he who is to receive them

39. *Sermon* 42:9; Eales, 264.   40. *Sermon* 16:10; CF4, 121.

should be humbled by reproof, that he may deserve them by humility. Do you then, when you see yourself humbled, take it as a sign, and even as a certain proof, that some grace from God is drawing near to thee. For as *pride goes before destruction,* so before honour comes humility.[41]

Humility, said Bernard, justifies us. He made a clear distinction here, between humility and humiliation. Humiliation only has merit if we respond to it with a positive attitude. We may be humiliated without being humble. We might be bitter and grudging about a humiliation. It is good to bear it with patience. It is better to bear it willingly. Humility is the perfection of righteousness, and if we can say that it is good for us to be humbled, we are truly humble. [42]

One virtue which Bernard saw as being essential to spiritual development and the reception of grace was obedience. In *Sermon* 19 he complained of novices who refused to obey their superiors, preferring to go their own ways in seeking perfection. They felt that the fasts were not strict enough, the vigils were not long enough. They were dissatisfied with the rules of the monastery and with the amounts of food and clothing they were allotted. They did not want to share in common but wanted to go their own private ways. They came to the monastery in a spirit of obedience, but now they have taken self-will for their master. They will not yield to reason, respect their seniors, or obey their abbot. They fail to understand that obedience is better than sacrifice.[43]

Bernard told his monks that it is clearly more difficult, though perhaps more meritorious, to live a good life under the constraining influence of one's own will. Many people who are able to live a good life of peace under the guidance of a competent director would not be able to do so if released from the obligation of obedience. "But I should regard him as the highest in character," said Bernard, ". . . who is obedient to those above him. . . ."[44]

41. *Sermon* 34:1; Eales, 225.
42. *Sermon* 34:3; Eales, 226.
43. *Sermon* 19:7; CF4, 145.
44. *Sermon* 23:8; Eales, 136.

There is a strong relationship between obedience and contemplation. True contemplation is built on obedience. Bernard said that "the taste of contemplation is not due except to obedience to God's commandments."[45] Again, the example is Christ: "He who is so great a lover of obedience that He preferred to die rather than not to obey, will assuredly not bestow His gifts upon one who is disobedient."[46]

Another essential virtue of the spiritual life is thanksgiving. It is important that we honestly evaluate our lives, that we confess our sins with genuine contrition. However, Bernard said that sorrow for sin "should not be an endless preoccupation."[47] We must also give much thought to the mercy of God; otherwise we will be driven to despair. The mercy of God is greater than all iniquity. The just man will begin his prayers by accusing himself, but will conclude with praise and thanksgiving for God's goodness.

Focusing on the goodness of God produces many benefits:

> Those . . . who are employed in the work of thanksgiving are contemplating and thinking about God alone, and so they cannot help but dwell in unity. That which they do is good because they offer to God the glory that is most rightly his; and it is also pleasant, since of its very nature it gives delight.[48]

We must be careful, however, that our thanksgiving is genuine and not false. Bernard told his monks that God listens only to that thanksgiving which comes "from a pure and genuine simplicity of heart."[49] When we give thanks to God while at the same time involving ourselves in evil, our thanksgiving is not genuine. Many people give thanks for the wrong things: a thief for his loot, an adulterer for his conquest, or a murderer for his victim. The Pharisee offers thanks to God with his lips, but inwardly praises himself for his own accomplishments.

45. *Sermon* 46:5; Eales, 283.   48. *Sermon* 11:1; CF4, 69.
46. *Sermon* 46:5; Eales, 284.   49. *Sermon* 13:3; CF4, 89.
47. *Sermon* 11:2; CF4, 70.

Bernard also warned against the vice of ingratitude:

> Ingratitude is the enemy of the soul, the starving of merits, the dissipation of virtues, and the loss of the benefits that God has bestowed upon us. Ingratitude is a burning wind, which dries up for itself the fountain of goodness, the dew of mercy, the flowing streams of grace.[50]

We must learn to be quick in rendering thanks to God for each of his gifts to us, no matter how great or small. Otherwise, all of the benefits we have received from God will be lost, "for is not that *lost* which is bestowed upon an ungrateful receiver?"[51]

A virtue that we would expect to find preached to monks is a contempt for the world and its values. What the world has to offer, said Bernard, is at very best only temporary. It is like a grape. Once pressed it can never produce liquid again. "Everything in the world indeed will come to an end, an end from which there is no return."[52] It is foolish for man to seek those values which will not last.

Worldliness is something that men, even with very good intentions, find difficult to give up. Even after entering the religious life, some men maintain traces of worldliness:

> ... we do sometimes hear men who have committed themselves to religious life and wear the religious habit, shamelessly boasting as they recall their past misdeeds: the duels they fought, their cunning in literary debate or other kinds of vain display that worldlings cherish, behavior of its nature pernicious and injurious, so opposed to spiritual well-being. These are signs of a mind still worldly, and the humble habit worn by religious of this kind serves but as a cloak for their old sinfulness rather than as proof of their renewal in holiness.[53]

An attachment to worldly things enslaves men and inhibits their freedom to develop spiritually. If we cannot give up such things for the sake of religious progress then they have become our master and we their slave. We are only their

---

50. *Sermon* 51:6; Eales, 311.
51. *Sermon* 51:6; Eales, 311.
52. *Sermon* 9:10; CF4, 60.
53. *Sermon* 16:9; CF4, 120-121.

keeper, not their possessor. A free man will be able to endure abundance and penury because he knows that spiritual strength is his greatest possession:[54]

> What again, shall I say of that soul, which affords, as it were, spacious avenues in which the grace of God may move without constraint? Assuredly, it is not tunnelled with the windings of worldly interests and secular cares, nor occupied with luxuries and sensual pleasures; nor with curiosity about the affairs of others; nor is it filled with tumid pride, nor the desire to rule. For it is essential in the first place that a soul should be free from all things like this, that it may become a heaven, and be the dwelling place of God.[55]

A final virtue to be discussed, although many more are mentioned in the sermons, is the ability to overcome temptation. Temptation is an ever present reality for anyone, even the most pious and faithful:

> As long as the soul is clothed in flesh, its course lies among thorns; nor can it avoid having to bear the inquietude of temptation, and the sharp piercing of troubles. If the Bride is a lily, according to the words of the Bridegroom, let her understand with what vigilance and care she ought to watch over her conduct, surrounded as she is on all sides with thorns, of which the sharp points encounter her everywhere. For the tender substance of a flower is unable to endure the slightest puncture of a thorn without injury.[56]

In another *Sermon* Bernard used the image of the vineyard. We must take constant care of our vineyard. Those evil tendencies which we cut down will quickly shoot up again. It does not help to prune only once, we must prune frequently. We commit grave error if, on having made significant spiritual progress, we think that sin and vice are dead within us. "Virtue cannot increase at the same time with vice; and if the one flourish, it will not suffer the other to increase."[57]

In *Sermon* 33 Bernard described four kinds of temptations.

---

54. *Sermon* 21:7; Eales, 120.
55. *Sermon* 27:10; Eales, 174.
56. *Sermon* 48:1; Eales, 292.
57. *Sermon* 58:10; Eales, 353.

The first is fear, the fear of the unforeseen sufferings we might have to face in the religious life as we strive for perfection. Bernard reminded his monks of the words of Paul, "For the sufferings of this present time are not worthy to be compared with the glory which shall be revealed in us."[58] The second temptation against which we must arm ourselves is vainglory. Here our greatest danger is the praise of men. It is a very serious problem for monks because most men admire the monastic life. Jesus faced similar temptations in the desert, and we must resist them as he did. The third major temptation is hypocrisy. Its source is ambition. The final temptation besets the most saintly, those who have overcome major temptations and have achieved a very high degree of religious development. Here the temptor comes disguised as good and attempts to convince the pious soul that what might appear to be evil is actually good. Bernard warned that "the higher anyone seems to have attained, the more careful and watchful let him learn to be against the attacks of the demon of noonday."[59]

When we give into temptation we set up a series of walls between God and ourselves. Bernard described them:

> Of these the first is concupiscence; the second, consent of the will; the third, the actual fact, the fourth, the habit of sin; the fifth, hardened indifference and contempt. Be careful, then, to resist with all your might the first approach of concupiscence, so that it may not draw you into an inward consent, and then the whole fabric of evil will disappear; nor is there anything to hinder the drawing near to you of the Lord, who is the Bridegroom, except only the barrier formed by your body. . . .[60]

There is a fascinating passage in Sermon 63 where Bernard preached about the temptations of novices. He described what happened when novices, characterized by an early enthusiasm, give in to temptation, which he called a frost or a chilling north wind. The effects of such a wind are:

---

58. Rom 8:8 as quoted in Eales.
59. *Sermon* 33:13; Eales, 222.

60. *Sermon* 56:6; Eales, 338-339.

... it stuns and paralyzes good dispositions, it closes up the avenues by which good advice might come, it troubles the light of judgment, it fetters the impulses of the spirit, ... its vigour is relaxed, a languour creeps over its powers, a horror of austerity is continually intensified, the fear of poverty troubles it more and more ... grace ebbs away from it, life becomes wearisome, the reason is stupefied, the courage stifled, the recent fervour of the man rapidly grows cold. ...

The law is evaded, righteousness is rejected, obligation proscribed, the fear of the Lord abandoned altogether. Finally, such a person yields himself to the last degree of shamelessness, he makes a leap which is rashness itself ... from the sky into the abyss, from the pavement of a palace into a dunghill, from a throne into the gutter, from heaven into a swamp of mire, from the cloister into the outer world—yea, from paradise into hell.[61]

These, then, are some of the virtues which Bernard urged upon the monks of Clairvaux in charting the course of the spiritual pilgrimage. A deepening knowledge of God was not built only upon prayer, liturgy, silence, or solitude. We could practice these things and still miss the mark by a wide margin. Our spiritual progress must be built upon a solid growth in virtue. Among other things we must seek to develop charity, humility, obedience, thanksgiving, a contempt for the world, and the ability to resist temptation. Knowing that Christ is the source of all virtue we must seek to imitate him and hope for his grace. In *Sermon* 50 Bernard gave a summary of the virtuous life:

Give me a man who, before all things, loves God with all his being, who loves both himself and his neighbour in the same degree in which each loves God; who loves his enemy as one who may perhaps at some time in the future turn to the love of God, ... who despises the earth and looks upward to heaven; who uses this world as not abusing it, and knows how to distinguish ... between things which are to be chosen and loved, and those which are merely to be

61. *Sermon* 63:6; Eales, 381-382.

used, . . . show me, I say, a man such as this, and I will boldly pronounce him wise. . . .[62]

William O. Paulsell

Atlantic Christian College
Wilson, North Carolina

62. *Sermon* 50:8; Eales, 307.

CARITAS IN THE INITIAL LETTERS
OF ST BERNARD

THIS ESSAY HAS AS ITS INTENT the explication of one idea found in a small number of texts, an idea that is fundamental to the whole of St Bernard's thought. Its basis is 1 John 4:16: *Deus caritas est.*

St Bernard's concept of *caritas* in the first twenty-one *Letters* is an explanation of his ecclesiology. Indeed, the *Letters* as a whole are the selected notes of a man of the Church. In them we may discern a theology of the Church that is as rich and as moving as Bernard's *Sermon on the Song of Songs.* Some authors such as Fr Yves Congar have held that the *Letters* were edited after Bernard had composed the *Sermons,* but this can no longer be simply maintained.[1]

We may see these first twenty-one *Letters* placed at the beginning of the corpus as a form of preface. They form a theological unity and contain ideas that Bernard wished the

1. In his article, "L'Ecclesiologie de S. Bernard," ASOC 9 (1953) p. 137, Fr Congar states that the *Sermons* were begun in 1135. At the same time he holds to the chronology of the *Letters* as it is in Migne. However, in the light of the subsequent work of Fr Leclercq (see n. 2) on the composition and editions of the letters, this no longer can be maintained. The first edition of the Letters, *B,* was compiled between 1126 and 1145; the second, *L,* shortly before Bernard's death. Throughout this time therefore, that is, during the composition of both *Letters* and the *Sermons on the Canticle,* the notion of the *sponsa Christi* was not the lens through which Bernard viewed the Church. Rather, the lens used was *caritas.* This is of special import with regard to the *L* edition, the final collection, finished after the *Sermons* had been begun. If Bernard had wished to use the image of the *sponsa Christi* in these prefatory letters, it would have been evident in this edition. However it is not.

reader to see developing throughout the cursus of the *Letters*. However, this is true only of the *Longior* (*L*) collection edited by St Bernard a few years before his death.[2] A shorter edition was made by him sometime between 1126 and 1145 which is known as *Brevis* (*B*). In this edition the initial order of the texts was: *Letters* 65, 78, 254, 11, 12, 2, 1, 107, etc.[3] It is most interesting to note in this collection that those *Letters* that form a part (and a most important part) of the *L* collection are also present in *B*; that is *Letters* 11, 12, 2, and 1—those concerning the monastic life. Even more notable is the fact that all these *Letters* are concerned with the monastic life and its reform, whether it be the reform of St Denis under Abbot Suger (Ep 78) or another house (as in Ep 254), or the Carthusian life. There are also the *Letters* of encouragement to young men or ex-monks to embrace the Cistercian life (Ep 1, 2, and 107). In general, then, the prefatory *Letters* of the *B* edition concern the monastic life and, in particular, the Cistercian reform. However, we are concerned here with the *L* text.

In the *L* edition *Letters* 1 to 44 form the first section of the corpus (and in the *P* [*Perfectus*] text as well[4]). The *Longior* text was edited by Bernard and was the final edition of the *Letters* that he wished to be published and known to the world. In its completed form, as the study of Jean Leclercq already cited has shown, it is a work no less labored and no less polished, no less rich in thought and religious experience than the other works of St Bernard.

A very important metaphor in the ecclesiology of Bernard, as in the whole of his mystical theology, is that of the Spouse. It was not until 1135, however, according to the chronology of the *Letters* (if that is reliable), that this idea was imposed.[5] It does not appear in those *Letters* with which

---

2. Jean Leclercq, "Lettres de S. Bernard: Histoire ou Littérature? " *Studi Medievali* 12 (1971) p. 22. Also see his "Recherches sur la collection des épîtres de saint Bernard," *Cahiers de civilisation médiévale* 14 (1971) 205-19; and earlier, *Etudes sur Saint Bernard et le texte de ses écrits* ASOC 9 (1953) 87ff.

3. "Lettres," p. 21.

4. Composed after Bernard's death. See Leclercq, "Lettres," pp. 23, 73.

5. Congar, "L'ecclesiologie," p. 137, n. 1.

we are concerned, nor does it appear in the tract *De moribus et officio episcoporum*, written in 1126. However, this image of the *Sponsa Christi* is frequently applied to the Church in the *Letters*.[6] Its cognate, *amici Sponsi*, is also found, applied exclusively to bishops and the Pope.[7] It is significant, however, that this image is not found in the first twenty-one *Letters*. We must look elsewhere for the dominant theme of these *Letters* and, indeed, of the entire corpus.

The fundamental concept ruling the first twenty-one *Letters* is *caritas*. This is not surprising for it is the one concept fundamental to all Bernard's thought. In these *Letters* we find Bernard explaining *caritas* in both a monastic and an ecclesiastical context. Of special note in this selection of *Letters* for the preface is the inclusion of *Letter Eleven* (to the Carthusians). This *Letter* comprises chapters twelve to fifteen of the *De diligendo Deo*. Its place in these *Letters* is meant as a sign-post of the import of the corpus.[8] St Bernard is concerned to present an apologia for his actions. He desires us to see that all his pleadings, warnings, advice, decisions, the whole range of his ecclesiastical dealings, were animated by the same life that he eloquently described in the *Sermon on the Song of Songs*: a life of mystical union with the Bridegroom Christ. It is a life fundamentally and totally animated by *caritas*. There is thus a bridge from the earlier *Letters* to the later ones. The concept of *caritas* receives its full development in the later ones (99 to 112).

Caritas is most fully developed and explained in those *Letters* addressed to monks expounding the virtues of the monastic life. In the first twenty-one *Letters*, not one is addressed to a layman; all are addressed either to monks, canons or clerics.

6. Ep 170:2 (PL 182:330; cited by column only in the following); 187(350); 191(358); 238(428); 244:2(442); 330(536); 331(536); 341(554); 348(552); 358(560); 395(604); 467(672); 468(673).

7. Ep 187(350); 191:2(358); 195(363); 246:3(464); 331(536); 351(554); 358(560); 395(605). This expression is also found in Csi 3, 5, 20; OB 3:448.

8. Leclercq, "Recherches," p. 213: "A lui seul, ce dossier 'monastique,' à cause de la longuer de ses exposés doctrinaux, occupe environ un huitième de tout le corpus: ce fait indique suffisament son importance. Bernard a voulu, dès le début, donner le ton, orienter toute la suite."

Letters 1 to 12 are addressed to monks and other regulars and *Letters* 13 to 21 are addressed to Roman prelates. The first series is concerned with the theology of the monastic life and the second with the life of the Church. The *Letters* are first and foremost literary documents, not an historical record. They are a record of a doctrinal view-point based on religious experience.[9] Fr Leclercq has shown that the same editorial process of polishing and perfecting of style that St Bernard applied to his other works went into the publication of the *Longior* corpus. The first twelve *Letters* are concerned with the monastic problem, "with the ideal and with the practical manner of its realisation."[10]

At the beginning of the *B* corpus, as at the beginning of the *L* text with which we are concerned, *Letters* 11, 12, 2, and 1 are found. But in the *B* text those *Letters* dealing with the monastic life are preceeded by three others that are found elsewhere in *L*, i.e., *Letters* 65, 78, and 254, all of which deal with the reform of monastic houses, and they are followed by *Letter* 107, an encouragement to a young man to follow the observance of Clairvaux to which he is promised. Several *Letters* found in *L* are not found in *B*, i.e., nos. 3, 5, 6, 7, 8, and 10. The emphasis in *B* is clearly on the Cistercian observance and its excellence (in St Bernard's eyes) in comparison with the un-reformed monastic houses. In *L* the emphasis is rather upon the theology and practice of the monastic or regular life.

In the *Longior* text then, following Fr Leclercq, we may see the following divisions: on the whole two main subdivisions, already noted, firstly, *Letters* 1 to 12 concerning the monastic life, and secondly, *Letters* 13 to 21 concerning the interests of the Church universal. These two divisions mark out the concerns of the entire corpus. The first subdivision is composed of several sections. *Letters* 1 and 2 are

9. Leclercq, "Recherches," pp. 41-2, 48.
10. Ibid., p. 213.
11. The order of the remainder of the *Longior* is given by Leclercq, ibid., pp. 214-5.

personal in tone and extol the values and ideals of the Cistercian calling. *Letter Three* forms the second section, concern-ing a *transitus* from one observance to another (from a group of canons regular to the Cistercians). The third group (*Letters* 4 to 7) is more explicitly concerned with monastic law in the case of a *fugitivus,* Abbot Arnold of Morimond, who illegally relinquished his office and made an attempt to go to the Holy Land. The *Letters* give a good picture of the case, its consequences and Bernard's attempts at solution. The fourth group is addressed to Bruno, the archbishop of Cologne, and to Guigo, prior of the Grande Chartreuse.

In the second sub-division the *Letters* may be divided into two sections. The first, *Letters* 14 and 15, are addressed to Pope Honorius II and the second, 16 to 21, to members of the Roman Curia."

Having briefly outlined the place of these *Letters* in the collection edited by St Bernard, we may now consider the role of *caritas* in them. In the first twenty-one letters there are approximately fifty occurances of the word *caritas.* [12] Of these only seven occur in the *Letters* of the second sub-division addressed to the Pope and the Roman Curia; the remaining occurances are found in those *Letters* concerned with the monastic life. In *Letter 11* alone there are twenty occurances of *caritas.* I shall set them forth and comment on them, trying to note Bernard's sources wherever possible, as they are very important and far more numerous than it first seems, far more than I can hope to notice.

Ep 1:3 (72A)

In setting this *Letter* to his cousin Robert at the head of the corpus it would seem that Bernard was concerned to point out the role of the Abbot in governing the monastery. This would be in accordance with the hierarchical ordering of the corpus—he starts at the top and works his way down. When we reach the *Letters* addressed to the Carthusians, we are dealing with the life of the individual monk in relation to

---

12. This is based on a count in Migne.

Christ. In the same way we find the *Letters* on the Church universal headed by those addressed to the Pope.[13]

St Bernard's conception of the abbot is drawn from Romans 8:15: *non in spiritu servitutis iterum in timore, sed spiritu adopitionis filiorum, in quo clamare et tu non confundaris, Abba, Pater.* Bernard expresses sorrow that by being overly strict he has driven Robert away from Clairvaux, but also stresses that the opportunity is now open for Robert to return as he, Bernard, has had a change of heart. The text from Lk 25:32: *Mortuus fuerat et revixit, perierat et inventus est,* is the basis for this new attitude. St Bernard takes on the role of the father who welcomes back his son, but, at the same time, repents of his own errors that lead to the misunderstanding.

Bernard furthermore links *caritas* with an attitude characterized by *non timore*. In this we see an echo of the later teaching of Bernard. In the mystical life one is led on, not as a servant, not by fear, but in sonship, by *caritas* with a boldness that he calls *fiducia*. The *Letter* is an exhoration to the Cistercian life and an explanation of it in Bernardine terms, in high rhetoric and sharp contrast. The Cluniac life is derided for not being based on Scripture. Above all, in this case, the charity that the Cluniacs have shown to Robert is called by Bernard *O molesta charitas! O dura necessitudo!* (76C). It is such that Bernard is greatly hurt at Robert's defection: because it is ultimately to Robert's ruin to prefer a soft way of life to a strict.

This *Letter* is, of course, a shot fired in the dispute between the Cistercians and the Cluniacs. It was for this reason that it was included in the beginning of *B,* and given the use it was to have in *P.* Here in *L,* however, it functions in a different manner. It is a personal letter and is meant not so much as an attack on the Cluniac observance as a setting forth of the

---

13. On some of the relationships of the Cistercians with the papacy and notable bishops, see B. D. Hill, "Archbishop Thomas Becket and the Cistercian Order," ASOC 27 (1971) 64-80. Cf Bernard's *Apologia,* 4:8, OB 3:88: "There are many orders in one Church... Further their unity consists here as there in one charity."

ideals of the monastic life and, in the *corpus epistolarum,* as a program for the practical realization of those ends. In this Bernard presents the action of the abbot as that of the prodigal's father in the Gospel parable. It is important to note that the charity that urges a soft way of life, in Bernard's eyes, only leads to ultimate destruction.[14]

Ep 2:1 (79D-80C)

This *Letter,* also written to encourage a young man towards the monastic life, is very rich in its explanation of *caritas.* The basic Scripture text used here is 1 Cor 13:5: *caritas non quaerit quae sua sunt.* This section of the *Letter* may be seen as an exegesis of the passage from 1 Cor 13. Charity is the mother of all virtue. It is meek, sincere, loving, patient, placating and reconciling God and man; it is the root of the fraternal life of the community:*habitare facit unius moris in domo* (Ps 68:7).[15] Indeed, it is the mother of the "sweet bread broken" (*dulces capiebas cibos*) in the community. Charity is a most flexible mother, *diversis diversa exhibens.* In anger it is patient, indignant yet not proud, in scolding meek, in consolation sincere.[16]

Bernard appeals to the love of God in Fulk to return to the monastic life to which he has vowed himself. In the last section of the letter Bernard makes use of the image of the *Militia Christi,* an image borrowed from St Jerome.[17] It is this *caritas Dei* that enables Bernard to speak with such profound forcefulness and emotion. It gives him authority in the Church and society. While he does not wish to argue with the hierarchy, it allows him to speak on matters that technically fall outside of his jurisdiction. To Bernard's mind Fulk's salvation lies in keeping the vows he has made, in his fighting the battle of asceticism and not giving way to urbane fashions. Bernard's thought is that to love God is to love him

14. See Leclercq, "Documents sur les 'fugitifs'," *Studia Anselmiana* 54 (1965) 95-6.
15. Cf Leclercq, "Lettres," p. 59.
16. Cf IV HM 9, OB 5:62-3.
17. Leclercq, "Lettres," p. 64 and n. 163.

alone, to live the monastic life. To break monastic vows made
to Christ is to break a vow made to the Spouse—a grave
offense indeed.

Bernard holds forth the *bona mater caritas* as the law of the
monastic life—it is again the role of the abbot to exhibit that
law. He makes a contrast between his own counsel in charity
and that of Fulk's uncle, who counsels from material motives. Bernard again makes allusion to the parable of the prodigal son (Lk 25:32) in 80C. A strong undercurrent of emotional appeal is made to the Last Judgement. Bernard is not
only concerned to stir up the love of God in Fulk, but also
and chiefly the fear of God.

These two *Letters* are exhortations to the monastic life.
They were not intended by Bernard to be matters for controversy, but rather spiritual enrichment. The place that *caritas*
occupies in them is simply this: charity is shown to the
young who may wish to enter—it is at the call of *caritas* itself
that the monastic way is taken up. It is the vivifying force
throughout the life and it is also the one thing that sustains
even the lapsed, for it is none other than Christ himself.
Caritas is the monastic life. [18]

These *Letters* also contain Bernard's teaching on the role of
the abbot, for he is the first element in the monastic program, the master and exemplar of the life of the *via caritatis*.
For Bernard, the fundamental attitude of the abbot is humility.

Ep 3 (88-89A)

This same theme is carried over into this *Letter* and Bernard simply asks the canons to practise what he himself has
been expounding. Again, and more clearly, the role of humility is stressed. Bernard emphasizes that the direction of monastic charity is not toward glory or comfort for oneself but the
glory of Christ alone.

---

18. Cf Ep. 142 (279C): "Ordo noster est . . . super omina excellentiorem viam
tenere, quae est caritas, porro in his omnibus proficere de die in diem, et in ipsis
perseverare usque ad ultimum diem." Cf J. Leclercq, "St Bernard and the Rule of
St Benedict," CS 12, pp. 151-167.

Ep 7 (93D-94C)

This *Letter*, also known as the tract *De discretione obedientiae* in a manuscript noted by Mabillon, was addressed to the monk Adam. Written about 1126 according to the tradition, it is also titled *Sermo Bernhardi de concordia fratrum*.[19] It develops the theme that the unity of the monastic community is founded on charity. The letter concerns the disobedience of Arnold and is an attempt to move the addressee from following the ruinious plans of that abbot. Bernard is concerned to point out to Adam the great scandal that the actions of Arnold have led to and to attempt to show to Adam the path that he should follow. He first must not offend charity, and secondly, must follow a proper obedience. In this connexion it is interesting to note that Origen in his Prologue to the *Commentary on the Song of Songs*, (PG 13:76 A-B) sees obedience as exemplified by Abraham, as the first step on the scale of perfection.

"Charity would not offend charity" (93D), charity "loves (*diligit*) peace, rejoices in unity" (94A). Furthermore, it is "it alone which begets unity . . . in the bonds of peace. Wherever charity is, there too is peace" (94A). These three, charity, unity and peace proceed from one another and together they form the substance of monastic community. In this they echo the Holy Trinity, as Bernard points out: "Charity is one (Eph 2:14). In the Trinity unity is greatly honored. He who understands charity, peace and unity to be irritated, what does he have in the Kingdom of Christ and God? "

In connecting unity and charity, Bernard might have been influenced by Augustine.[20] In his *De Baptismo* 3, 16, 21, Augustine also makes reference to Bernard's two favorite texts on *caritas*, Rom 5:5 and 1 Cor 13:

> . . those who do not love the unity of the Church, however, do not have the charity of God; and from this it is

---

19. Leclercq, "Lettres," p. 43.
20. See Y. Congar, *Ecclésiologie du haut Moyen Âge* (Paris: Cerf, 1968), pp. 92-3 for the influence of Augustine in linking charity and unity; also see n. 23 below.

rightly understood how it is said that the Holy Spirit is received on in the Catholic Church.[21]

St Bernard is concerned to show that the offense of the monk Adam (and of his abbot, Arnold) is against charity: that the act of disobedience is against God himself (*caritas ipse Deus est*). He is at particular pains to stress the relationship between charity and unity. Unity, following the Trinitarian model, can not be separated from charity. Charity "cannot be divided against herself or deny her own nature." Perhaps here Bernard has in mind the text from 2 Tim 2:13: "if we are faithless, he remains faithful, for he cannot deny himself."

Addressing the issue at hand, Bernard places charity above all else (following 2 Cor 13). He states that even obedience to an abbot cannot interfere with charity or with the unity of the community. The whole passage is close in its language to Bernard's sermon for Wednesday in Holy Week.[22]

Ep 8-9 (105B-107A, 107B-108A)

Letter Eight is addressed to Bruno and, although Bernard expresses some doubt about his qualifications for the office of bishop, Bruno eventually became a bishop. Bernard exhorts Bruno to penance for his past life. Here he quotes from Eccles 30:24. In this he is following an old pattern of using *Ecclesiastes* as the book of penance, fear, contrition and hope, *Proverbs* as the book of devotion and perseverance, and the *Song of Songs* as the book of the higher knowledge of the Divine Being.[23]

---

21. PL 43:148: " . . . non autem habet Dei charitatem, qui Ecclesiae non diligunt unitatem: ac per hoc recte intellegitur dici non accipi nisi in [Ecclesia] Catholica Spiritus sanctus."

22. IV HM 9, OB 5:62-3.

23. See Origen, Prologue, *Commentary on the Song of Songs*, PG 13: 73A, 76. This is the distinction of the Fathers among πρακτική, φυσική and θεωρητική, or, as Origen terms it in his other works πίστις, γνῶσις, and σοφία: *Contra Celsum*, PG 11:1309C; cf *In Epist. ad Rom 1:18* (PG 14:866A); *De Principiis*, III, 4, 3 (PG11:323B). This is further brought out by Bernard in the first twelve SC: see J. Morson and H. Costello, *Guerric of Igny, Liturgical Sermons*, 2 vols. CF 8, 32 (Spencer, Mass.: Cistercian Publications, 1970-1) 1:xlix-l; M. Basil Pennington,

What Bernard wishes, significantly, to establish is *rectus ordo*. Bernard is a master of the spiritual life, of the training of men to become saints, and he demonstrates this here. The letter is furthermore interesting in that it shows Bernard's conception of the role of the bishop. The primary function of the bishop is to love. In order to do this, he must be a man fully in control of his own heart, soul and passions. For Bernard this is *caritas ordinata*.

Even on the personal level, Bernard states, one cannot love another person without first having that spiritual love of self (*diligere*), that is, a right order of charity.[24] "If, however, you should first learn to love (*diligere*) yourself, then, perhaps you will know how to love (*amare*) me."

Bernard then goes on to answer the objections that might be raised by Bruno to his thesis in the form of historical figures, Mary Magdalen, Matthew and Paul. These are exceptions. No analogy will bring them to evidence in favor of the case of Bruno. Mary Magdalen is an interesting example for "she without the labor of many penances" had her sins forgiven, "for she loved (*dilexit*) much" (Lk 8:37-50). So, in a short time she merited the *latitudinem caritatis*, that which "covers a multitude of sins" (1 Pet 4:8).

In *Letter* 10 Bernard uses the word *caritas* in a sense that may at first seem strange, if not satirical, but actually it is a matter of using the word to gain a hearing. He writes this *Letter* to admonish Bruno, now Bishop of Cologne. Bernard's advice, for bishops, abbots, and all in high places, is to "walk with the humble, and fear." Bruno is still in the first stages of the program of *caritas ordinata*.

"Three stages of Spitirual Growth according to St. Bernard," *Studia Monastica* 11 (1969) p. 326. The trilogy is developed by Bernard in the stages of ascent to *caritas*. Penance is the first stage for entry into the monastic life and, indeed, is the evangelical call of John the Baptist.

24. See H. Pétrè, *Caritas, étude sur le vocabulaire latin de la charité Chrétienne*, pp. 79-98. Bernard seems to follow Ambrose and Augustine in his use of *diligere, amare, caritas,* and *amor* rather than the earlier Fathers studied by Pétrè. The usage here seems to follow that of the passage in Jn 21:15 where Jesus questions Peter, "*diligas me? ... amas me?* and the comment of Ambrose (*Exp. Ev. sec. Luc*; X, 176 [PL 15:184 8C], noted by her on p. 81.

Ep 11 (108C-115C)

This *Letter* is the most rich of this whole collection of twenty-one *Letters* in its use of *caritas*. It is in fact a short treatise on *caritas*, setting out in full Bernard's thought and teaching. Much has been written about this letter and more generally about the place of *caritas* in the mystical theology of St Bernard. But I wish to dwell on the place of *caritas* not only in this *Letter* but in the collection, and as such it is this *Letter* that provides the key to the understanding of the whole.

In this *Letter* Bernard responds to the charity that Guigo, prior of the Grande Chartreuse, has shown in writing to him. In that same spirit of charity, Bernard responds, "Truly, what I would not dare do, charity does dare" (109C). Charity is the *amicitiarum matrem*. But it is in section three (110C) that Bernard comes to the heart of his matter, the hierarchy of love. Here he makes his famous distinction between the three types of subjects of the Father: the slave, the hireling, and the son.[25] The characteristic of the first is fear; that of the second, greed for reward. All participate in the economy of the Father's will, they can all serve the ends of goodness. Nonetheless, it is only the third who loves disinterestedly, who loves the Father for his own sake, recalling the quotation from 1 Cor 13:5: *caritas non quaerit quae sua sunt* (111A). One of the marks of this "true and sincere charity," proceeding from an all pure heart, a good conscience and an unwavering faith, is that "we love (*diligimus*) the good of our neighbor equally as our own" (110C).

25. Cf Gregory of Nyssa, *In Cant. Cant.* (ed. Langerbeck, pp. 15-6): "For He, 'Who will have all men to be saved, and to come to the knowledge of the truth,' shows us in this book the most perfect and glorious path of salvation, I mean by way of love. For some are saved by fear, as for example, when we break from sin because we have our eyes fixed on the threatened punishment of hell. There are others too, who live lives of virtue because of the rewards promised to the good; and these possess their goal not by charity but by their hope of reward. But he who runs in the Spirit to reach perfection, casts out fear. For it is the attitude of a slave, who does not stay with his master out of love and simply does not run away for fear he will be punished. The truly virtuous man even despises rewards, lest he give the impression that he esteems the gift more than the giver."
But most importantly, see Cassian, *Conferences*, XI, 6, 7, where this same metaphor occurs. It is evangelical, as this passage shows.

Bernard interprets the words from Ps 18:8, *Lex Domini
immaculata, convertens animas,* as refering to the attitude of
the son, who alone has charity because he has faith in the
Lord who is goodness itself (*quoniam simpliciter bonus est*).
The first two types of affection are motivated by self-concern, not by disinterestedness. Only *caritas* can convert the
soul, because it alone is disinterested. He then gives a long
and rather "Scholastic" interpretation of the idea that even
God himself is ruled by the law of charity. But this is not law
in the sense that it is applied to mankind, rather it is the
divine substance itself (*substantiam illam divinam,* 111C).
Here again, as in *Letters* 1 and 7, it is stated that God is
charity, and that charity is the bond of peace and unity in
the Holy Trinity. Furthermore, "it is rightly said that *caritas*
is God and the gift of God. Thus Charity gives charity, the
substance gives the accident. When the Giver is meant, the
name is the substance, when the gift is meant, the quality.
This is the eternal law, the creator and ruler of the universe . . . and nothing remains without a law, so the law of all
things is not without a law; however, it is not different from
itself, for though it did not create itself, nonetheless, it does
rule."

Bernard wishes to establish a system of *rectus ordo* in the
spiritual life. In order to do this the first principle must be
sound. For him the first rule of the spiritual life is the Law of
God, any other man-made law bears with it its own consequences. But the Law of God is nothing other than God
himself, *caritas.* So the law of the slave and the law of the
hireling (that is, any solely human *modus vivendi*) are still
subject to the Divine Law. The result of the slave's law is
fear; that of *caritas, fiducia.* The result of the law of the
hireling is greed, self-interest; the result of *caritas* is fraternal
love, disinterestedness (selflessness). The one ruled by charity
is under a light yoke (*sub levi onere,* 112C). The prevailing
movement in the Law of Charity is that of the Holy Spirit,
spiritus libertatis. As one of the sons of God, one is in this
world; by participation in the Divine Life, in *caritas,* one is as
God in this world.

As the logical conclusion to the postulate that God is ruled by a law, that of charity, is that of the sons of God not without a law. This law of the son is not fearful, but *a spiritu libertatis data in suavitate.* The just are not bound by the law because they are not *in timore,* but they are not without the law of charity because they are "adopted sons." The reason for their freedom is that the Law of God is not imposed from without, but offered freely, either to be accepted or rejected. To those who will not accept the Law, God says, ". . . take it if you wish. Otherwise you will not find rest but labor for your souls" (113A).

Herein is not a rigid system of "either/or"—it is not a hard and fast scheme that is complete, but it allows for movement within itself. Bernard states that the law of charity "lightens" the burden of the law of the slave and the hireling as well, taking as his text Matt 5:7: "I have not come to destroy the law, but to perfect it." The law of the slave (fear) is given devotion, thus taking away anguish (*poena*). The law of the hireling is rightly ordered (*recte ordinatur*); so that first evil is rejected, the better is prefered to the merely good, and good only because of what is better.

Bernard distinguishes four stages in this spiritual growth in the law of charity. We are creatures of the earth, of flesh and blood, we are born of the desire of the flesh, but if correctly directed (*si recto ordine dirigitur*), we develop by grace, until we are consumed by the Spirit. First, a man loves himself. Secondly, realizing his own finitude, man begins to seek God by faith and to love him, but again, in a selfish way. Thirdly, by meditation, reading, praying and obedience (*cogitando, legendo, orando, obediendo*), that is, by the Benedictine formula, he comes to love God for his own sake.[26] The fourth stage, Bernard says, is outside his own experience, that is, when a man loves himself for God's sake. At this stage man enters fully into the life of the Holy Trinity; he is outside

26. Cf SC 50:4 (OB 2:80).

himself, *inebriatus*, and with God, *ei unus spiritus erit*. It is the state known in the Patristic age as *theosis*.[27]

There is then a right order to the spiritual life. For Bernard this right order should be reflected in the lives and actions of the members of the Church, especially those in authority and monks.

Ep 13 (116C) and *Ep 14* (117B)

There is one occurence of *caritas* in each of these *Letters* addressed to Pope Honorius. The usage is both polite and at the same time reveals two facts. For Bernard states that he dares to write to the Pope because of the urging of *domina caritas* (117B) who rules both of them, and that charity suffices (116C). This is an expression of Bernard's ecclesiology and reveals the supreme and at the same time gently feminine character he ascribes to *caritas*, which he elsewhere calls *bona mater* (Ep 2).

Ep 18:2, 3 (121 C,D)

In the first section of this letter, addressed to Peter, Cardinal Deacon,[28] charity is seen in its relation to faith, know-

27. On the connexion between *theosis* and charity, see Gregory Nazianzus, *Carm.* 1. 2. 34. 160-1 (PG 37:957A) and especially Maximus the Confessor, Ep 2 (PG 91:393B). It would be interesting to study the transmission and history of this connexion. Does it come through Cassian (cf *Institutes*, V, 38, 2; IX, 11; XII, 31; XII, 32, 1; *Conferences*, I, 6, 7, 10; XI. 6 (SC, 54:107); XI, 7: "tertium *(caritatem) specialiter dei est et eorum qui in sese imaginem dei ac similitudinem recepterunt*;" and XVI, 13) or through Benedict (RB 7:67; cf 2:19-22; Prologue 45-8; from Evagrius (cf S. Marsili, *Giovanni Cassiano ed Evagrio Pontico*, pp. 23-4; 68-9; 106-10; 116-7) or did Bernard know Maximus the Confessor through translations? He need not have, as the doctrine of Maximus is heavily dependent on Evagrius (cf M. Viller, "Aux sources de la spiritualité de Saint Maxime. Les oeuvres d'Evagre le Pontique" RAM, 11 (1930) 156-84, 239-68, 331-6. I think it more likely that the influence is through Cassian, or directly from Origen, whom Bernard knew in translation. On Cassian and his relationship to RB on this point, see the magnificent work of A. de Vogüé, *La Régle de Saint Benoît*, 6 vols., S. Ch 181-6 (Paris: Cerf, 1971-2), 4:344-52. Also see J. E. Bamberger, "Introduction," Evagrius Ponticus, *Prakitikos - Chapters on Prayer*, CS 4 (Spencer, Mass.: Cistercian Publications 1970) p. lxxxvi: "The content of the Evagrian *apatheia* is fully Christian beyond all cavil, both in its inspiration and in its aim. It is the art of achieving the right order of charity, as the medieval monks would speak of it, that Evagrius describes when he writes on attaining the *apatheia*."

28. See D. van den Eynde OFM, "Les Premiers écrits de saint Bernard" in J. Leclercq, *Recueil, d'études sur saint Bernard et ses écrits III* (Rome, 1969), pp. 343-348.

ledge and desire. The soul begins by faith and desire for God and reaches its culmination in understanding and love (*intellectus et amor*). Desire leads to *perfecta dilectio,* and as it is a desire, it leads to the perfection of charity (*perfectio caritatis*). It is the desire of the just man which reaches the height of its fulfillment "in joy drinking from the fountains of the Saviour," delighting in the plenitude of charity. The important step in the argument is that justice proceeds from faith, thus in judgment it is full understanding. Without faith there is no true understanding. *Caritas,* too, is the fruit of faith. In this world the just live by faith, but in heaven by understanding, then charity will attain its fullness.

In the second section dealing with *caritas* Bernard shows that these two, understanding and love (*intellectus et amor*) are eternity; *caritas,* power and wisdom, Christ himself, for *Deus caritas est.* The factor that obscures things and makes it impossible for us to love God as he is, is human vanity which makes us desire praise and unwilling to praise others, even God, when they deserve it.

All this was written by Bernard as a quick letter to establish that he does not deserve the praise of the Cardinal-deacon. This theme occurs often in these letters and thus may be seen to be a pointer to something that Bernard wishes to say by way of apology: that it is not he himself who is deserving of praise or adulation, but only God himself, for God alone is the perfection of love, and the cause of all love, and thus, only he is deserving of our love for his own sake. An important corollary to this is fraternal charity.

Ep 20 (123B)

This usage of *caritas* is similar to that in *Letter 14.* It is used as a polite way of entering a plea. The use here linking *caritas* to truth and justice may be a clue to the reason for the inclusion in the collection of this *Letter* as well as *Letter 21* which is addressed to another high ecclesiastic, Matthew, a papal legate, as adjuncts to this section dealing with the Church universal.

Conclusion

Bernard's use of *caritas* in these *Letters* presents a rather unified and complete picture of his thought on the matter. The systematic approach to this important theological concept is quite startling. Yet, it is not an abstract discussion. Bernard relates it to the life and practice of the monk, the bishop and the abbot, to all in authority in the Church. The prime consideration in all this is *rectus ordo*, not only of the Church but of the spiritual life of the individual as well; Bernard sees these two as intimately linked. It is this connexion that gives force to the use of *caritas* in the first two *Letters* dealing with the role of the abbot and perhaps a sense that the same issue was ultimately at stake lead Bernard to include the *Letter* addressed to Adam (7). The list at the beginning of this essay outlines the various sections within this group of twenty-one *Letters*. It is important to note that in each of the sections dealing with a different hierarchy within the Church *caritas* occurs. The concept covers the Church universal.[29]

Yet, in order for Bernard to present this concept, already latent in the *B* collection in *Letters* 11, 12, 2, and 1, he had to expand the collection of *Letters* in *Longior*. A sense of context may have lead him to the inclusion of such *Letters* as 4, 5, 6 (dealing with Abbot Arnold), *Letter* 10 (dealing with Bruno of Cologne), *Letter* 15 (dealing with the same case as *Letter* 14) and *Letter* 16 either because it deals with the same case as *Letters* 14 and 15 or because it is addressed to Peter, Cardinal-deacon, as are *Letters* 17, 18, and 19. *Letter* 17 itself is introduced because of its relationship to *Letter* 18.[30] *Letter* 19 because of its relationship to *Letter* 20, and so also *Letter* 21. Thus we can see that the doctrine of *caritas* is intimately linked to the actual life and daily problems of the government of the Church, the monastery and to the indi-

29. See A. de Vogüé, "Le monastere, Eglise du Christ," *Studia Anselmiana* 42 (Rome, 1957) 25-46, esp. p. 36. It is the ancient concept of the unity of monastery and Church that is expressed in these letters of Bernard and it is to this type of literature, studied by de Vogüé, that these initial twenty-one letters belong.

30. See n. 28 above.

vidual spiritual life of their members. This is perhaps precisely what Bernard wished to emphasize.

The *Letters* present then a study of charity (*caritas*) in the individual soul and in the Church universal. Bernard pays close attention to the foundations and to the development of true charity in his three stations of fear, selfishness and unselfishness. These correspond to the movement from ignorance to faith, from faith to understanding, and thence to charity as outlined in *Letter* 18. The soul moves in the same way from obedience to humility and then to fraternal love, and then to *caritas,* to God Himself.

Further, we can see a type of editorial arrangement of the *Letters* corresponding to the three sets of stages in the movement toward *caritas*. It is to be noted that each set leads to a fourth stage, of which Bernard will not speak. These three stages are set forth in the *Letters* in a particular order. First, we find in *Letter* 7 the explication and summation of the doctrine of the preceeding six *Letters*: the role of *caritas* in the monastic life. This is the movement that we have outlined as being from obedience to humility to fraternal love. It is noteworthy that in this same *Letter* the Trinitarian model is used (94A) and the colon is made of unity, peace, and charity. The second colon is found in *Letter 11* dealing with the ascent of the individual soul on the *scala caritatis,* namely the famous division of the hireling (fear), the servant (self-concern) and finally, the son (disinterested love—*caritas*). It is here that Bernard explicitly states that there is a fourth stage which he believes to be impossible to reach in this life (114A) but which some may have experienced. It is the state that is the reward of the "good and faithful servant," the state of *inebritatus* and of being one in spirit with God. Finally, in *Letter 18* he speaks of the trilogy of faith and desire, understanding (true judgment) and *caritas*. Noteworthy here is the final stage of this movement, that by which those in heaven live, understanding and love (*intellectus et amor*), that is to say eternity, *caritas,* power and wisdom, Christ himself, for *Deus caritas est.*

Thus we see in *Letters* 1 to 21 three colons of degrees of

perfection or virtue leading to *Caritas,* each of these three colons is consummated in a fourth degree or state which itself forms a fourth and culminating colon, corresponding to the Trinity itself and about which Bernard is silent. Thus we see obedience, fear and faith forming the first degree; and humility, self-concern and desire forming the second. The third degree is formed by fraternal love, disinterested love and true understanding based on the judgment formed by charity. The consummation of all these is in God himself, *Caritas.*

This arrangement is surely not accidental and is, I posit, evidence of the editorial processes that Bernard employed in making the collection *Longior.* It shows us the prime motive for this revised collection and also the intent of the author—to present a unified and complete doctrine of *caritas* as the sole factor that he held to be essential in the life of the Church. He attempts to include under this supreme virtue the other virtues, both moral and intellectual, that go to make the whole man, formed in the image of God, to wit, obedience, humility, fraternal love, fear, self-desire, disinterestedness, faith, intellectual desire and discernment (true understanding). All these are subject to the will of God and are used by him to lead the soul, the whole man, the monk and indeed the whole Church on to the "joy from the fountains of the Saviour," delighting in the plenitude of charity, in the life of the Trinity itself.

G. L. J. Smerillo

Pembroke College
Oxford

TWO TREATISES ON LOVE

WHENEVER ONE SPEAKS of William of St Thierry
one immediately thinks of Bernard of Clairvaux.
And I think Bernard would be happy if whenever
one spoke of Bernard of Clairvaux, William came to mind. At
least Bernard's letters give us a strong basis for saying this.[1]
The lives of these two twelfth-century monks, alike and unlike in so many ways, were intimately intertwined.[2] At their
very first meeting[3] they seem to have discovered "another

1. See Bernard's Letters to William of St Thierry: Ep 85 and 86; PL
182:206-210; tr. Bruno Scott James, *The Letters of St. Bernard of Clairvaux,*
Letters 87 and 88, pp. 124-128, where we read such passages as: "I love you as
much as I can according to the power that has been given to me." "It was you
who gave me this formula of greeting when you wrote 'To his friend all that a
friend could wish.' Receive back what is your own, and in doing so realize that
my soul is not far from one with whom I share a common language." James
includes as Letter 89 (pp. 128-129) one that might have been addressed to William at the time he went to Signy against Bernard's will. Here we read Bernard
writing of William: "I do not ask for my friend back, because I am confident that
I hold him. I do not receive him back, because I have never lost him. I cling to
him, and there is no one who can take him from me."

2. I hesitate to say "Cistercians" since over half the time William and Bernard
were friends, William was a Black Monk, as he was for the greater part of his
monastic life. Yet William is spoken of as one of the "Four Evangelists of
Cîteaux."

3. We can not say for certain exactly when William first visited Bernard. Jean-
Marie Déchanet, *William of St Thierry: The Man and his Work,* CS 10, tr. Richard
Strachen (Spencer, Massachusetts: Cistercian Publications, 1972) p. 24, says: "To-
ward the end of the year 1118, when he was still a monk at St Nicaise. . . ." But
Stanislaus Ceglar, who explores the question extensively (*William of Saint
Thierry: The Chronology of his Life with a Study of his Treatise* On the Nature of
Love, *His Authorship of the* Brevis Commentatio, *the* In Lacu, *and the* Reply to
Cardinal Matthew [Ann Arbor, Michigan: University Microfilms, 1971] pp. 33-40)
gives the opinions of all the authors and himself concludes: "If, then, one puts the

137

self" in each other, and no matter what popular notions about monks and friendship might expect,[4] these two undoubtedly totally dedicated and saintly monks did not hesitate to take even extraordinary measures to foster and enjoy their friendship.[5]

Until fairly recently it was assumed that Bernard was wholly the master, William the admiring disciple.[6] However, more recently, as William has come more into his own, this has been more and more questioned. Dom Jean Leclercq has clearly established William's influence on Bernard's *Apologia*[7] and his *Adversus Abaelardum.*[8] In the one case it is perhaps more extrinsic; in the other William clearly acts as Bernard's theologian.[9] But the matter is not so clear when we

probable approximate time of our William's first visit to Clairvaux in the early spring of 1120, one could hardly be more than five months wrong."—p. 40.

4. For a thorough study of the attitude of the early Cistercians on friendship see M. Adele Fiske, *Friends and Friendship in the Monastic Tradition,* CIDOC Cuaderno 51 (Cuernavaca: CIDOC, 1970).

5. In his life of Bernard, William candidly admits that after their first encounter he became a frequent visitor: "It was about this time that I myself began to be a frequent visitor to him and his monastery." (Vita Bern I, 7, 32-4; PL 185:246). And Bernard himself took an active part in developing the friendship. William writes: "I was unwell at St Thierry, drained of strength and quite worn out by an illness that dragged on and on. When the man of God heard the news he sent his brother Gerard, of blessed memory, to bid me come to Clairvaux. . . . Bernard's illness itself worked for my good, while I lay ill beside him. Flat on our backs, the two of us, we spent the livelong day talking. . . ." (Vita Bern, I, 12, 59; PL 185:259).

6. See note 14 below.

7. See Jean Leclercq's Introduction to the *Apologia* in *Sancti Bernardi Opera* 9 vols. (Rome: Editiones Cistercienses, 1957-1973 [Hereafter OB]), 3:63-7.

8. Jean Leclercq, "Les lettres de Guillaume de Saint-Thierry à saint Bernard," *R Ben* 79 (1969) 375-82. Leclercq concludes: " . . . il ressort que la dépendance de Bernard à l'égard de Guillaume est, non seulement manifeste, mais très étroite, beaucoup plus qu'on aurait pu s'y attendre de la part de saint Bernard."

9. See Edward Little, "Bernard and Abelard at the Council of Sens, 1140," in *Bernard of Clairvaux: Studies presented to Dom Jean Leclercq* (Washington, D.C.: Cistercian Publications, 1973) pp. 35-51; especially the Appendix where Little lists the Nineteen Propositions of Bernard and the Thirteen Propositions of William, stating: "Bernard's nineteen propositions are a re-working of a list of thirteen, which William of St-Thierry had included in a letter he had written to Bernard and to Bishop Geoffrey of Chartres. Bernard took some of William's propositions unchanged (William's no. 3, 5); he altered some (William's no. 4, 6, 7, 8, 10, 11, 13); he omitted some (William's no. 1, 2, 9, 12); he added some of his own. . . ." (pp. 50-51). See also Jean Leclercq, "Les forms succesives de la lettre-traité de saint Bernard contre Abélard," *R Ben* 78 (1968) 86-105.

come to their spiritual doctrine. All sorts of conjectures have been made in the light of the *Brevis commentatio*.[10] My aim in this brief paper is not so ambitious as to try to solve this extremely complicated question, but rather to make a very modest contribution to the study of it by comparing, under certain aspects, the rather brief and relatively early treatises on love which each of these monks has left us.[11]

Even though we cannot date either piece with certitude, the chronology is fairly well established. William's treatise seem quite certainly the earlier. Most would date it around 1120.[12] It may be conjectured that it is substantially composed of chapter talks William gave to his community in his early days as abbot of St Thierry. We might further fill out this conjecture by suggesting the following development:

William, as a significant member of the community of St Nicaise, accompanied his abbot on a trip south.[13] On their way back they broke their journey to see the young abbot of

10. Ceglar studies the question at length (*William of St Thierry*, Chap. IX: "William's Part in the *Brevis Commentatio*," pp. 350-379) and concludes: "It can be taken for certain that *BC* is a more or less faithful literary record of the spiritual conversations of the two friends, as described by William in the *Vita Bernardi*, xii, 59." (p. 352). See also, J. Hourlier, "Guillaume de Saint-Thierry et la *'Brevis commentatio in Cantica'*," ASOC 12 (1956) 105-114; Jean Leclercq, "Le commentaire bref du Cantique attribué à St Bernard," in *Etudes sur St Bernard et le texte de ses écrits*, ASOC 9 (1953) 105-124.

11. Dom Hourlier has already done a comparative study of these two treatises: "Saint Bernard and Guillaume de Saint-Thierry dans le *'Liber de Amore'*," in *Saint Bernard Théologien: Actes du Congrès de Dijon, 15-19 september 1953*, ASOC 9 (1953) 223-233. It is hoped that the additional ideas presented here will complement that study and bring the whole question a step forward.

12. Déchanet in *William of St Thierry* (p. 11) says: "Written between 1119 and 1122. . . ." and in his chronological listing in *Oeuvres choisies du Guillaume de Saint-Thierry* (Paris: Aubier, 1944) says "Vers 1120" (p. 39). Ceglar says Hourlier accepts this (Ceglar, *William of St Thierry*, p. 377) but this is not clear in the text of Hourlier (*La contemplation de Dieu*, SCh 61 [Paris: Cerf, 1959] pp. 15-17). Ceglar himself studies the question and concludes: " . . . Déchanet's dating . . . is certainly wrong." (p. 377); "In short, there are no cogent reasons to date *CD* and *NDA* [the treatise we are considering] before the mid-twenties of the XII century (1124-26)." (p. 378). A. Wilmart ("La série et la date des ouvrages de Guillaume de Saint-Thierry," *Revue Mabillon* 14 [1924] 156-167) holds for around 1120.

13. Admittedly, it is not clear from the text that the abbot in question is his own abbot: " . . . when I first went to see him with a certain other abbot. . . ." —*St. Bernard of Clairvaux*, tr. Geoffrey Webb and Adrian Walker (Westminster, Maryland: Newman Press, 1960) p. 56.

Clairvaux whose reputation was already rapidly growing. That Bernard made a profound impression on William at that first encounter cannot be doubted. Some thirty years later, William would still speak of it with awe:

> It was about this time that I myself began to be a frequent visitor to him and his monastery. . . . Going into the hovel which had become a palace by his presence in it, and thinking what a wonderful person dwelt in such a despicable place, I was filled with such awe of the hut itself that I felt as if I were approaching the very altar of God. And the sweetness of his character so attracted me to him and filled me with desire to share his life amid such poverty and simplicity, that if the chance had then been given to me I should have asked nothing more than to be allowed to remain with him always, looking after him and ministering to his needs. . . . But it is not really true to say that he was alone, for God was with him, and the holy angels came to console and watch over him. . . . Although unworthy of so great a privilege, I remained with him for a few days, and as I looked about me I thought that I was gazing on a new heaven and a new earth, for it seemed as though there were tracks freshly made by men of our own day in the path that had first been trodden by our fathers, the Egyptian monks of long ago.[14]

Undoubtedly William returned home inspired to seek a more truly contemplative life. But the way was not to be easy for him, for he was very soon elected abbot of the not insignificant abbey of St Thierry. Something of his struggle, one that would grow and be reflected in all his writings until it was resolved by his resignation in 1136, is expressed in his earliest extent work, the soliloquy, *On Contemplating God*.[15] In this William poured out his longing for that contemplative experience which he saw irradiating the life and countenance of his

14. Ibid., pp. 56-58.
15. The critical edition of this was published by Hourlier, SCh 61 (See note 12 above). An English translation is available in the Cistercian Fathers Series: Sister Penelope [Lawson] CSMV, *The Works of William of St Thierry*, Vol. 1: *On Contemplating God, Prayer, Meditations*, CF 3 (Spencer, Massachusetts: Cistercian Publications, 1971) pp. 36-64.

recently acquired friend. He perceived that the experience is to be obtained essentially through desire and is found in love. This naturally leads to his investigation of the *Nature and Dignity of Love.*[16]

Bernard's treatise, *On Loving God,*[17] as a whole certainly was written later. The inclusion of the *Letter to the Carthusians*[18] and the fact that Cardinal Haimeric, to whom the treatise is addressed, became chancellor only in 1126 makes that year the earliest possible date for the treatise's composition. The death of the Cardinal determines the other extreme: 1141.[19] But chronological succession does not settle the question of dependency nor even throw much light on it. William probably visited Clairvaux more than once before he wrote his treatise.[20] We could well imagine the neophyte abbot, on his visits, carefully listening to his renowned friend's talks to his community and taking mental, if not actual, notes which he would make use of when he returned home and spoke to his own community.

We have perhaps some evidence of this if we compare sections 18-24 of his treatise[21] with Bernard's *Tenth Occasional Sermon.*[22] These *Sermones de diversis* are probably in good part some of the ordinary chapter talks that Bernard gave his community. From its position toward the beginning of the series, it can be surmised that *Sermon Ten* was

16. Perhaps the best edition of Nat am is that of Robert Thomas, Pain de Cîteaux 24 (Chambarand, 1965). A critical edition is presently being prepared by John Cummings of Wilson College, Chambersberg, Pennsylvania, who is also preparing a translation for the Cistercian Fathers Series. Webb and Walker published a translation in 1956 (*On the Nature and Dignity of Love* [London: Mowbrays, 1956]) based on the Migne edition (PL 184:379-408) and on that of M.-M. Davy (*Deux traités de l'amour de Dieu: De la contemplation de Dieu, De la nature et la dignité de l'amour* [Paris: Vrin, 1953]) who employed only a very limited number of manuscripts in the preparation of her edition.

17. OB 3:119-154; *On the Love of God,* tr. A Religious of CSMV [Sr Penelope Lawson] (London: Mowbray, 1950).

18. OB 3:148-154. This section is not found in the translation cited.

19. See Leclercq's Introduction, OB 3:111-112.

20. See note 5 above.

21. Davy, *Deux traités,* pp. 96-100; Webb and Walker, *On the Nature,* pp. 30-33.

22. OB 6-2:121-124. There is so far no published translation of these *Sermones de diversis,* but one is in preparation for the Cistercian Fathers Series.

preached and/or written early in Bernard's career, at a date
perhaps not too far distant from the time William spoke in
the same vein to his community. There is a certain amount of
conjecture here, but if we read the two passages we will see
that they are undoubtedly related: [23]

23.   *Sermo 10*

Porro dilectionem quidem multipli-
cem, si diligenter advertas, et fortasse
secundum quinque corporis sensus
quinquepertitam poteris invenire.

Denique, si curiosius considerare de-
lectat, non immerito fortasse videbi-
tur primus, id est parentum amor,
tactui convenire, quod hic sensus sola
proxima et corpori iuncta percipiat,
quemadmodum amor ille nullis exhi-
betur nisi proximis carnis nostrae.
Sed nec illud quidem discrepat a ratione similitudinis, quod hic solus e
sensibus per corpus diffunditur uni-
versum, quoniam et amor ille naturalis est omni carni, adeo ut ipsa quoque animalia bruta et diligant fetus
suos, et diligantur ab eis.

Amor quoque socialis videre licet
quam proprie dicatur gustui convenire, ob maiorem profecto dulcedinem, et quoniam solus hic sensus est,
quo magis eget humana vita. Nec vi-
deo qua ratione vivere dicendus sit,
saltem hac communi vita, qui non eos
diligit inter quos vivit.

Amor autem generalis, quo videlicet
omnes homines diliguntur, odoratus
habet similitudinem, in eo utique

Nat am

Per quinque sensus corporis, mediante vita, corpus anime conjungitur: per
quinque sensus spirituales, mediante
caritate, anima Deo consociatur.

Tactui comparatur amor parentum:
quia affectus iste promptus omnibus,
et quodammodo grossus et palpabilis,
sic se omnibus naturali quodam oc-
cursu prebet et ingerit, ut effugere
eum non possis, etiam si velis. Tactus
enim sensus et totus corporalis qui ex
quorumlibet corporum conjunctione
conficitur. . . .

Secundo, gustui comparatur amor socialis, amor fratrum, amor sancte et
catholice Ecclesie. . . . Gustus etiam
licet corporaliter exerceatur saporem
tamen introrsum generat, quo anima
afficitur. Propter quod corporalis quidem sensus hic maxime, sed tamen ex
parte aliqua etiam animales esse com-
probatur. Sic et amor socialis, quia ex
corporali cohabitatione in unum, ex
similitudine professionum, ex parili-
tate studiorum, aliisque hujusmodi
causis, confederatur mutuisque offi-
ciis enutritur, maxime animalis esse
videtur. Sed tamen ex magna parte
etiam spiritualis est, quia sicut sapor
est in gustu, sic affectus fraterne caritatis flagrat in affectu. . . .

Tertio, odori comparatur amor naturalis, qui naturaliter ex ipsius nature
similitudine et consortio absque omni

quod hic sensus iam remotiora percipiat, et quod non ex toto carnalis delectationis expers, eo tamen tenuiorem eam habeat, quo diffusiorem.

Auditus autem multo magis remotiora capit, nec inter homines ab amante quisquam remotior est quam non amans. Denique cum in ceteris sensibus nonnulla carnis ipsius oblectatio sit, et ad carnem magis pertinere videantur, auditus paene totus exit a carne, et ei dilectioni non immerito convenire videtur, cuius tota causa oboedientia est, quam pertinere ad auditum satis evidens est, cum ceterarum, ut diximus, dilectionum nonnulla a carne sumatur occasio.

Porro visus quidem in eo sibi vindicat amoris divini similitudinem, quod ceteris omnibus excellentior et singularis cuiusdam naturae, perspicacior quoque ceteris invenitur, et discernit multo remotiora. Denique odoratus quidem et auditus videntur utique remota sentire; sed ad se magis quem sentiant aerem creduntur attrahere. Visus autem non ita, sed magis ipse exire videtur et ad remota procedere. Sic et in dilectionibus est. Quodammodo enim attrahimus proximos, quos tamquam nosipsos diligimus: Attrahimus et inimicos, quos ad hoc diligimus, ut sint et ipsi sicut nos, id est ut sint amici. Deum vero si, ut dignum est, tota virtute, tota anima, toto corde diligimus, ipsi magis in eum pergimus, et tota festinatione in eum, qui ineffabiliter supra nos est, properamus. / Iam vero et id manifestum est, quoniam in corporis sensibus visus quidem ceteris omnibus, auditus vero reliquis tribus dignior est; ordoratus quoque et gustum, et tactum, etsi non utilitate, dignitate tamen su-

spe recompensationis omnem hominem diligit. . . . Sic et amor naturalis magis spiritualis esse videtur quam animalis; quia, preter solum connaturalis humanitatis respectum, non consanguinitas, non societas, nec aliqua omnino in eo necessitudo hujusmodi consideratur.

Quarto, auditui comparatur amor spiritualis, amor inimicorum. Auditus enim nichil interius, id est intra corpus operatur, sed exterius quodammodo, id est ad aures pulsans, animam evocat ut exeat et audiat. Sic et amorem inimicorum in corde nulla vis nature, nullius alicujus necessitudinis suscitat affectus sed sola obedientia, que per auditum significatur.

Quinto, visui comparatur amor divinus. Visus enim principalis est sensus: sicut inter omnes affectiones principatum obtinet amor divinus. . . . Visus in eminenti corporis arce et insigni capitis loco positus etiam secundum ipsius corporis formam infra se habet et ordine, et dignitate, et virtutis potentia omnia ceterorum sensuum instrumenta, ipsosque sensus, quos, ut ita dicam, animaliores, propinquiores, quos vero corporaliores, remotiores. Infimus enim omnium et ceteris ignobilior tactus, licet communis videatur esse totius corporis, tamen proprie manuum est. Sic mens que caput est anime, et principale ipsius mentis, sedes esse debet amoris Dei, ut sub se habeat et regat et illustret ceteros amores, nec sit in eis quod se abscondat a calore et lumine ejus; quos spiritua);iores, habens propinquiores, quos animaliores vel carnaliores, remotiores: cum dilexerimus Dominum Deum nostrum et extoto corde nostro, et ex tota anima nostra et ex omnibus veribus nostris et post

Sermon Ten

If you consider the matter carefully you can see that love is a multifold thing, and perhaps is fivefold like the five senses of the body. . . .

Then, if you care to examine the matter more carefully you will perhaps see that, indeed, the first form of love, love of one's own relatives, is like the sense of touch. This sense perceives only what is closest to it and is joined to the body, and so also is that love given to those closest to our own flesh. And this also enters into the likeness: this sense alone is found in every body, because this love is natural to all flesh. . . .

The Nature and Dignity of Love

There are, as we have said, five bodily senses, and by means of these the soul gives sense-life to the body. Likewise there are five spiritual senses by means of which charity gives life to the soul. . . .

The love of near relatives is compared to the sense of touch, for this disposition is inherent in all men and we think of it as common and somehow tangible. It wells up in everyone in the most natural way, and there is no way of stopping it. The sense of touch is wholly corporeal, and it comes about by the contact of any two bodies. Contact will engender touch in any body which is alive.

Sermo

perare videtur, et gustus tactui superexcellere, quod manifestat etiam dispositio ipsa membrorum. Oculis siquidem in summitate locatis, aures inferiores esse quis nesciat? Sic et auribus nares, et naribus fauces, ipsis quoque faucibus manus pariter et reliquas corporis partes, ad quas pertinet tactus, subesse manifestum est. Secundum hunc ergo modum, et in sensibus animae considerare licet alterum altero digniorem, quod, quia facile iam potestis advetere, brevitatis causa praetereo. Illud quoque vestrae nihilominus diligentiae consederandum relinquo. . . . —OB 6-1:122-123.

Nat am

proximum nostrum sicut nos ipsos. —Nat am 18-24; Davy, *Deux traités,* pp. 96-100; Webb and Walker, *On the Nature,* pp. 29-32.

Sermon Ten

We can see how much social love is like the sense of taste, both because of the greater sweetness it brings into one's life and because this is the particular sense of which human life stands more in need. I cannot see how one can be said to live, at least in this common life, if he does not love those among whom he lives.

The Nature and Dignity of Love

Social love is compared to the sense of taste. This is brotherly love, the love of the holy catholic church. . . . Taste is admittedly a corporeal function, but its purpose is to bring about the savouring of food within the body, which savouring is for the soul's appreciation. So we may say that this sense is mainly a bodily thing, but quite evidently it also belongs in some measure to the soul. This is equally true of social love, which comes as the result of people living together and of sharing the same profession, or studies, or such like things. It provides a common bond and grows through mutual help and exchange. It would seem to belong to the soul considered in its relationship with the body (being based on physical cohabitation and common material interests), but it is in large part spiritual. For just as flavor is in tasting, so does brotherly love yield that love. . . .

General love, by which all men are loved, is like the sense of smell in this, that this sense perceives more

To the sense of smell we can compare natural love, by which we mean that love which causes us to love

Sermon Ten

distant things and while it is
not wholly divorced from
bodily pleasure, it nevertheless experiences it less insofar as it is more extended.

Hearing for its part per-
ceives things much more re-
mote, and among men no
one is so far removed from
the lover as the one who
does not love. While in the
other senses the flesh has
some share in the pleasure,
and they seem to belong
more to the flesh, hearing is
almost wholly outside the
realm of the flesh. And
hearing rightly seems to
apply to that love which a-
rises from obedience, for
that quite evidently belongs
to hearing. . . .

Finally, sight is like divine
love. It is more excellent
than the others and of a
rather unique nature. It is
more perceptive and dis-
cerns things at greater dis-
tances. Certainly smell and

*The Nature and Dignity
of Love*

every man in virtue of our
sharing in the same nature,
and to ask for nothing in return. . . . Natural love then
belongs more to the spirit
than to the soul which vivi-
fies the body, for it considers only the human conna-
turality of the loved one,
and has no respect for con-
sanguinity, society, or any
other kind of obligation.

Spiritual love we compare
to the sense of hearing. By
spiritual love we understand
the love of our enemies.
Hearing, instead of pro-
ducing its effect within the
body, works after an ex-
terior fashion. That is to
say, it knocks on the ear
and calls on the soul to
come out and hear. Like-
wise the love of our enemies
is not stirred in our hearts
by any power of nature, nor
by any spontaneous affec-
tion, but by obedience a-
lone, which hearing signi-
fies.

Divine love is compared to
sight, for sight is the highest
sense, and divine love is the
highest of all the affec-
tions. . . . The power of seeing is located in the highest
part of the body, and be-

hearing do seem to perceive distant objects but they are believed to do this through air which they take in. But this is not the case with sight which rather seems to go out and approach objects. So it is in the matter of love. In a certain sense we take to ourselves our neighbor whom we love as ourselves, and also our enemies whom we love, so that they might be as we are, friends of God. But if we love God, as he deserves, with all our strength, all our soul and all our hearts, it is more of a question of going out to him, and with all speed seeking to approach him who is inexpressibly above us. Indeed it is true and manifest that sight excels all the other bodily senses, and hearing has greater dignity than the other three. The sense of smell seems more eminent, if not more useful than taste and touch; and taste excels touch. This is manifest from the disposition of the various members of the body. The eyes have the highest place, the ears just a bit lower. The nostrils are lower than the ears, the lips below the nose, and the cause of this it has all the other instruments of sense beneath it. Those which belong rather to the soul are nearer to it than those which belong more to the body. The least of the senses, and the lowest, is touch, which is most proper to the hand although it is common to the whole body. The mind, which is the head of the soul, must be the seat of the love of God, so that from this position it may illumine, govern, and guard all the loves below itself, giving them of its own warmth and light. The more spiritual loves will be nearer to it than the more carnal ones, when we have learned to love God with all our heart and soul and strength, and when we really love our neighbor as ourselves.

Sermon Ten

hands and the other parts of
the body which pertain to
touch are clearly below the
mouth. In this way the relative dignity of the various
senses of the soul can be
considered, but, since you
can already easily see this,
because of the lack of time
I will move on. I will leave
that to your diligence to re-
flect on. . . .

The whole of these two texts should actually be read and
compared but the excerpts given here clearly demonstrate the
similarity of thought and construction. William's treatment is
more developed and many Scripture texts are brought forth.
Did he respond to Bernard's concluding invitation and dili-
gently consider the matter, developing it in his own presentation? Or was Bernard excerpting the essence of William's
text? It does not seem likely he would have invited his
hearers to develop the theme on their own if he and they
already had at hand a text written by William. Unless they
are drawing from some common source, I think we would
have to affirm some interdependency. And I would be inclined to say it is William who is developing Bernard as he has
been invited to do.

Let us consider another factor. A summary of Bernard's
treatise is to be found in an earlier letter, which Bernard did
not hesitate to add to his treatise (even though it includes
some relatively unrelated material[24]). This indicates that the
ideas were long in his mind. This letter was not an important

24. Most notably the development of the stages of fear, par. 36, OB 3:150-151.
The last seven par. of this treatise are not found in the translation of Sister
Penelope (St Bernard, *On the Love of God*, tr. by A Religious of CSMV [London:
Mowbray, 1950]), but will be found in CF 13 which is at the printer's at this
writing.

piece of writing and therefore did not call for a particular literary endeavor to be creative. When Bernard wrote to the Carthusians in 1125 he probably used ideas that were already in his mind, ideas he could well have discussed with his fellow abbot as they recuperated together. William tells us explicitly that they discoursed on the *Song of Songs,*[25] and Bernard does connect the consummation of his degrees of love with the *Song.*[26]

It is significant that the passage in the two treatises that most closely relates them is in the case of Bernard to be found in the earlier letter. It is in the central passage on the essential nature of charity. Compare the two:

On Loving God	The Nature and Dignity of Love
God is charity. Therefore it is rightly said, charity is God, and the gift of God. Thus charity gives charity, the substance produces the quality. Where the one giving is signified, the name stands for a substance; where it is a question of the gift, it stands for a quality.	Charity is God, and "God is charity." A short praise for charity, but it sums up everything. Whatever can be said of God can also be said of charity. Considered according to the nature of gift and giver, the name of the substance of charity is in the giver, the name of the quality of charity is in the gift.[27]

25. "It was then, so far as the length of my illness allowed, that he expounded the Song of Songs to me; though only in its moral sense, without launching upon the mysteries with which the book abounds. This is what I hoped for, what I had asked him to do."—Vita Bern, I, 12, 59; PL 185:259.

26. Par. 31-33; OB 3:145-147.

27.

Dil	*Nat am*
Deus caritas est. Dicitur ergo recte caritas, et Deus, et Dei donum. Itaque caritas dat caritatem, substantiva accidentalem. Ubi dantem significat, nomen substantiae est; ubi donum, qualitatis.—Par. 35; OB 3:149.	Caritas autem Deus est: Deus, inquit, caritas est. Brevis laus, sed concludens omnia. Quicquid de Deo dici potest, potest dici et de caritate; sic tamen ut, considerata secundum naturas doni et dantis, in dante nomen sit substantie, in dato qualitatis. . . . —Par. 15; Davy, *Deux traités,* p. 88; Webb and Walker, *On the Nature,* p. 24.

Again, unless a common source can be affirmed, the dependency of one upon the other is clear. But, again, it is not easy to affirm in which direction the dependency lies.

The most obvious general similarity between the two treatises is that they both trace out four stages in the development of love. But the categories they employ are in fact quite different. William is more allegorical. He compares man's growth in love with his natural growth, passing from infancy (*voluntas* — choice), through youth (*amor* — love) and manhood (*caritas* — charity) to old age (*sapientia* — wisdom).[28] These stages provide the whole context of his treatise.

Not so for Bernard. The stages or degrees of love are only introduced after a long treatment of the motive, measure and profit of love.[29] His presentation of the degrees and indeed the whole treatise is more philosophical than William's Maybe he means to warn us that this is to be the case by his allusion in the Prologue to his being considered a philosopher.[30] It is not that William despises philosophy or a philosophical approach. He draws on philosophy in developing his treatise.[31] In his earlier work he points to the "true and divine philosophy" that is found in the teaching of the Lord Jesus to his disciples.[32] Bernard actually does not depart from William in this. If he does begin his treatise with rather precise synthetic distinctions as he develops his initial thought, he quickly moves into the patristic style to which he is more accustomed. His tender love for our Lord is very much in evidence. And the same is true of his friend. William's long *excursus* on Christ during his treatment of "old age" is truly a work of beauty, the fruit of a deep, personal and tender love.[33]

---

28. Par. 4; Davy, *Deux traités*, p. 74; Webb and Walker, *On the Nature*, p. 14.
29. Par. 23; OB 3:138; Sr Penelope tr., p. 56.
30. Prologue; OB 3:119; Sr Penelope tr., p. 11: " . . . lest I be deemed a philosopher because I hold my tongue."
31. Par. 49; Davy, *Deux traités*, p. 128; Webb and Walker, *On the Nature*, p. 54.
32. Contemp 12; SCh 61:110; CF3:60.
33. Par. 40-46; Davy, *Deux traités*, pp. 118-126; Webb and Walker, *On the Nature*, pp. 46-51.

The way the two monks developed their theme is quite different, the *way*, but there is actually not much difference in their approach.[34] What of the content?

As we have already seen, in the expression of the essence of charity, of love, they are at one. Can their respective four stages be identified? It is difficult to equate them. William's whole ladder is set a bit below Bernard's. His first step is naked will, image of God, free, moving toward the initial choice that leads it on to the second step of love. Here he joins Bernard's first step, carnal love, and touches the under-part of his second, where the soul begins to love God for the benefits it has received. William's third step of charity is found on Bernard's second and most fully on his third, where God is loved because of his own goodness. Wisdom, the savor of God, William's "old age," is already found in Bernard's third degree of love, but as it reaches out beyond, it parallels Bernard's fourth—love of self and all else only for God's sake. While all the elements are there, William's treatment seems to lack the richness and depth found in Bernard. William honestly says:

> This is the wisdom which the Apostle "speaks among the perfect," and which we also speak who have heard but not seen. . . . And if we had actually seen it, we would be able to say more than we do, describing it more fully.[35]

Here I believe is a fundamental difference. Both are essentially existential writers in the best sense of that word, writing out of their own lived experience. But William has been but recently drawn into the contemplative way. His description of the way is much fuller than Bernard's, more helpful to the young, no doubt. But when he gets to the heights his treatment is more speculative, more a thing of hearsay and

---

34. This in part explains how this treatise of William could have come to be united to that of Bernard and commonly offered together with it as being the work of Bernard.

35. Par. 47; Davy, *Deux traités*, p. 126; Webb and Walker, *On the Nature*, pp. 52f.

desire.[36] But Bernard writes more from personal experience. William just touches on rapture in passing;[37] Bernard writes on it at length.[38] William adapts the first great commandment to his four stages;[39] Bernard declares it can only be fulfilled in the resurrection of the body.[40] William does not fail to speak of the eschaton;[41] but again it does not form a significant part of the fabric of his fourth degree as it does for Bernard.[42]

I would say in conclusion that while there are touch points between Bernard and William in these two treatises, there is a very great independence. In many incidents where similar themes are touched on, they are handled in very different ways.[43] William's explicit use of liturgical texts[44] and pagan authors[45] finds no echo in Bernard, while Bernard's very traditional presentation of the three kinds of fear, which is developed at length, is not mirrored in William's text even though occasions offered themselves to its introduction.[46]

Where a textual relationship is present I do not think that a study of these texts alone establishes in which direction the

---

36. William's later and more mature work stands in marked contrast to the present work in this regard: *Exposition on the Song of Songs*, J.-M. Déchanet, ed., *Exposé sur le Cantique des cantiques*, SCh 82 (Paris: Cerf, 1962); Sr Columba Hart, tr., *The Works of William of St Thierry*, vol. 2, CF 6 (Spencer, Massachusetts: Cistercian Publications, 1969).

37. Par. 8; Davy, *Deux traités*, p. 80; Webb and Walker, *On the Nature*, p. 17.

38. Par. 27; OB 3:142; Sr Penelope, tr., p. 64.

39. Par. 33; Davy, *Deux traités*, p. 110; Webb and Walker, *On the Nature*, p. 42.

40. Par. 29; OB 3:143f; Sr Penelope, tr., p. 67.

41. Par. 52f; Davy, *Deux traités*, pp. 134-136; Webb and Walker, *On the Nature*, pp. 58-60.

42. Par. 30-33; OB 3:144-147; Sr Penelope, tr., pp. 64-76. Bernard's strong, clear affirmation for the resurrection of the body stands out here.

43. Besides those noted above, p. 000, we might also note their respective treatment of fear.

44. E.g., in proving his point concerning the mediation of Christ, he brings in the text used by the Church in concluding all prayers: "Through Jesus Christ our Lord"; Par. 36, Davy, *Deux traités*, p. 114; Webb and Walker, *On the Nature*, p. 44.

45. E.g., Terence in par. 21 (Davy, p. 98; Webb and Walker, p. 31), Horace in par. 39 (Davy, p. 108; Webb and Walker, p. 39), Juvenal in par. 32 (Davy, p. 110; Webb and Walker, p. 41).

46. See par. 7, Davy, *Deux traités*, p. 78; Webb and Walker, *On the Nature*, p. 16; par. 41-42, Davy, pp. 120-122; Webb and Walker, pp. 49-50.

dependence lay. Bernard could have read his friend's treatise and used ideas from it in speaking to his community (*Sermon Ten*) and in writing to the Carthusians. Just as readily, as we conjectured above, William could have heard *Sermon Ten* while visiting Clairvaux and Bernard could have shared his thoughts with him on the nature of charity, and then William could have used these ideas in talks at home and in his treatise. The more general argument coming from William's idolization of Bernard and Bernard's leadership qualities I do not think proves William the disciple in every case. William, too, was a leader.[47] Moreover, we have evidence of the dependence of Bernard on William as a theologian.[48] Indeed, this fact might argue strongly for Bernard's dependence on William in the case of the clear distinction concerning the essence of charity as an accidental quality. This was a still disputed question at this period. And Bernard's contemporary and friend, the Master of the Sentences, Peter Lombard, held the opposing position[49] and had to be refuted by Aquinas.[50] Again, though, the argument is far from being apodictic.

As I said at the beginning, this is meant to be but a very modest contribution to the much more extensive study that must take place before we can hope to have anything like a satisfying understanding—if we can ever have it—of the ways and degree in which these two great monks influenced each other's thought.[51] While a comparison of the two treatises does show a commonness of spirit between the friends and some kind of interdependence, it does not establish a depen-

47. Besides being the abbot of a prominent abbey, William exercised a leadership role in the reform of the Black Monks; see Ceglar, *William of St Thierry*, pp. 400-404, V. Berlière, ed., *Documents inedits pour servir à l'histoire ecclésiastique de la Belgique*, 2 vols. (Maredsous, 1894) 1:91-110.

48. See above, notes 8 and 9. R. Javelet, *Image et ressemblance au douzième siècle*, 2 vols. (Paris, 1967) notes the influence of William on Bernard in regard to his doctrine on grace and free choice (1:196-197).

49. *Sententiarum*, Lib. I, distc. xvii, cap. 1; QR 1:106.

50. *Summa theologica*, 2-2, q. 23, a. 2 c.

51. Certainly William's *Exposition on the Song of Songs* would have to be carefully compared with Bernard's *Sermons on the Song of Songs*; e.g. Cant 4 with SC 79:1.

dence on the part of William, at least at the time of this writing—a significant fact, given the adulation he heaped upon Bernard. This conclusion may depend more on my lack of perception than on the actual facts. I suspect William had Bernard in mind when he wrote: "The wise have a way of speaking to one another by means of their mutual love, and this they communicate to each other by means of a glance . . . a language strange to the stranger."[52]

M. Basil Pennington OCSO

St Joseph's Abbey
Spencer, Massachusetts

---

52. Nat am, 51; Davy, *Deux traités*, p. 132; Webb and Walker, *On the Nature*, p. 56.

RELATIONS BETWEEN ST BERNARD
AND ABELARD BEFORE 1139

I T IS OFTEN ASSUMED that St Bernard and Peter Abelard were enemies of some sort prior to their conflict of
1139 and 1140. The latest example of this is Professor
Robertson's new book, *Abelard and Heloise.*[1] Tradition has
it that St Bernard was one of the two "new apostles" perse-
cuting him, to whom Abelard refers in *Historia calamitatum;*[2] and that Abelard is the unnamed "inventor" about
whom St Bernard wrote to Hugh of St Victor in his *De
baptismo*[3] These events occurred in the 1120's, long before
the conflict at Sens. From them, largely in retrospect with
the eventual collision, the earlier is inferred. The situation
deserves amimosity close and specific scrutiny to determine
whether these inferences are justified.

Let us first examine the best modern scholarship on the
question, and then review the sources.

Much of the modern scholarship seems to focus on the
aforementioned question of the two "new apostles." It began
with the first printed editions of Abelard's works, those of
d'Amboise and Duchesne in 1616.[4] The *Censura doctorum*

1. D. W. Robertson, Jr., *Abelard and Heloise* (N.Y.: The Dial Press, 1972), pp.
62, 78-79.
2. Ed. J. T. Muckle, *Mediaeval Studies* 12 (1950): 202; ed. J. Monfrin, (Paris: J.
Vrin, 1962), p. 97.
3. Bernard, *Ad Hugonem de Sancto Victore epistola seu tractatus de baptismo
aliisque quaestionibus ab ipso propositis;* PL 182:1031-46.
4. *Petri Abaelardi . . . Opera* (Paris: Nicolas Buon, 1616); a double edition (see
description in Monfrin, *op. cit.,* p. 31-46.

Parisiensium, printed in the d'Amboise edition, specifically identified the two "new apostles" as Bernard and Norbert.[5] A note of Duchesne's in the two editions did likewise.[6] This was the beginning of the modern tradition. There is little need now to trace all the intervening steps. Recently several scholars have spoken of the unanimity of the tradition,[7] but it is not unanimous. As early as 1881 Vacandard expressed some doubt about the designation.[8] If, he said, Abelard really did mean Bernard, he was gravely mistaken, since at the time in question (toward 1125) Bernard was not running around the world. It was probably due to Abelard's somber melancholy and his troubled imagination. In any case Vacandard's reservation, "if," should not escape our notice. J. G. Sikes in 1932 appears to have followed Vacandard's line of thought on the matter in part, but he also appears to have contradicted himself. First he said, "That Abailard was here referring to St Norbert . . . and to St Bernard cannot be doubted, but it is equally clear that at this period neither of these two men was actively engaged in attacking him. . . . Very probably the sense of some impending danger was

5. Reprinted in PL 178:109A: *Col. 163, cap. 12, Historiae calamit. Paulo acerbius conqueritur Abaelardus, etsi tacito nomine, de DD. Bernardo et Norberto, qui ejus erroribus magis quam ipsi fuere infensi.*

6. Note 47, to page 28, reprinted in *Petrus Abaelardus, Opera,* ed. Cousin, Jourdain and Despois, vol. 1 (Paris: A. Durand, 1849), pp. 63-4. Duchesne quoted the *Chronicon Lemovicense* (Limoges) *ad annum 1130* on the widespread activity of the Praemonstratensians and Cistercians at that time, and he charged Norbert and Bernard with "gall and acrimony against our Abelard, as is clear from the letters alone that Bernard wrote to Pope Innocent and the cardinals, against him." Note the anachronism of that.

7. Notably, Arno Borst, "Abälard und Bernhard," *Historische Zeitschrift* 186 (1958) 502: *Die Forschung ist einmütig;* and Damien Van Den Eynde, "Détails biographiques sur Pierre Abélard," *Antonianum* 38 (1963): 221: *Depuis toujours tous les auteurs ont identifié les deux "nouveaux apôtres" avec saint Norbert et saint Bernard,* etc.

8. Vacandard, *Abélard, sa lutte avec saint Bernard, sa doctrine, sa méthode* (Paris: Maison Jouby et Roger, 1881), p. 48, note 1: *Pour ce qui regarde saint Bernard, nous verrons plus loin qu'Abélard (s'il désigne réellement notre saint) s'est gravement trompé. A cette époque, c'est-à-dire vers l'an 1125, l'abbé de Clairvaux ne courait pas encore le monde.* Above, same page: *Abélard tomba dans une sombre mélancolie; et son imagination troublée ne lui montra bientôt plus autour de lui que des ennemis déclarés . . . saint Norbert et saint Bernard.* Vacandard also noted their good relations at Morigny in 1131.

merely the hallucination of a nervous man who had already suffered so much at the hands of his enemies."[9] Sikes also wrote of "the suspicion he [Abelard] entertained that St Bernard and St Norbert were working for his destruction . . . the feeling which haunted him that Bernard and Norbert had been enrolled among his enemies," and "the constant, though unfounded dread that St Bernard and Norbert were working to effect his ruin."[10] But elsewhere he noted that: "Since the chronicler of Morigny does not mention any noticeable estrangement between the two men during their stay at his abbey, and as Abailard in defending the exegesis of the nuns does not refer to any difference of opinion between St Bernard and himself,[11] it seems safe to conclude that Bernard's hostility towards Abailard and his views dates from a period shortly before the meeting at Sens."[12] This is no real contradiction. It appears that Sikes' position was that Abelard meant St Bernard and St Norbert, but that the accusation was based more on fancy than on fact. This is an echo of Vacandard's position, except for the more positive designation of St Bernard and St Norbert as the two "new apostles" of Abelard's text. It would argue for enmity on one side between Abelard and St Bernard (however fancied), but not on the other. Let us continue.

J. T. Muckle is the scholar presently credited with first raising difficulties with the traditional view that St Norbert and St Bernard were the two "new apostles."[13] This was in

---

9. J. G. Sikes, M.A., *Peter Abailard* (Cambridge: Cambridge University Press, 1932) pp. 21-2. Note also that Sikes here also cast doubt on the theory that Bernard's *De baptismo* was directed against Abelard, a question which will be returned to below.

10. Ibid., pp. 46, 47, 254.

11. The reference is to Abelard's *Letter 10* to Bernard, concerning the use of the Lord's Prayer at Paraclete, in PL 178:335-40, to be discussed below.

12. Sikes, op. cit., p. 224.

13. See, for example, Borst, op. cit., p. 502; Van Den Eynde, p. 221; Chrysogonus Waddell, "Peter Abelard's Letter 10 and Cistercian Liturgical Reform," paper delivered at the Conference on Medieval Studies, Western Michigan University, May 2, 1972 (to be published in *Studies in Medieval Cistercian History*, II, CS 24), note 3. Muckle's comments were appended to his edition of Abelard's *Historia calamitatum*: "Abelard's Letter of Consolation to a Friend," *Mediaeval Studies* 12 (1950): pp. 212-13.

1950. The several difficulties he raised were:

1. There is no record of attacks on Abelard by St Norbert and St Bernard at this time. This however, Muckle admitted is not compelling: there could have been sermons that have not been preserved.

2. "It appears that St Bernard was not too familiar with Abelard's works until he received the letter of William of St. Thierry, calling attention to his errors and complaining of St Bernard's silence regarding such a grave matter."[14]

3. "In St. Bernard's reply to William, he makes no mention of any part he had already taken in opposition to Abelard, and distinctly states that up to that time he knew nothing of most, if not all, of these matters."[15]

4. The letter of the bishops to Pope Innocent, after the Council of Sens, states "that St. Bernard had frequently heard of Abelard's errors from various sources and especially in 'the aforementioned book of theology' and in other works ... and that having inspected them carefully, he had had meetings with Abelard, first in private and then before witnesses, and had in a kindly and friendly manner admonished him. ... All this certainly implies that St. Bernard's activity against Abelard was recent."[16]

5. Abelard's *Letter 10* to St Bernard, about the use of the Lord's Prayer at the Paraclete, contains "nothing which suggests estrangement based upon St. Bernard's having preached against him."[17]

6. In Abelard's Letter, *Dilectissimis sociis suis,*[18] which "must have been written just before the council of Sens ... [and] directed against St. Bernard, Abelard states that although for a long time St. Bernard had been secretly against him, yet up to the present he had pretended to be very friendly. In other words, St. Bernard had not yet openly bro-

14. Muckle, p. 212, cites William of St Thierry, *Letter 326*; PL 182:531-3.
15. Muckle, p. 212, cites St Bernard, *Letter 327*; PL 182:533.
16. Muckle, pp. 212-13. The reference is to *Letter 337: Ad Innocentium pontificum in persona Franciae episcoporum*; PL 182:540-1.
17. Muckle, p. 213. See note 11 above.
18. Ed. J. Leclercq, ASOC 9 (1953) 104-5; and Raymond Klibansky, *Mediaeval and Renaissance Studies* 5 (1961) 1-27.

ken with Abelard, much less preached against him. . . . ." [19]

Several of these difficulties were answered by Damien Van Den Eynde in 1963, who explicitly took issue with Muckle.

1. Van Den Eynde claimed that the text of *Historia calamitatum* does not say, as Muckle supposed, that Norbert and Bernard were preaching against him. In reading the text, *Hii praedicando per mundum discurrentes et me impudenter quantum poterant corrodentes, non modice tam ecclesiasticis quibusdam quam secularibus potestatibus contemptibilem ad tempus effecerunt, et de mea tam fide quam vita adeo sinistra disseminaverunt, ut . . . etc.,* [20] he seems to have read *praedicando* as restricted in its use to modify the opening phrase only. That is to say, Norbert and Bernard were going around preaching, but it was not their preaching that was directed against Abelard; rather it was occasional criticism. This seems to me to be a pretty fine bit of interpretation, and the best that can be claimed about the text is a possibility of ambiguity.

2. Van Den Eynde said of Muckle's third point, that Bernard's profession of ignorance of Abelard's errors, in his 1139 reply to William of St Thierry, is only related to the specific errors that William had raised. This seems to be a sounder objection on the part of Van Den Eynde. For that matter, the same objection could also be made to Muckle's difficulties 2, 4, and 6, raised with regard to William's letter, the bishops' report, and Abelard's letter to his associates. It is quite possible that all those remarks can be read as referring only to the immediate matters of the controversy of 1139-40. Nevertheless one cannot be certain.

3. Van Den Eynde was silent on Abelard's *Letter 10* to Bernard, although, as we will later see, there might be evidence to support argument there, too. But he on his part brought up a document ignored by Muckle, St Bernard's letter to Hugh of St Victor, *De baptismo,* written in the mid-1120's. "Although, following Hugh's example, the Abbé

19. Muckle, p. 213.
20. Abelard, *Historia calamitatum,* ed. Monfrin, p. 97.

of Clairvaux does not pronounce there the name of Abelard, he expresses himself no less severely on his teaching, his thirst for success, and his tendency toward novelties."[21] It has already been noted (note 9) that Sikes cast doubt on this.

It was Van Den Eynde's conclusion that it was only St Norbert and St Bernard that Abelard could have meant by the respective titles of "a reformer of canons regular" and "a reformer of monks," and the explanation of all the problems raised lay in Muckle's failure to distinguish between historic facts and Abelard's subjective interpretation. If St Norbert and St Bernard clearly fit Abelard's description in *Historia calamitatum,* but if Bernard at least was not active at that time against Abelard, and if he also appeared to be in good relations with him at several later times, the explanation lay in the activity of Abelard's imagination.[22] This was similar to the explanations of Vacandard and Sikes. It neatly solved the major problem about the relations of St Bernard and Abelard, that has perplexed many of us. *C'est joli pourvu que ça dure.*

In the meantime Arthur Landgraf in 1953,[23] Raymond

---

21. Van Den Eynde, p. 222, as is the case with the preceding quotations.
22. Van Den Eynde, p. 222: *"J. T. Muckle ne fait pas de distinction assez nette entre les faits historiques et l'interprétation subjective qu'Abélard en présente. Les faits sont les suivants: vers la fin de son séjour au Paraclet, Maître Pierre prend conscience que sa personne et sa doctrine sont vivement critiquées dans beaucoup de milieux et par des personnes aussi influentes que saint Norbert et saint Bernard. Comment expliquer cette hostilité croissante? Pour tout esprit non prévenu, elle s'explique par les prétensions et les hardiesses du Maître du Palet. Mais ce dernier est incapable de reconnaître son tort. . . . Comme à l'époque de sa condemnation à Soissons en 1121, il fera donc remonter l'opposition dont il est l'óbjet à la jalousie de ses adversaires de longue date, Albéric de Reims et Lutolphe de Novare. Par eux-mêmes—au moins affecte-t-il de le croire—ces personnages sont insignifiants. Mais il sait qu'ils sont liés d'amitié avec Norbert et Bernard, qui, eux, se meuvent dans les milieux les plus divers et jouissent d'un crédit immense. Pour Abélard tout est clair: Albéric et Lutolphe ont instigué Norbert et Bernard, et ceux-ci ont monté l'opinion contre lui."*
23. Arthur Landgraf, "Der Heilige Bernhard in seinem Verhältnis zur Theologie des zwölften Jahrhunderts," *Bernhard von Clairvaux, Internationaler Bernhardkongress Mainz 1953,* ed. Joseph Lortz (Wiesbaden: Franz Steiner Verlag, 1955) p. 45. No reason is given.

Oursel in 1959,[24] and Raymond Klibansky in 1961,[25] had all identified St Bernard as one of the two persecutors mentioned by Abelard.

However, another scholar, Arno Borst had come up with a strikingly different view in 1958.[26] It was indeed unique.

Borst, as if anticipating Van Den Eynde's disfavor with some of Muckle's arguments, wrote that Muckle's protest was "somewhat timid" and his "argument sounded poor."

> Nevertheless Muckle was right! Unlike Norbert, Bernard was, around 1125 anything but a wandering preacher. . . . That this is what Norbert was, is shown from the story that Abelard told about him and his "co-apostle" Farsitus in one of his sermons. . . . The whole sermon [27] drips scorn

24. Raymond Oursel, *La dispute et la grace* (Paris: Société Les Belles Lettres, 1959) pp. 32-4, said that "the explanation is a bit vague, but it is hardly imaginable that the affair was limited to some speeches and insinuations, or intellectual polemics. If that were all, Abelard would hardly have failed to respond to them in his autobiography, confident as he was of his dialectic and his orthodoxy. It seems as though, aside from doctrinal matters, the moral atmosphere at Paraclete was in question. It is not hard to imagine that that was not entirely peaceful." He referred to the poem of Hilarius as evidence (PL 178:1855). "We don't know the tenor of Bernard's attacks, but other letters of his enable us to imagine." Although Oursel is imaginatively reconstructing the scene here, his reference to Hilarius is not idle. Note too the reference to later correspondence of Bernard.

25. Raymond Klibansky, p. 6, line 15 and note thereto, p. 20, including note 3 (which erroneously stated that Heloise referred to Bernard; she mentioned no name in the text cited). No reason is given.

26. Cited above, n. 7.

27. Abelard, *Sermo 33*; PL 178:605. *Ad majora veniam, et summa illa miracula de resuscitandis quoque mortuis inanita tentata. Quod quidem nuper praesumpsisse Norbertum, et coapostolum ejus Farsitum mirati fuimus, et risimus: qui diu pariter in oratione coram populo prostrati, et de sua praesumptione frustrati, cum a proposito confusi deciderent, objurgare populum impudenter coeperunt, quod devotioni suae et constanti fidei infidelitas eorum obsisteret.*

A reading of Abelard's *Sermon 33* does seem to me to support, though not prove, Borst's contention, that it was all written with St Norbert and the Praemonstratensians in mind. After addressing his fellow monks, and taking as his text *Job* 39:5, and glossing this text, Abelard states his theme: the principle of monasticism illustrated by St John and the wild ass, withdrawal from the world. There is a long "digression" (the word is Abelard's: 596B) on monks who engage in church affairs, would-be performers of miracles, and those who would become bishops (588B-96B). After a brief return to St John and the etymology of "monk" (596B-8C), Abelard (in his typical fashion) goes back to his "digression": more

for Norbert. . . . Abelard calls the Praemonstratensians here monks.

Norbert is the reformer of the monks [mentioned by Abelard in *Historia calamitatum*] . . . The reformer of the canons regular is Farsitus: Hugh of Fosses! Hugh was Norbert's oldest associate and successor as Abbot of Premontré. It is he and Norbert, whom Abelard meant as the two "new apostles." That Hugh of Fosses is the same as Hugh Farsitus has more recently been a matter of scholarly argument.

The latter was a common name: Hugh the Fat. Mabillon identified five, and considered that Abelard's Farsitus (one of the five) was Hugh of Fosses.[28] "Those in the know, having read the *Sermon 33,*" Borst went on to say, "were well aware whom Abelard meant in *Historia calamitatum.* This included Heloise, it seems, who also mentioned the two 'pseudo-apostoli' in her reply."[29]

If Borst is right we may eliminate consideration of Abelard's remarks about the two "new apostles" from our study of the relations of Bernard and Abelard before 1139. Even if Van Den Eynde is right we may all but eliminate consideration of them as momentary aberrations of Abelard's active imagination. Muckle, Sikes, and Vacandard would also fall more or less in either of these two categories. These are the

about monks and bishops (598C-604B). The applicability of all this to the Praemonstratensians and Norbert (elected Bishop of Magdeburg in 1126) is obvious. One might ask if it were not also applicable to many others at that time, of course. But the explicit reference to Norbert (605C) seems to clinch the matter. The cat is out of the bag, as it were.

28. PL 182:141-2 (note 128); St Bernard, *Opera* (Venice, 1781), 1:40, note: *Plures invenio per id tempus Hugones Farsitos. Duos monachos, alterum Latiniacensem . . . alterum S. Luciani apud Bellovacos . . . Tertium lego Hugonem Farsitum, Canonicum regularem S. Joannis de Vineis, laudatum in Necrologio ecclesiae Suessionensis. Quartum suggerit Farsitum Abaelardus in sermone de S. Joanne Baptista pag. 967 ubi Norbertum et coapostolum ejus Farsitum memorat, forsan Hugonem Praemonstrati abbatem, Ordinisque praepositum post Norbertum, cujus primus ac praecipuus discipulus fuit.* The fifth was Hugh, abbot of St John in the Valley near Chartres.

29. Heloise, *Letter 1, Domino suo immo patri,* ed. Muckle, *Mediaeval Studies* 15 (1953) p. 68.

scholars who seem to have addressed themselves most assid-
uously to the problem raised by d'Amboise and Duchesne
and the Parisian Doctors.

If we have pursued this matter at length and in detail, it is
only because this particular text of Abelard in the *Historia
calamitatum* has always dominated discussion of the relations
between Bernard and Abelard before 1139. It now seems safe
to set it aside, and to take a fresh look at the sources.

The sources may be classified as follows (some of them
have already been mentioned in passing):

1. A group of three *Letters* of 1139 and 1140 which contain comments upon the former friendship of St Bernard and
Abelard: a. William of St Thierry, *Letter* 326, to Geoffrey of
Chartres and Bernard of Clairvaux (the letter that began the
controversy at Sens);[30] b. St Bernard, *Letter 327,* the reply
to William;[31] and c. Abelard's letter, *Dilectissimis sociis suis,*
just before the council.[32]

2. A letter of St Bernard to Hugh of St Victor, *De baptismo
aliisque quaestionibus ab ipso propositis,* written about
1125.[33]

3. The *Chronicon Mauriniacense* for the year 1130 (by our
calendar, 1131).[34]

4. Abelard, *Letter 10,* to St Bernard, on the use of the
Lord's Prayer at the Paraclete.[35]

Let us inspect them one at a time.

1. *The three letters*:

a. In his letter to Geoffrey and St Bernard, William said,
"Since you and others who should speak out have been
silent, I am forced to speak to you" (*silentibus vobis, et
aliis, quorum erat loqui, cogor vos alloqui*), and again, "I
tell you, with danger you are silent" (*Dico vobis, periculose*

30. PL 182:531-3.
31. PL 182:533.
32. Ed. J. Leclercq, ASOC 9 (1953): 104-5; and ed. R. Klibansky, *Mediaeval and
Renaissance Studies* 5 (1961) 1-27.
33. PL 182:1031-46.
34. MGH SS 26 (1882) p. 40-1.
35. *Venerabili atque in Christo dilectissimo fratri Bernardo,* PL 178:335-40.

siletis) . . . "close your eyes, and whom will he fear? "
(*claudite oculos: quem timebit?*).

b. St Bernard, replying, said "Up to now, I have not known
of most, or nearly all of these things" (*horum plurima et
pene omnia hucusque nescierim*).

c. Abelard later wrote of Bernard to his associates, "That
long hidden enemy, who up to now has pretended to be
friendly, indeed most friendly" (*Ille quippe occultus iam-
dudum inimicus, qui se huc usque amicum, immo amicissi-
mum simulavit*).[36]

The difficulty with all this evidence is that it could apply
only to the matters and events shortly before the council in
1140. *a.* William could be speaking of the two little books he
had just read and the thirteen propositions he had culled
from them, or to Abelard's renewed activity in general (*iterum nova docet, nova scribit*), and *b.*, St Bernard could be
doing likewise. So *c.*, could Abelard, since, at the time he
wrote his letter to his associates, St Bernard had just make an
effort to settle the matters in a friendly and familiar
fashion. [37] That St Bernard followed up this conference with
a sermon to the scholars of Paris, and that this irked Abelard,
lends some weight to this observation.

These three letters do not compel us to infer that St Bernard had for a long time been silent about, or ignorant of,
Abelard's activities, or that he and Abelard had long maintained friendly relations. As Muckle and Van Den Eynde have
shown, they can be read either way. Other evidence is
needed.

---

36. Abelard, to be sure, does not name Bernard in this letter, but the circum-
stantial evidence of the ascription is overwhelming, and St Bernard appears to
verify the fact in his *Letter 189*, PL 182:355D: *Quae de me ad discipulos suos
scripserit, dicere non curo.* See also the report of the bishops to Pope Innocent,
Letter 337, PL 182:541C.

37. Letter 337; PL 182:541 A-B: *Verum dominus abbas Clarae-Vallis . . .
secreto prius, ac deinde secum duobus aut tribus adhibitis testibus, juxta evangeli-
cum praeceptum, hominem convenit: et ut auditores suos a talibus compesceret,
librosque suos corrigeret, amicabiliter satis ac familiariter illum admonuit.* St Bernard's next move, a talk with the students (*De conversione ad clericos*, PL
182:833-56), seems to have changed Abelard's attitude, according to the bishops'
report.

2. St Bernard's letter to Hugh of St Victor, *De baptismo*, about 1125, is widely considered to have been directed against doctrines of Abelard, even though neither Hugh nor St Bernard named the author of the doctrines in question. *Scribis,* wrote St Bernard to Hugh, *itaque quemdam asserere nescio quem (nam non nominas). . . . Is ergo, cujus me respondere assertionibus jubes, et nomen taces.*[38] The silence with regard to the name could indeed be interpreted as evidence of a desire to maintain good personal relations in a matter of professional difference. *De homine tamen qui ista loquitur (pace ipsius dico paucis quod sentio), videtur mihi plus novitatis curiosus, quam studiosus veritatis.*[39] *Sed miror admodum, si novus iste novarum inventor assertionum, et assertor inventionum. . . .*[40] *Ipse ejus inventor, in sua superiori sententia ipsam per se satis impugnet, sibimetipsi contratius.*[41] It sounds like Abelard well enough, considering familiar echoes in William's and St Bernard's 1139 and 1140 letters,[42] but these were common epithets of the time, liberally used. In that intellectually turbulent age we find quite a few "inventors" of "novelties." If anything of the above were especially revealing, it would be the words, *in sua superiori sententia.* But there is nothing explicit to suggest with any certainty that this refers to Abelard.

In fact the position, objected to by St Bernard, taken by the unknown glossator of the Nicodemus text (Jn 3) is not in agreement with positions known from his writings to have been taken by Abelard. Sikes pointed this out, although his particular supporting citation of Abelard's *Commentary on Paul's Letter to the Romans* lacks cogency when one considers that that *Commentary* was written over ten years after the events now being considered. Another citation might have been better.[43]

38. PL 182:1031.
39. Ibid., 1038C.
40. Ibid., 1035C.
41. Ibid., 1041C.
42. Ibid., 531, 535-36, 1056A, for some examples.
43. Sikes, p. 214, incl. note 5; Abelard, *Commentaria in epistolam Pauli ad Romanos* in *Petri Abaelardi, Opera theologica,* I, ed. E. M. Buytaert, Corpus

The position taken by St Bernard himself in his letter to Hugh seems at first sight somewhat ironically similar to the position ascribed to Abelard in the ninth proposition at Sens.[44] Everything is indeed mixed up.

Still, there is nothing to prevent the claim that Abelard could have been the unnamed glossator of the Nicodemus text. There exists here too the possibility of lost or oral sources. It is also worthwhile to point out that the position is typical of the nascent, exploratory theological arguments of the schools of that time, and of Abelard himself at times. It also could have been an argument of one of his scholars, as Sikes pointed out. He had crowds of them. All sorts of viewpoints were being debated and explored for the sake of clarifying innumerable questions, and this would hardly have been unusual. But if Hugh and St Bernard's objections were directed against Abelard, St Bernard was being very correct in his relation, professional in the best sense. If we disagree, but refrain from being personal, it argues for rather good relations.

3. The Chronicle of Morigny reported that in February, 1131, St Bernard and Abelard were both present at the consecration of the altar there by Pope Innocent. *Inter eas venerabiles personas . . . Bernardus abbas Clararum-vallium, qui tum temporis in Gallia divini verbi famosissimus praedicator*

christianorum, continuatio mediaevalis, XI (Turnhout: Brepols, 1969) pp. 118-21. *Theologia christiana,* II, 112-5, ed. Buytaert, *Opera,* II, CCCM XII, pp. 182-4, might be better evidence. Although it seems less clear and forceful, the first redaction is more or less contemporary with St Bernard's letter. Although this redaction in the extant Durham manuscript lacks Book II and the following books, the editor leaves us little doubt about the existence of our text, much the same as in later redactions.

44. *Excusari poterant, si non audissent* (1033A); *inobedientiae culpam ignorantia nihilominus excusaret* (1033C). Compare with proposition 9: *. . . quod non sit culpae ascribendum quidquid fit per ignorantiam.* Of course it must be pointed out that St Bernard goes on to make some distinctions in *cap.* iv: ignorance does not always excuse guilt. *Verendum tamen ne securius spargat seminarium vecordiae in auribus insipientium. . . . Is forsitan qui asserit non posse peccari per ignorantiam prophetam irrideat. . . . Si ignorantia numquam peccatum est . . . etc.* (1041D-1042A). Because ignorance excuses some unbaptized, does not mean that it excuses all sinners. St Bernard is here giving a distinction in the best scholastic tradition, whether consciously or not. As John Sommerfeldt has pointed out, he was quite capable (there is a passage in *cap. iii,* 11, 1038C-39A, which exhibits classical dialectical form: the *aut . . . aut* is like the *éi . . . éi* of Proclus).

erat, Petrus Abailardus monachus et abbas, et ipse vir religio-
sus, excellentissimarum rector scolarum, ad quas pene de tota
Latinitate viri litterati confluebant. The skeptic might argue
that all this proves is that they had the good manners not to
carry on their quarrel in another's house and on such an
occasion, but this seems to push skepticism a bit far. It seems
that, had there been any great difficulty between two such
notable personalities at the time, remarks would have been
made here and elsewhere. It is sure that they met, and that
their meeting occasioned no special comment, other than on
their fame. This seems significant.

4. Abelard's *Letter 10* to St Bernard, written between 1131
and 1135, seems especially significant, because it has to do
with a disagreement between them: the use (recommended
by Abelard) of the word *supersubstantialem* in place of *coti-*
dianum in the Lord's Prayer by the nuns at the Paraclete.
Chrysogonus Waddell, ocso, has recently described this letter
and its context, and there is no need to repeat his description.[45] For our purposes it is, however, important to note
Abelard's remark that St Bernard "had been moved by that
love with which you have especially embraced me," *vos ea*
charitate, qua me praecipue amplectimini, aliquantulum com-
motum esse.[46] "Having heard this, I decided to write you my
excuse for this, especially since I would be grieved at your offense more than all others, as is fitting," *maxime cum ves-*
tram minus quam caeteras omnes dolerem, ut decet, offensi-
onem.[47]

What follows, however, might not seem so friendly. Abelard's argument is not only strong, it is filled with ironies,
turning St Bernard's charge of *novitas* (335C) into *vetustas*
(338A), and chiding St Bernard for his own novelties: *vos*
quippe quasi noviter exorti (339A) *vestra novitas* (339B,
340A). At times Abelard sounds as though he is really need-
ling St Bernard. He lays it on in a fashion that sounds almost
personal, particularly in his criticism of Cistercian liturgical

45. See note 13 above.
46. PL 178:335B.
47. Ibid., 335C; also Cousin, p. 619, who notes that *minus* perhaps should be
read *magis*.

novelties (e.g.: *dirisione moventur,* 339C, *quasi vos suffragiis sanctorum minus egeatis*). But it should be commencing to dawn upon us that this was a custom of the schools of those days, a more or less accepted way of life that we have overlooked too long, and should not make too much of.

In short there is no sure evidence that St Bernard and Abelard were at odds, other than professionally in some particulars, before 1139, and there is some slight evidence that their relations were surely correct, and probably friendly.

Edward F. Little

Claremont, California

EPISTEMOLOGY, EDUCATION, AND SOCIAL THEORY IN THE THOUGHT OF BERNARD OF CLAIRVAUX

TO "UNDERSTAND AN AGE" would seem a hopeless task, even in the case of an age as relatively unified and consistent as the early twelfth century. Nevertheless, we historians persist in that task, and there is, I believe, an approach which is useful—perhaps the most useful—in our endeavor. I believe that most fundamental to the understanding of the *Weltanschauung* of an age is a study of the means to truth of that culture, for one's whole way of life is inextricably bound up with the way one seeks to solve the secrets of one's environment and attempts to obtain at least a measure of consistency.

It would, of course, be too much to expect that the average monk, cleric, or layman of the early twelfth century could systematize his view of his entire culture or social order, or have a comprehensive view of the epistemological presuppositions of that culture and social order. Indeed, it is amazing that there should be anyone, regardless of his genius, who could enjoy such far-ranging understanding. And yet I think there was such a man, Bernard of Clairvaux.

Bernard's position on the epistemological questions so fundamental to any culture was self-conscious. In his First Sermon on the *Song of Songs*, Bernard prefaced a great mystical exposition with a statement indicating a difference in mode and level of comprehension between members of different social groups:

169

What I shall say to you, my brothers, will differ from what I should say to people in the world, at least the manner will be different. Since he who follows St Paul's method of teaching will give them milk to drink, not solid food, likewise he will serve a more nourishing diet to those who are spiritually enlightened. "We teach," he said, "not with the persuasive words of human wisdom, but in the way that the Spirit teaches us; we teach spiritual things spiritually." And again: "We speak wisdom among the perfect," in whose company, I feel assured, you are to be found, unless in vain you have occupied yourselves so long with divine teaching, mortified your senses, and meditated day and night on God's law. Therefore, make your jaws ready for bread rather than milk.[1]

Bernard not only distinguished different levels of knowledge appropriate to the various states of life, he also associated with them different epistemological methods. Monks had as their primary means of attaining knowledge the contemplation of Truth in the mystical experience, and this I have discussed elsewhere.[2] The epistemological methods appropriate to the secular clergy and the laity will now be investigated.

THE SECULAR CLERGY

Bernard referred directly to the education of the secular clergy and implicitly to the epistemological method underlying it when he exclaimed:

Who will give me learned [*litterati*] and holy men as pastors presiding in the Church of God, if not everywhere or even in many places, at least in some?[3]

Here Bernard referred to properly qualified secular clergy as *litterati*. He also referred to them as *docti* and associated that description with the word *litterati*:

1. SC 1:1; PL 183:785; OB 1:3; CF 4:1.
2. "The Epistemological Value of Mysticism in the Thought of Bernard of Clairvaux," *Studies in Medieval Culture* 1 (1964) 48-58.
3. Ep 250:2; PL 182:450.

Perhaps you think I go too far in scorning knowledge, as if to censure the learned [*doctos*] and condemn the study of literature. Far from it! I am not ignorant of how much her learned members [*litterati*] have benefitted and still do benefit the Church, whether by refuting her opponents or by instructing the ignorant. And I have read: "Because you have rejected knowledge, I will reject you, that you not function as priest for me." I have read: "Those who are learned [*docti*] shall shine as the splendor of the firmament, and those that instruct many in justice as stars for all eternity."[4]

This identification of *docti* with *litterati* becomes all the more important when one remembers that *docti* is the word Bernard used to distinguish those monks who had been enlightened by the contemplative experience.[5]

Thus we can see that Bernard thought one was learned when one had been trained in the epistemological method appropriate to one's state of life. Indeed, Bernard found support in the sanction of the Scriptures for his positive attitude toward those whose learning he associated with the study of literature, a study not an essential part of the mystical program of the monk.[6] Bernard associated this "literary" learning with the office of priesthood and described the function of one who has such learning in terms of the duties of the secular clergy.

Bernard made a great point of the need for opposing the enemies of the Church with rational arguments. In writing to Pope Eugenius III, he made the point clear:

It is important, therefore, to do your best to convert unbelievers to the faith, to keep the converted from falling away, to bring back the fallen-away, further, that the perverse be directed toward righteousness, and the subverted recalled to the truth, that the subverters may be convinced by irrefutable reason, so that, if possible, they may either

4. SC 36:2; PL 183:967-68; OB 2:4.
5. SC 23:14; PL 183:891; OB 1:147.
6. There are qualifications which must be made to this statement. I shall try to make them in an article now in preparation.

change their ways or, if that may not be, they may loose their authority and the power of subverting other men.[7]

Bernard not only urged that reason be employed against heretics, but, in response to the entreaties of Eberwin, provost of Steinfeld, he himself used rational argument against them. Eberwin wrote:

I entreat you then, Father, to distinguish between all the parts of the heresy of those who have come to your notice and, by opposing them with the reasons and authorities of our faith, destroy them.[8]

Bernard's commentary on the positions of the Rhineland heretics whom Eberwin described made distinctions which, while maintaining Biblical authority, were independent of it and based on reason. For example:

Certain among them dissenting from the others, declare that marriage is permitted only between those who are virgins. . . . "These [Adam and Eve]," they say, "were both virgins whom God joined together, and it was not then lawful to separate them; however, no union of those who are not virgins can be presumed to be from God." But who has told you that they were joined together by God because they were virgins? . . . . They were; but it is not the same to unite those who were virgins and to unite them because they were virgins.[9]

Bernard expected the secular clergy to be versed in dialectics to carry out their responsibilities toward the faithful, too. Learning was not only necessary in presenting doctrine, but also in formulating the teachings of the Church in terms intelligible to the age. Bernard himself made use of dialectic in answering a question put to him on the relationship between grace and free will.[10] The resulting treatise is an excel-

---

7. Csi 3, 1, 3; PL 182:759; OB 3:433.
8. Eberwin, provost of Steinfeld, *Epistola ad s. Bernardum* (*inter s. Bernardi*) 472, 1; PL 182:677.
9. SC 66:4; PL 183:1095-96; OB 2:180-81. Bernard also advocated the use of reason rather than force in dealing with Jews (Ep 365:2; PL 182:571).
10. Gra 1:1; PL 182:1001; OB 3:165.

lent example of the application of reason in reconciling opposing positions drawn from the Scriptures. [11]

It is apparent, then, that Bernard saw a twofold use for dialectic. It was a means of communicating the truths of Christianity to those both inside and outside the Church; it was also a legitimate and necessary epistemological method through which theological truth could be discovered or clarified.[12]

The same dual function belonged to literature according to Bernard:

> I am not saying that knowledge of letters is to be despised. Such learning adorns and instructs the mind and even enables us to instruct others.[13]

Bernard's biographer, William of St Thierry, tells us that as a boy Bernard ". . . gave himself over to the study of letters by which he might learn about God and know him in the Scriptures."[14] In addition, when one considers the frequency with which Bernard cited classical authors,[15] it surely seems that he considered at least some of the *content* of classical literature of use, if not in discovering truth, then at least in the communication of ideas.

If Bernard thought both dialectics and literature were useful in discovering and disseminating the truths of theology—the task of the secular clergy—what was the educational process by which to obtain mastery of these tools? I have tried to give a detailed account of Bernard's answer elsewhere.[16] This answer can be summed up easily and, I suppose, obviously by saying that Bernard encouraged atten-

---

11. A particularly fine example of close reasoning is Gra 11:36-37; PL 182:1020-21; OB 3:191-2.

12. See my "Bernard of Clairvaux and Scholasticism," *Papers of the Michigan Academy of Science, Arts, and Letters* 48 (1963) 265-77, especially pp. 270-72.

13. SC 37:2; PL 183:971; OB 2:9.

14. Vita Bern I, 1, 3; PL 185:228.

15. See Bernard Jacqueline, "Répertoire des citations d'auteurs profanes dans les oeuvres de saint Bernard," CHOC, *Bernard de Clairvaux* (Paris, 1953) Appendice IV, pp. 549-54.

16. "Bernard of Clairvaux and Scholasticism," pp. 266-70.

dance at the schools of his time. Bernard fostered the education of many young students, praised the erudition of many scholars, and befriended many whom he acknowledged were skilled in intellectual pursuits. But, in each of these cases, Bernard's patronage or friendship was for a member of the secular clergy or for one preparing for this state of life. Peter Lombard became bishop of Paris, John of Salisbury bishop of Chartres, and Robert Pullan a cardinal. Bernard attempted to obtain the bishopric of Châlons-sur-Marne for Alberich, master of the cathedral school at Reims; though this bid was unsuccessful, Alberich did later become archbishop of Bourges. Bernard praised the erudition of Geoffrey of Loreto who later became archbishop of Bordeaux, and Gilbert, whom Bernard praised for ". . . taking pleasure in all the books and studies of the wise men of the world . . . ,"[17] was bishop of London when Bernard wrote his cordial letter to him.

Bernard's epistemological, educational, and social theories were consistent on this point. The duties of the secular clergy were such that the training in literature and dialectics which one obtained in the contemporary schools was highly desirable for the secular clergy. Hence, for the secular clergy intellectual endeavor was the proper means to the truth.

Bernard's linking of epistemological and social theory is none the less real with regard to the laity of his time, but there is much less material with which the historian can work. Similarly, Bernard said very little on the education of the laity, so clues from this area are few too. Bernard described the office of the prince in this way:

> The King of kings has set you up as a prince on earth so that under him and for him you may encourage the good, restrain the evil, defend the poor, and give justice to those who suffer injury. If you do this you will be performing the work of princes and can hope that God will increase and strengthen your principality.[18]

17. Ep 24; PL 182:129.
18. Ep 279; PL 182:485.

My concern here is not so much the duties of the prince as the means by which he was to obtain the knowledge necessary to perform those duties well. Bernard thought one of the means to knowledge available to the ruler was counsel; he wrote to Melisande, queen of Jerusalem:

> ... Andrew [writes] ... that you are behaving peacefully and kindly, [and] that you are ruling yourself and your kingdom wisely with the advice of wise men.[19]

Counsel by wise advisors was particularly appropriate in Bernard's time since temporal law was largely customary; Bernard did not attempt to change existing social institutions, but rather to make them consistent with their true purpose.[20] The normal means of obtaining the knowledge necessary to govern he thought legitimate.

To be sure, Bernard recognized the limitations of this method of discovering the standards by which the ruler should govern. He wrote, for example, to Conrad, king of the Romans:

> I do not know how the wise men and princes of the realm advise you on this matter, but I, speaking in my folly, shall not keep silent but speak out. . . . Since I am an obscure and mean person, it is foolish of me to thrust myself forward on a great matter into counsels of such weight and wisdom, as if I were a person of some consequence. But the more obscure and lowly I am, the more free I am to utter what love suggests. And so, in my folly, I will add this: if anyone else should try to persuade you to anything different from what I have said to you (which I do not think anyone will do), certainly he is either one who does not love the king, or he understands little of what becomes the king's majesty, or he is shown not to care for the interests of God or the king.[21]

---

19. Ep 289:1; PL 182:495.
20. See my "The Social Theory of Bernard of Clairvaux," *Studies in Medieval Cistercian History Presented to Jeremiah F. O'Sullivan* (CS 13; Spencer, Massachusetts, 1971) p. 45. See also Jean Leclercq, "St. Bernard's Attitude Toward War," soon to appear in *Studies in Medieval Cistercian History, II* (CS 24).
21. Ep 244:2-3; PL 182:441-42.

The problem is, then, that the counsel on which the ruler must rely is fallible. The wise men of the council do not have an unerring source of knowledge in custom; furthermore, their advice may not be honest.

Bernard did offer a partial solution to this problem, of course, in making himself available for consultation. His letters[22] and the advice he gave in person provided counsel from one whom his contemporaries thought to be close to the very Source of all truth and justice.[23] However, the problem still remained, for the twelfth-century prince could hardly have turned to the mystic to solve all the problems of his land.

Another aspect of Bernard's view of the epistemological methods open to the laity is also found in his letter to Queen Melisande:

> . . . Andrew [writes] . . . that . . . according to the wisdom given you by God, you are providently and wisely meeting the dangers which threaten your land.[24]

Here there is a new element—the divine help which the ruler must have. Bernard also referred to God's help in a letter to Louis VII of France; Bernard urged him to bestow the *regalia* on the new Cistercian bishop of Langres and warned Louis:

> . . . If you think otherwise, this also he [God] will reveal to you, and he will instruct your heart in wisdom.[25]

This infusion of wisdom by grace also poses a problem, in that Bernard provides no guidelines for the ruler to ascertain just what line of action is in accord with God's wishes. The appeal to the mystic is, again, efficacious, but not always practical.

22. The following are letters to the high nobility and royalty: Epp 31, 37, 38, 39, 40, 41, 92, 97, 116, 117, 119, 120, 121, 137, 138, 139, 140, 170, 183, 206, 207, 208, 209, 220, 221, 226, 241, 244, 255, 271, 279, 282, 289, 299, 300, 301, 303, 304, 308, 315, 354, 355, 375, 449, 455, and 468.
23. The implications of this are discussed in my "Charismatic and Gregorian Leadership in the Thought of Bernard of Clairvaux," *Bernard of Clairvaux: Studies Presented to Dom Jean Leclercq* (CS 24; Washington, D.C., 1973) pp. 73-90.
24. Ep 289:1; PL 182:495.
25. Ep 170:2; PL 182:331.

Bernard did, however, acknowledge the efficacy of a sort of elementary reasoning to meet the problems of the world. Here I think it important to say that Bernard considered sense data the basis for most kinds of knowledge, even the more exalted:

> Therefore, the soul, even though it is a spiritual creature, has need of a body. Without it the soul could by no means attain to that knowledge by which it ascends to the contemplation of truths essential to happiness.[26]

Bernard affirmed that all men, not only philosophers or theologians, were capable of knowing of the existence of God by reasoning from nature.[27] Even wicked men have the power to arrive at truth by reason:

> You need not wonder that sometimes the souls of wicked men are aware of the truth and yet are devoid of love, since in some bodies also you find life without sensitivity. . . . In the same way the souls of wicked men also are aware of the truth by natural reason and are sometimes helped by grace, although in no way animated thereby.[28]

The sort of everyday reasoning to which it seems Bernard was referring in this passage might be best described as common-sense reasoning in which sense data is taken at face value and elementary deductions made from it. Here there is no question of syllogisms, subtle comparisons or distinctions, or close scrutiny. This is a method open to all people.

And indeed, all people—not just rulers—were to avail themselves of ordinary means of attaining the truths necessary to the proper discharge of their office.[29] A passage from Bernard's moving lamentation over the death of his brother Gerard shows this--as well as Bernard's respect for the dignity of all sorts of occupations:

26. SC 5:1; PL 183:799; OB 1:21-22; CF 4:25.
27. SC 31:3; PL 183:941-42; OB 1:221.
28. Div 10:1; PL 183:567; OB 6/1:121-22.
29. See Ep 31, 92, 97, 120, 129, 139, 175, 206, 288, 308, and 363 for letters about knights and their role. Some letters which mention merchants are Ep 119, 363, and 375.

Both in the greatest things and in the least he was the greatest. For instance, in building, in agriculture, in horticulture, in waterworks, indeed in all the different arts and trades of country life, was there anything, I ask, to which Gerard's skill and resources were not equal? He could easily be the teacher of the quarrymen, the workers in wood and iron, the farm laborers, the gardeners, the shoemakers, and the weavers. And while all judged him wisest, in his own eyes alone he was not wise.[30]

Two elements appear to support one in one's everyday occupation: skill, which is the product of normal training in an activity, and resource, which seems to be the same sort of common-sense reasoning Bernard urged on the ruler.

If, as I have said, Bernard's references to lay occupations and the means of dealing with them are fewer than those to monks and secular clergy, it is surely true—and understandable—that the epistemology which he associated with the laity is both obvious and unsure. We might describe the layman's means to truth as common sense. But common sense is a fallible guide, less trustworthy in Bernard's eyes than the mystical contemplation of the monk and the dialectical exposition of the secular cleric.

There were areas of life in which Bernard would not have allowed a guide of such doubtful certainty as common sense. We have skirted these areas in discussing the activities of the ruler, for the justice which the ruler was to dispense involved ethical and moral decisions. How was the twelfth-century layman to obtain knowledge of those things essential to the good life—knowledge of what to believe and what to do? I have already pointed out that the layman could have recourse to the mystic. But there was a more readily accessible source of information on questions of belief and morality, the secular clergy. As we know, Bernard saw the task of the secular clergy as the refutation of heresy and the instruction of the people. He wrote to the people of Toulouse:

Obey the bishop, other superiors, and teachers of the church. . . . And I also remind you, my dear friends, of

30. SC 26:7; PL 183:908; OB 1:175.

what I have said when I was with you, that you should not receive any outside or unknown preacher, unless he should be sent by the Supreme Pontiff or have permission to preach from your bishop, for "how shall they preach unless they are sent."[31]

The secular clergy were to be the normal source of the information necessary to the salvation of the laity.

CONCLUSION

Bernard's epistemological and social theories were consistent and corresponded to one another. The monastic, clerical, and lay ways of life had as their proper means of obtaining truth mystical contemplation, scholarship, and common sense. Bernard's educational theory stemmed from this association of states of life with epistemological methods; the monk was to be trained through asceticism, the cleric in dialectic and literature, and the layman in his trade.

Much that seems inconsistent in Bernard's thought makes sense when one remembers this association of epistemological, social, and educational theories. How could Bernard have supported dialectical training in the schools and yet exclude it from the monastery? [32] Because an epistemological tool and its study may be appropriate to one state of life and not to another.

Bernard's approval of widely differing means to the truth— some of which had mutually exclusive educational systems— is consistent even though complex. Bernard could assume a leadership role in so many phases of twelfth-century European life because he had a consistent concept of their place and importance in the culture of his time.

John R. Sommerfeldt

Western Michigan University
Kalamazoo, Michigan

31. Ep 242:2-3; PL 182:437.
32. SC 36:2 and 5; PL 183:968-69; OB 2:4 and 6-7.

A PLEA FOR THE *INSTITUTIO SANCTI BERNARDI QUOMODO CANTARE ET PSALLERE DEBEAMUS*

IN 1963 FATHER JEAN LECLERCQ published a minor Bernardine text so minuscule as to be all but lost among the treatises and *opuscula* which make up Volume Three of the monumental *S Bernardi Opera*. Still, for musicologists and others interested in Cistercian chant, the publication of a critical edition of Saint Bernard's *Prologus in antiphonarium quod cistercienses canunt ecclesiae* was a significant event, even though the text runs to scarcely thirty lines.[1] It was the first item in what one hopes will soon be a rather complete series of critical editions of Cistercian chant treatises and related documents.

The signs augur well for the future. Fr Francis Guentner SJ of Saint Louis University has recently finished work on his edition of the treatise for which Saint Bernard's *Prologus* served as an introduction—*Cantum quem Cisterciensis Ordinis*;[2] and Cecily Sweeney, of the University of California, Los Angeles, has even more recently completed a doctoral dissertation on, and edition of, a lengthy late thirteenth or early fourteenth-century treatise formerly attributed to John Wylde, but now restored to an Anonymous who was much beholden to the principles operative in the Cistercian chant reform effected under Saint Bernard's aegis in the middle of the twelfth century. Among other chant treatises awaiting

1. (Rome, 1963), pp. 515-6; introductory notes, pp. 511-3.
2. To be published in the *Corpus Scriptorum de Musica,* under the general direction of Gilbert Reaney.

the editorial attention of Dr Sweeney are the *Regulae de arte musica* attributed to Guy, Abbot of Cherlieu—a work much used by the theorists active in the just mentioned Cistercian chant reform;[3] a *Tonale* (a sort of catechism of chant) often attributed to Saint Bernard, and extant in several different redactions;[4] a preface to the reformed Cistercian *graduale*;[5] a late thirteenth-century treatise authored at Heilsbronn Abbey, near Erlangen, Germany;[6] and an hitherto unknown early thirteenth-century anonymous work discovered by Dr Sweeney in the British Museum manuscript, Arundel 25.

One of the purposes of this article is to draw attention to yet another item which should be included in the canon of Cistercian chant writings: the *Institutio Sancti Bernardi abbatis Claraevallis quomodo cantare et psallere debeamus.* So slender is this *opusculum* (and admittedly of such minor importance), it might easily be overlooked. And this would be unfortunate. In its own way it has much better reason for being attributed to Saint Bernard than do a number of other chant writings often attributed in times past to the Abbot of Clairvaux. Further, the *Institutio* was at an early date invested with something of an "official" character, as we shall soon see.

Not that the *Institutio* is unknown to musicologists. It figured rather massively in two studies by the late Fr S. A. van Dijk OFM.[7] The first of these, "Saint Bernard and the *Instituta Patrum* of Saint Gall," was printed in 1950, in *Musica Disciplina* 4, pp. 99-109, where the author, profiting by the earlier research by Fr J. Smits van Waesberghe, SJ,[8] left

3. The edition of the *Regulae* in Coussemaker's *Scriptorum de musica medii aevi nova series,* T.II, pp. 150-91, is almost too defective to be of practical use to the scholar.

4. The most accessible of the many printed versions is in PL 182:1153-66.

5. Also in PL 182:1151-4.

6. Identified by H. Hüschen in his article "Zisterzienser," *Die Musik in Geschichte und Gegenwart* 14 (1968) col. 918; the manuscript is now in the Universitätsbibliothek, Erlangen, where it is catalogued as ms. 193.

7. Fr van Dijk also used the initials S. J. P. van Dijk.

8. "Verklaring der lettertekens (litterae significativae) in het Gregoriaansche neumenschrift van Saint Gallen," *Muziekgeschiedenis der Middeleeuwen* 2 (Tilburg, 1939-1942) 197 ff.

intact precious little of the reputation once enjoyed by the so-called *Instituta Patrum* of Saint Gall. In 1754 Antonio Francesco Vezzosi had drawn attention to the text by editing it in Volume Four of his edition of the *Opera omnia* of the Roman cardinal and liturgist, the Bl Giussepe Thomasi (or Tommasi or Tomasi); and two decades later, the German Benedictine, Martin Gerbert, made the text even more accessible by including it in his famous collection of treatises on ecclesiastical music, *De cantu et musica sacra a prima Ecclesiae aetate usque ad praesens tempus.*[9] Erring by the margin of a mere near-millenium, Gerbert decided that the *Instituta Patrum* was all but co-eval with the emergence of the Church from the catacombs, and placed it third in his series of treatises arranged according to chronological order. A date closer to the early thirteenth century would be more accurate, as Fr Smits van Waesberghe has convincingly demonstrated; and, more likely than not, the author was the wordy dean of Saint Gall, Ekkehard V (died ca. 1220), about whose literary qualities no one seems able to say anything kind. Fr van Dijk's contribution consisted in his showing that, beneath the minuscule *Instituta Patrum* lay an even more minuscule source—the *Institutio Sancti Bernardi.*[10] Not for a moment did Fr van Dijk take seriously the attribution to Saint Bernard; but neither did he hesitate to identify the character of the text as "unmistakably Cistercian."[11] This was not intended as a compliment. Fr van Dijk tended to view the twelfth-century Cistercian phenomenon with a somewhat jaundiced eye. Bland and innocuous though the *Institutio* might appear to us, it "is really full of criticism against Cluny. It is conceived and written in the spirit of reaction which is typical of the early Cistercian statutes. . . . ."[12]

The second of Fr van Dijk's articles in which the *Institutio* looms large bears the title "Medieval Terminology and Methods of Psalm Singing." Like its predecessor, it too

9. Sankt Blasien 1774, Vol. 1, p. 5 ff.
10. The mss differ considerably as to the precise title—as we shall see when we examine the text later in this article.
11. "Saint Bernard and the *Instituta Patrum*," p. 107.
12. *Ibid.*

appeared in *Musica Disciplina.*[13] The data marshalled together by the author spanned many centuries, and represented many different regions and many different ecclesiastical milieux. It was in this context that our *Institutio* appeared as the key document essential to an understanding of Cistercian psalm singing. Fr van Dijk's scope was modest, and he insisted that "The matter . . . collected is not intended to be a basis for definite conclusions."[14] And, in point of fact, nothing very definite did emerge for the general reader, other than the not particularly revolutionary idea that, in the Middle Ages, psalm singing was somewhat problematical as regards tempo, ensemble execution and general style.

It is admittedly remarkable that a document so unremarkable as the *Institutio* should have had so wide a circulation, and this at an early date. For the scribe, its chief usefulness perhaps lay in the fact that, given the extreme brevity of the text, it proved ideal as a space-filler for that blank half-column at the end of this or that manuscript—usually one relating to the liturgy. Medieval scribes had a horror of the void; and it is thanks to this horror that so much occasional verse and so many pieces of interesting (and not so interesting) literary and liturgical debris have been preserved for us.

When Fr van Dijk prepared his study, "Saint Bernard and the *Instituta Patrum* of Saint Gall," his acquaintance with the manuscript tradition was limited to material available at Oxford and in the London British Museum. Of the five original manuscripts collated by Fr van Dijk, only one—a fifteenth-century manuscript from Padua, but now in the Bodleian Library at Oxford[15]—hailed from outside England. The other manuscripts, all of which are now catalogued in the British Museum, included a fourteenth-century *opus* by John Beleth, Harley 5235;[16] a fourteenth-century manuscript of *varia*, Add. 16975;[17] a co-eval manuscript with a version of the

13. 6 (1952) 7-27.
14. "Medieval Terminology," p. 7.
15. Can. Patr. lat. 223; the *Institutio* is on f. 289v, where the full title reads: *Institutio bernardi abbatis quomodo psallere debeamus.*
16. F. 127r: *Modus canendi secundum Bernardum.*
17. F. 162r: *Modus psallendi in choro.*

Institutio too heavily interpolated to prove useful for our present purposes—Royal 5.A.VI;[18] and, finally, the front guard leaf of a thirteenth-century manuscript from Ramsey Abbey, Royal 8.D.III. This last mentioned version was too mutilated to be of help to Fr van Dijk in establishing his text of the *Institutio*. He had recourse, however, to secondary sources: the transcription published by W. H. Frere in his edition of the thirteenth-century Sarum Ordinal;[19] and the edition of a *ceremoniale* from Subiaco (Italy), first edited in 1902 by Leone Allodi OSB,[20] and a few years later, in 1905, by Bruno Albers OSB, in Volume Two of his well known edition of monastic customaries.[21] In the Subiaco *ceremoniale*, the text of the *Institutio* was quoted *in extenso* as part of a chapter touching on choir observances; a similar incorporation of the text took place in Denis the Carthusian's *opusculum*, "Contra inordinationem detestabilem cordis in Dei laudibus,"[22] and in John Cardinal Bona's *De divina psalmodia.*[23]

If, then, the *Institutio* really is, as Fr van Dijk claims, a text which "was certainly conceived by the Cistercians about the middle of the twelfth century,"[24] the direct manuscript evidence used by Fr van Dijk is remarkable neither for its antiquity nor for its geographical distribution.

My own version of the text has been established on the basis of five manuscripts not included in Fr van Dijk's list of sources. A careful survey of library holdings in western Europe and elsewhere would probably yield at least another

---

18. Here the title is: *Regula sancti Bernardi de modo psallendi et cantandi in ecclesia.*

19. *The Use of Sarum,* Vol. I: *The Sarum Customs* (Cambridge, 1898), p. 36.

20. *Consuetudines et caeremoniae regularis observantiae monasterii Sublacensis et venerabilis loci Specus S. Benedicti* (Sublaci 1902) p. 11.

21. *Consuetudines monasticae,* Vol. II (Typis Montis Casini, 1905) pp. 132-3.

22. *Opuscula aliqua quae ad theologiam mysticam egregie instituunt* (Monsterolii, 1894), p. 613.

23. Cap. XVIII: "De Cantu Ecclesiastico," Pars V, n. 1; p. 885 of the Antwerp edition of the Cardinal's *Opera omnia* printed in 1677; p. 540 of the Antwerp edition of 1694; and the same page in the later Antwerp edition of 1723.

24. "Medieval Terminology and Methods of Psalm Singing," p. 11.

fifty copies.[25] But the text in question, being of minor importance, hardly justifies the efforts required for so thorough a search, especially since there is nothing particularly mysterious or doubtful about the text as it emerges from the manuscript evidence already at hand.

MANUSCRIPTS AND ABBREVIATIONS

PARIS, Bibliotheque national, ms. nouv. acq. lat. 372, f. 66v, col. 2.

This ms. is a late twelfth-century collection of various works by Saint Bernard (*De diligendo Deo,* various sermons, *De ortu novae militiae . . .*) and by William of St Thierry (*Vita Sancti Bernard*). It was written at the Abbey of Eenaeme (or Einham), East Flanders, on the Scheldt. Originally a college of canons, it became Benedictine in 1063. The scribe's note at the bottom of f.lv identifies the place and the copyist: "Liber Sancti Salvatoris Einamensis ecclesiae . . . Hunc etiam librum Hugo scripsit. . . ." In the list of abbots of Eenaeme edited in *Gallia Christiana* V (Parisiis - Bruxellis, 1877), col. 34, we read under the entry for Giselbertus or Gislebertus II, a quotation from the *Chronicle of Afflighem*: An. 1169. *D. Giselbertus monachus Affligeniensis agens abbatem Eynamensem illam ecclesiam illustravit et in proventibus ampliavit; sed et tria ordinis Cisterciensis monasteria laudabiliter rexit. Depositus fuit, eo quod Enemenses nigros eiecerit, et Cistercienses introduxerit.* (Could the text of the *Institutio* have been introduced into this

---

25. Among these would be: Lisbon, Biblioteca Nacional, ms. CCCXXXIX/75 (14th-15th cc.), five ff. from the end; Rome, Biblioteca Vittorio Emmanuele, Fondo Sessoriano, ms. 75 (13th c.) f. 127r; Lilienfeld (Austria), ms. 108 (13th c.), f. 16r; Frauenfeld (Kanton Thurgau, Switzerland), ms. Y38 (14th-15th cc.), f.5v. This last version has been transcribed almost *in extenso*—though with a few errors—by Fr Bruno Griesser SOC, in his article "*Exordium, Carta Caritatis* und *Institutiones cap. gen.* in einer Salemer Handschrift," *Cistercienser-Chronik* 59 (1952): 23. I owe these references to Fr Raymond Milcamp OCSO, monk of Scourmont, whose unpublished bibliographies of Cistercian manuscripts have always been for me a goldmine of helpful information.

Benedictine abbey by the Cistercianophile Giselbertus?)
In the manuscript, the *Institutio* is in somewhat darker
ink, and in a hand different from that of the scribe
Hugo; but it belongs to roughly the same period to
which the rest of the manuscript belongs.

A   AARAU, Kantonsbibliothek, ms. Wett. 4° 5, f. 87r.

Late twelfth-century. The manuscript is an incomplete
copy of the *Liber Usuum* (i.e., *Ecclesiastica Officia,
Instituta, Usus Conversorum*), with a number of additions in various hands, and from various other manuscripts. For the section in which the *Institutio* appears,
the script seems to be late twelfth-century.
The manuscript comes from Wettingen (Switzerland),
founded in 1227 by Salem (line of Morimond). For an
analysis of the manuscript, see Jean Leclercq, "Manuscrits cisterciens dans diverses bibliothèques," ASOC 11
(1955) p. 144.

V   ROME, Biblioteca Vaticana, Ottoboniani latini ms. 176,
f. 119r.

Thirteenth-century martyrology and Rule, followed by
several folios of additions in various thirteenth-century
hands. From San Pietro della Canonica (Canonica S.
Petri), near Amalfi. Originally founded in 1212 as a
house of canons, it came into the Cistercian Order soon
after in 1214, in the filiation of Fossanova (line of Clairvaux). For a detailed description of the contents of the
manuscript, see Jean Leclercq, "Textes et manuscrits
cisterciens à la Bibliothèque Vaticane," ASOC 15
(1959) 87-9.

C   ROME, Biblioteca Casanatense, ms. 361, f. 68v.

A fourteenth-century *Ordinarium,* with a final chapter
purloined from the *Ecclesiastica Officia.* Provenance unknown; but for an analysis of the manuscript, see Jean
Leclercq, "Manuscrits cisterciens dans les bibliothèques
d'Italie," ASOC 5 (1949) 99-100.

U UPPSALA, Universitets Biblioteket, ms. C.203, f. 140r. A fifteenth-century collection of *varia* written at the mother abbey of the Bridgettine Order, Vadstena, on Lake Vättern, Östergötland, Sweden. This abbey had one of the largest libraries in Scandanavia. There were close contacts between Vadstena and the near-by Cistercian Abbey of Alvastra (originally Benedictine, but later Cistercian, line of Clairvaux, in 1143); the text of the *Institutio* may well have come to Vadstena by way of Alvastra. For an analysis of the Cistercian items in the final folios of this manuscript, see Jean Leclercq, "Textes et manuscrits cisterciens en Suéde," ASOC 6 (1950) p. 127.

TEXT OF THE INSTITUTIO

The following transcription is based on the above listed manuscripts. Modern punctuation has been inserted, but medieval orthography preserved. Minor orthographical variants between the manuscripts have been ignored, however, so as to leave the critical apparatus uncluttered by useless details. The division into paragraphs corresponds to the subject matter of the *Institutio*, but is not found in the manuscripts; the typographical divisions have been introduced with a view to the brief commentary which is to follow.

1   INSTITUTIO SANCTI BERNARDI ABBATIS CLAREUALLIS
     QUOMODO CANTARE ET PSALLERE DEBEAMUS

3   Venerabilis pater noster beatus Bernardus abbatis clareuallis precepit monachis hanc formam candendi tenere, affirmans hoc deo et angelis placere, ita dicens:

6   Psalmodiam non nimium protrahamus, sed rotonde et uiua uoce cantemus. Metrum et finem uersus simul intonemus et simul dimittamus. Punctum nullus teneat, sed
9   cito dimittat. Post metrum bonam pausam faciamus. Nullus ante alios incipire et nimis currere presumat, aut post alios nimium trahere uel punctum tenere. Simul
12 cantemus, simul pausemus, semper auscultando.

Quicumque incipit antiphonam aut psalmum aut
hymnum aut responsorium aut alleluia, unam aut duas
15 partes solus tractim dicat, aliis tacentibus; et ab eo loco
quo ille dimittit, alii incipiant, non repetentes quod ille
iam dixit. Similiter teneatur dum cantor reincipit anti-
18 phonam, alleluia, et responsorium. Hoc ubique seruetur,
ne alter redicat quod iam ab altero dictum est.

Dum hymnos, alleluia, aut responsorium cantemus, in
21 clausulis aliquantulum expectemus, maxime tamen in
festiuis diebus.

1-2 *Tit. om.* AU / INSTITUTIO] DE INSTITUTIONE c /
ABBATIS CLAREVALLIS] *om.* VC 3 noster] *om.* PU /
beatus] sanctus PCV 3-4 abbatis clarevallis] clarevallis
abbatis U 4 monachis] + suis V; *om.* C / formam] normam U
5 affirmans—placere] om. A / et angelis placere] placere et
angelis V 6 et] *supra lineam* A 8 et] *om.* V / nullus] nemo V;
ullus C 10 nimis] *om.* V 12 pausemus] + et C / auscultando]
auscultator C 13 aut psalmum] *om.* A 13-14 antiphonam—
alleluia] antiphonam alleluia et responsoriam aut psalmum
aut ymphum U / 14 aut responsorium aut] vel responsorium
vel A 14 aut[3]] vel A 15 solus] om. A 16 dimittit] dimittat U
/ good] que C 17 reincipit] incipit C; incipiat U 17-18 anti-
phanam, alleluia, et responsorium] antiphonam uel alleluia uel
responsoriam A 18 servatur] teneatur U 19 quod] que VC; quia
A/alter] alio A 20 hymnos] hymnum V/aut] uel A 21 tamen]
om. PV 22 festivis] festis U

The Title, Lines 1 - 2

Of the three manuscripts which include the title, all refer to
Bernard as *Saint* Bernard. This suggests that the title at least
is likely to be (though not necessarily) posterior to 1174, the
date of Bernard's canonization. On the other hand, the
opening lines of the body of the text refer to Bernard as
beatus in two of the manuscripts (A U); and this is the
reading retained in the above transcription, even though the
three other manuscripts read *sanctus*: it is easy enough to see

how a pre-1174 *beatus* would have been changed, after Bernard's canonization, to *sanctus*; but, on the contrary hypothesis that *sanctus* is original, there is absolutely no reason for any scribe to substitute *beatus* for *sanctus*. All of which suggests, though it certainly does not prove, that the *Institutio* in its earliest form might well have pre-dated Bernard's canonization. As for the title as a whole, the variants are too many (especially if we take into account the four variant titles found in the manuscripts referred to above, Notes 15-18) to justify our proposing a single reading as probably authentic.

Introductory Paragraph, Lines 3-5

The manuscripts fluctuate between *pater* and *pater noster* in line 3. Surely, the latter reading is correct. But why? Because the only two manuscripts which omit the *noster* are non-Cistercian, coming, in the one instance, from a Benedictine monastery (P), and from a Bridgettine abbey in the other instance (U). In neither case would Bernard have been referred to as "*our* father."

What about the explicit attribution of the *Institutio* to Saint Bernard? The manuscript evidence could not be more unanimous. This attribution might be more founded in fact than many of us would think likely, and it deserves at least a brief discussion.

In view of the meagre content-matter of the *Institutio,* no one would be seriously inclined to include the text in a *corpus* of the Saint's authentic writings. Evidently, Saint Bernard had to concern himself on occasion with the more prosaic details of day to day life at Clairvaux; but it *is* somewhat temerarious, perhaps even offensive to pious ears, to suggest that the declaimer of the *Sermons on the Song of Songs* could also have authored so devastatingly unmystical a set of practical norms for chanting such as we find in the *Institutio.* Still, we would do well to exercise a bit of caution in this regard, and not dissociate too completely Bernard's name from this set of rules.

It is a well known fact that, at the level of the Order at large, the Cistercian *Consuetudines* aimed at preserving and fostering an Order-wide mutual charity by means of a rather uniform observance even in much which involved only the practical organization of daily life. But these codified customs by no means provided, or intended to provide, norms for every conceivable situation; and there were obviously large areas where details had to be arranged at the local level, and as best suited the particular circumstances of a given community. Local customs and even collections of local house rules were by no means unknown.[26] And if Clairvaux were like any other normal Cistercian monastery of almost any period, there must have been any number of Cantors who, from time to time, drew up lists of practical rules of thumb for the sake of novices and others who had to be introduced to, or recalled to, the niceties of choir discipline and practice. Indeed, during my own years at Gethsemani, almost each Cantor in a long succession of Cantors, has authored similar texts, ranging from mere check-lists of particular points to be kept in mind (rather like the *Institutio*) to distressingly lengthy treatises of monumental proportions. Moreover, if Bernard were like most normal abbots, he probably had more than one occasion to make public remarks about this or that detail of choir performance. Indeed, in my own time I have heard abbots exhort their monks (sometimes much to the chagrin of the official Cantor) not to drag the tempo so excessively, or to make a good pause at the mediant, or to listen twice as much as they sing: all of which sounds suspiciously like "Psalmodiam . . . rotunde et viva voce cantemus . . . Post metrum bonam pausam faciamus . . . Simul cantemus, simul pausemus, semper auscultando." In point of fact, we do have from Bernard himself a vaguely

---

26. An interesting collection of the local customs followed at Cîteaux, and probably compiled around the middle of the 13th century, in part by a monk of Cîteaux, and in part by a visiting monk from some other Cistercian monastery, has been edited by Fr Bruno Griesser SOC, "Consuetudines domus Cisterciensis," ASOC 3 (1947) 138-46. Most of these customs or rules deal with questions of choir discipline and liturgical practice.

similar text of undoubted authenticity—a text, moreover, often found transcribed together with the *Institutio*:[27]

... Our Rule tells us that nothing ought to be preferred to the work of God. By this name of the "work of God" our holy Father St Benedict willed should be designated the solemn service of praise we daily discharge in our churches, and his purpose was to impress upon our minds the necessity of devoting ourselves with all earnestness to that great duty. Therefore, I exhort you, dearest brethren, to assist at every hour of the canonical office with zeal and recollection. You must be zealous in order to join fervently, yet reverently, in chanting the praises of God, not lazily, not drowsily, not yawningly, not sparing yourselves, not mutilating the words or omitting any, not with weak and mincing voices effeminately stammering or sounding through the nose; but singing with the manly fullness and sonorousness and the religious affection proper to songs which have been inspired by the Holy Ghost....[28]

The exact relationship between this text, which forms part of the conclusion to *Sermon Forty-Seven* on the *Song of Songs,* and any actual chapter exhortation delivered by the Saint is, of course, problematical. But there were certainly times when Bernard was not above descending to admittedly mundane but practical points of usage; and it would by no means be astonishing if, on one or another such occasion, some Clairvallian Cantor jotted down a set of practical norms for choir discipline, incorporating into his brief text a few of the remarks made by the illustrious Abbot of the place.

No matter how fanciful the hypothesis proposed, however, the fact remains that, somehow, Bernard's name got attached to the *Institutio* as early as the final decades of the twelfth century. Moreover, at an early date, the *Institutio* became invested with something of an *official* character. This point is

27. As in the case of Cardinal Bona (*supra,* Note 23), Denis the Carthusian (*supra,* Note 22), the Subiaco *Consuetudines et caeremoniae* (*supra,* Notes 20 and 21), and the Vadstena manuscript described above under the abbreviation (U).

28. SC 47:8; OB 2:66. tr "Priest of Mount Melleray" [Fr Ailbe Luddy OCSO], *St Bernard's Sermons on the Canticle of Canticles,* 2 vols. (Dublin, s.d. [1920]) p. 42.

clear in several of the visitation reports drawn up by one of
the most attractive of the Order's personalities in the thirteenth century, Stephen of Lexington, who was succesively
abbot of Stanley (in England), then of Savigny (in northern
France), and finally of Clairvaux itself.[29] We find, for instance, in a visitation card drawn up by Abbot Stephen for the
Abbey of Chaloché (diocese of Angers) in 1233, the following prescription:

> Item cantor et succentor studeant diligenter, quod in choro
> cantantes comptetentes (for *competenter*?) pausando con-
> corditer cantent alterutrum auscultantes secundum formam
> a beato Bernardo prescriptam.[30]

The allusion to the *Institutio* is patent, even if the editor of
the text, Fr Bruno Griesser soc, mistakenly referred the
reader to the finale of *Sermon Forty-Seven* on the *Song of
Songs* as the point of reference.[31] Abbot Stephen's prescription seems to have been ineffectual, since we find him repeating it in the visitation card drawn up for the same abbey
in 1235:

> Item inprimis precipitur, ut forma cantandi ab beato patre
> nostro Bernardo saepius in capitulo recitetur et in ecclesia
> teneatur.[32]

Here we read that the text of the *Institutio* is to be often
read out in chapter, exactly as other official texts emanating
from the General Chapter. There is yet another clear allusion
to the *Institutio* in Stephen's visitation card for Longvillers
(diocese of Thérouanne) sometime after 1131, where the
then Abbot of Savigny prescribes:

> Firmiter precipitur, ut servitium Dei in Ecclesia cum maiori
> reverentia et diligentia fiat et psalmodia cum bona pausa in
> metro. . . .[33]

29. A summary *curriculum vitae* of Stephen is given in pp. 4-8 of the *Registrum
Epistolarum Stephani de Lexinton,* ed and annotated by Fr Bruno Griesser SOC,
ASOC 2 (1946).
30. *Pars altera* of the work described in the preceding footnote, ASOC 8 (1952)
p. 217.
31. Ibid., Note 3.
32. Ibid., p. 218.
33. Ibid., p. 202.

The reference to the *Institutio* in the final phrase is unmistakable—at least in this corrected version of the editor's transcription, where the abbreviated form of *in metro* was wrongly extended as *i(m)metur,* and then "corrected" to read *himnetur.*

In summary, we cannot in any way be sure to what extent the *Institutio* really came from the Abbot of Clairvaux; but it would be as rash to exclude all mention of Bernard as it would be to make him the author of the text in the strict and immediate sense of the term "author." That Bernard's name was associated with the *Institutio* from an early date is certain; and there must have been a *fundamentum in re* behind this fact. Finally, the text enjoyed a quasi-official character, at least in the mind of Stephen of Lexington, who was probably not alone in accepting the *Institutio* as normative for Cistercian chant discipline.

The final phrase of the introductory paragraph deserves at least a passing comment. . . . *Affirmans hoc deo et angelis placere.* This inclusion of angels is a nice touch, and one rather typical of the twelfth-century Cistercian milieu. In Chapter 19 of the *Holy Rule,* "De disciplina psallendi," Saint Benedict concludes a series of biblical quotations with a text from *Psalm* 137:2: "In the sight of angels I will sing psalms to you." He then goes on immediately to draw from this text and the preceding ones a practical conclusion: "Let us then consider how we ought to behave ourselves in the presence of God and his angels. . . ." In many of the edifying stories of the early Cistercian period—stories such as abound in the huge collection which goes by the name of the *Exordium Magnum*—we see to what a great extent angels are part of the spiritual universe in which the average Cistercian monk moved. Indeed, one gets the impression at times that the celebration of the Office actually involved a kind of "concelebration" in which the monastic liturgy merely mirrored and participated imperfectly in the heavenly liturgy being celebrated by the angels—as when the monk Christian saw in a vision the community of Cîteaux standing in choir, and, "bathed in dazzling light, performing the praise of God with the utmost devotion. But above this community (he) saw yet another community: a community of the holy angels, each standing according to his rank; and from them streamed forth a far greater light of glory, and they seemed to be rejoicing at the devotion of the brethren (in the choir below)."[34] In *Distinctio* II of the same collection, Chapter 3 describes "How at Vigils, one night, Saint Bernard saw an angel standing beside each monk, writing down on parchment what each monk was chanting." The angels, we are told, wrote in gold, silver, ink or water, according to the degree of devotion of the monk assigned them. . . .[35] And the very next chapter in the same *Distinctio* shows us the angels doing all they can to stir the brethren to even greater fervor for the chanting of the *Te Deum*, a hymn for which, says Bernard, angels have a special fondness.[36] The list of such passages could be extended to considerable length.

The Body of the Text

The *Institutio* belongs to that category of practical treatises, the chief function of which was to take care of the practical problems involved in the chanting of the liturgy. In the twelfth century, it was generally taken as axiomatic that music was bound up with the very order of the universe. Centuries earlier, the Roman philosopher Boethius (d. 525) had adopted a tri-partite division of music which seems to have been everywhere accepted as normative. At the bottom level of the three kinds of music was the phenomenon of sound and rhythm (both instrumental and vocal) which we today call "music" without further qualification, but which Boethius dubbed *musica instrumentalis*. At a higher level was *musica humana*, which involved the harmony of man's physical being, as well as the concord between the body and soul. At the highest level stood the "music of the spheres," vari-

---

34. *Distinctio* I, Cap. 34, p. 95, lines 24-26, of the critical edition by Fr Bruno Griesser SOC, *Exordium Magnum Cisterciense . . .* , Series Scriptorum S. Ordinis Cisterciensis, 2 (Rome, 1961).
35. *Distinctio* II, Cap. III; pp. 100-1 of the Griesser edition.
36. Ibid., Cap. IV, p. 101.

ously designated as *musica mundana* or *musica caelestis.* This was a music rooted in the music of the *trisagion* chanted before God in glory, and it found its expression in the order of the universe, in the succession of the seasons, in the movements of the heavens and celestial bodies. Only the philosopher could be a musician in the deepest sense. But this lofty consideration was not always of practical help in getting the Office chanted with some semblance of dignity and beauty; so that we find quite a sizable collection of medieval treatises on music geared rather directly toward the monk in the choir-stall, whose immediate concern was chanting the Office without floundering about too much.[37] The *Institutio* attributed to Saint Bernard reaches the nadir of this type of treatise-genre, and consists simply of a series of practical norms governing:

1 - general style and unity in performance;
2 - intonations and reprises;
3 - pauses after cadences of certain types of chant.

The text of the body of the *Institutio* is accordingly divided into three paragraphs of unequal length, corresponding to these three chief topics.

Paragraph on General Style and Unity in Performance (lines 6-12)

Psalmodiam non nimium protrahamus, sed rotunde et viva voce cantemus. "We do not drag the tempo of the psalmody, but sing out full voice, and at a lively clip." The question of tempo is, of course, relative. If the term of comparison is a choir skipping through the psalmody at a fast and furious rate, then a normal, sedate but moving pace will as likely as not be felt and described as "slow"; whereas, if the term of

---

37. An excellent summary description of the various types of medieval treatises on music is to be found in Albert Seay, *Music in the Medieval World* (Englewood Cliffs, [New Jersey], 1965) pp. 22-3.

comparison is a choir plodding along with lugubrious solemnity, the very same normal, sedate but moving pace will be experienced as excessively fast. One can, of course, find isolated texts which describe the slow, solemn chanting of Cistercian monks, as in the description of the Vigil Office celebrated by the pioneer colony of monks from Clairvaux who founded Villers (in Brabant) in 1146. They spent the first night in Brabant at a private home, but rose as usual for Vigils, which they sang "according to rule" (*regulariter*) and extremely slowly (*et valde morose*). So devotional was the impact that the result was inevitable: the on-looking members of the household were struck with compunction, and gave themselves and their possessions into the hands of the visiting Cistercians (*compuncti se et sua in manibus eorum dederunt*).[38] Such can be the power of really devout psalm-singing. . . . But we have many texts which suggest that there were frequent occasions when the tempo adopted was rather on the lively side. In Chapter 115 of the *Ecclesiastica Officia*, the Cantor is authorized to speed up the singing either at a sign from the sacristan (who was one of the timekeepers of the community) or on his own initiative;[39] and a statute from the General Chapter of 1175 lays it down that, during periods of special work (sheep-shearing, harvest season, etc.), the Hours of the Office are to be sung at a faster tempo.[40] If, however, the thirteenth-century local house rules of Cîteaux, may be considered at all typical of the practice not only at Cîteaux, but elsewhere in the Order, there were yet other occasions when a faster tempo was the norm. In the edition

38. *Historia Monasterii Villariensis*, Lib. I, Cap. I; ed. Martène-Durand, *Thesaurus Novus Anecdotorum*, T. III (Lutetiae Parisiorum) col. 1270.

39. P. Guignard, *Les monuments primitifs de la Règle Cistercienne* (Dijon, 1878) p. 236. It should be noted that the earliest version of the *Ecclesiastica Officia*, extant in a manuscript written in the early 1130's, authorizes the Cantor to speed up the psalmody only at a node from the sacristan; see Fr Bruno Griesser SOC, *Die "Ecclesiastica Officia Cisterciensis Ordinis" des Cod. 1711 von Trient*, ASOC 12 (1956) 274.

40. J. Canivez, ed., *Statuta Capitulorum Generalium Ordinis Cisterciensis*, 8 vols. (Louvain, 1933-41) Anno 1175/22, 1:83: "Tempore quo conventus infra terminos laborat, ore citius cantent[ur]."

prepared by Fr Bruno Griesser soc, we find prescriptions such as the following ones here reproduced in their original orthography:[41]

18— In cena domini et parasceue et sequenti sabbato uesperas festinanter canimus.

20— In die sancto pasche et tribus sequentibus diebus laudes festinanter cantamus. Similiter in pentecoste et omnibus sollempnitatibus quibus habetur sermo in capitulo et quando defunctus est in ecclesia. Insuper diebus quibus conuersi laborant et intersunt priori misse. . . .

21— In tonsione ouium post pascha prior primam, cantor nonam et completorium accelrant.

22— Similiter tempore secationis. Messionis uero tempore priuatis diebus duos primos psalmos primi nocturni trahimus, cetera omnia festinanter.

23— Dominicis diebus et festis a secundo nocturno incipimus festinare, ut eo minus fratres dormiant.

24— Ipsis diebus absque nutu sacriste cantor primam et terciam acceleret.

So far as I know, the only official reference to an expressly slower tempo occurs in the *Ecclesiastica Officia,* and, even here, only in a later redaction dating from around the middle of the twelfth century. In the chapter on Vigils, we find a slower tempo designated for the opening versicle and response of the Office. We thus read:

Dicto itaque *deus in adiutorium meum intende,* morose et trahendo a sacerdote, cancellatis manibus incuruentur profunde, donec ad *adiuuandum me festina,* sed eadem morositate et grauitate compleatur.[42]

---

41. Pp. 141-142 of the edition described above, Note 26. The numbers attached to the various prescriptions are editorial additions by Fr Griesser.
42. Ms. 31, from the University Library, Laibach (Yugoslavia), as transcribed by Fr Canisius Noschitzka SOC, ASOC 6 (1950) p. 79.

A still later redaction of the same text, from around 1182, adds several lines extending the slow performance of the opening versicle and response to all the Hours, and introducing a pause before the *Gloria Patri* and the *Sicut erat* of the doxology which followed:

> Sed et omni tempore quando conuentus est in ecclesia, ad omnes horas reuerenter et morose dicatur a sacerdote *Deus in adiutorium meum intende,* et a conuentu subiungatur *Domine ad adiuuandum me festina* et cetera, facta pausatione ante *Gloria patri* et ante *Sicut erat.* . . . [43]

From all of which emerges the impression that an intentionally laborious pace was meant to be the exception, although the general tempo was still slow enough to allow for speeding up when circumstances (such as extra work, a sermon after Prime, or a drowsy community) seemed to warrant it.

Viva voce cantemus. "We sing out with full voice." This is a point made by Bernard in a text already quoted—the one from the conclusion to his *Sermon Forty-Seven* on the *Song of Songs,* where he told his monks that they must "be zealous in order to join fervently, yet reverently, in chanting the praises of God, not lazily, not drowsily, not yawningly, not sparing yourselves, not mutilating the words or omitting any, not with weak and mincing voices effeminately stammering or sounding through the nose; but singing with the manly fullness and sonorousness and the religious affection proper to songs which have been inspired by the Holy Ghost."

Bernard, in brief, calls for a tempo which allows the text to be articulated correctly, and for a general style which is straightforward and unpretentious. This question of an honest, virile style seems to have been a rather general preoccupation of twelfth-century Cistercians; and, *pace* Fr van Dijk, it was not the singers of Cluny envisaged by such texts, but the monks of the celebrated Order of Cîteaux. There is, for example, a statute of one of the General Chapters held

---

43. Dijon, Bibl. municipale, ms. 114 (82); as transcribed and edited by P. Guignard, in *Les monuments* . . . , p. 162.

almost certainly around the time the Cistercian chant reform, which, under Saint Bernard's leadership, was terminated around 1147.[44] The statute in question is no. 73 in a long series of similar *statuta* generally designated as the *Instituta Generalis apud Cistercium,* and wrongly edited under the year 1134 by J. Canivez ocso, in Volume One of *Statuta Capitulorum Generalium Ordinis Cisterciensis.* Scholars are now in general agreement that these *Instituta* were issued over a fairly long period which ended before 1151; and the evidence rather inclines one to see the collection as arranged in chronological order. Details relative to the precise date of any individual statute will probably always be a matter of dispute. Still, Fr Jean-Baptiste van Damme ocso, has made out a good case for an approximate dating of statutes which precede or follow Statute 73;[45] and a year around 1147 would fit this statute admirably into a logical chronological sequence, which would suggest that it was issued in the context of the chant reform which terminated around 1147. The text reads:

LXXIII. *De falsis vocibus*
Viros decet virili voce cantare, et non more femineo tinnulis, vel ut vulgo dicitur falsis vocibus veluti histrionicam imitari lasciviam. Et ideo constituimus mediocritatem servari in cantu, ut et gravitatem redoleat, et devotio conservetur.[46]

The prohibition, then, seems to be against overly precious modes of voice production (falsetto singing?), and against what might nowadays be called an "operatic" rendition of plainsong. At just about the same time this statute was being formulated, the gentle English abbot, Aelred of Rievaulx, was inveighing mightily against the same abuse:

44. For the date of this reform, see Chrysogonus Waddell OCSO, "The Origin and Early Evolution of the Cistercian Antiphonary: Reflections on Two Cistercian Chant Reforms," *The Cistercian Spirit,* ed. M. B. Pennington, CS 3 (Spencer, Mass.: Cistercian Publications, 1970) pp. 192-3, n. 5.
45. "Genèse des *Instituta Generalis Capituli*", in *Cîteaux: Comentarii Cistercienses* 12 (1961) pp. 58-59.
46. Canivez, *Statuta,* 1:30.

What is the meaning of these chokings and sudden breaks in
the singer's voice? . . . At one moment the voices are loud
and shrill, the next they subside; now they speed onward,
now they linger in long-drawn sounds. Sometimes—the
shame of it! —a singer seems to imitate the neigh of a
horse, sometimes he will exchange his manly tones for the
piercing shrillness of a woman's, and sometimes we have a
wonderful weaving and unweaving of the notes that reminds
one of the circumvolutions of a serpent. Nay, you may
sometimes see a soloist with his mouth wide open as if
about to expire for lack of breath; you cannot hear a sound
from him—he has interrupted his singing with a sudden
silence as if all were over; but in a moment you shall hear
him mimicking the cries and groans of the agonizing or the
rapturous outbursts of the blessed. All this is accompanied
with histrionic gestures. The singers twist their lips, roll
their eyes, bend their shoulders, and move their fingers in
time with the music. . . .[47]

From Aelred's description, one might surmise that the
twelfth century had something which corresponded quite
precisely to our twentieth century rock-and-roll or "soul
music." It is likely that the above graphic description was
meant for an audience wider than just the Cistercian family.
So, even though it will necessarily come as something of an
anti-climax, it might be well to allude to a text which describes the same phenomenon as something which not only
could, but *did* happen in Cistercian monasteries. When Conrad, monk of Clairvaux, but later abbot of Eberbach, assembled from various sources a vast collection of edifying accounts for his *Exordium Magnum,* sometime early in the
thirteenth century, he found it advisable to include in *Distinctio* V a hair-raising chapter "On the Danger Incurred by
Those Who, in the Service of God, Presume to Sing in a
Lascivious Manner, or in a Way Calculated to Win Ap-

---

47. *Speculum caritatis,* Lib. II, Cap. 23; PL 196:571. The translation is by Fr
Ailbe Luddy OCSO, and is taken from his *Life and Teaching of St Bernard*
(Dublin, 1927), pp. 258-9. This earliest extant treatise by St Aelred was written
around 1142-3; cf. Anselme Hoste, OSB, *Bibliotheca Aelrediana* (Steenbrugge,
1962) p. 39 and p. 41.

plause."[48] Included in this chapter were texts culled from the end of Saint Bernard's *Sermon Forty-Seven* on the *Song of Songs* already twice quoted in the course of this article, and from the *statuta* of the General Chapter. But pride of place was given to the true-to-life tale of the Cistercian monk who used to coddle his Caruso-like voice by refusing to chant along with the other brethren, so as to muster all his vocal reserves for the showy solo passages assigned him for feast-day responsories. His fate was a horrible one. Also included in the same chapter was the account transmitted to Conrad by the Lord Abbot of Cîteaux, who once had occasion to query a visionary about the weak points in the Order's religious observance. "Know, my Lord and Father," she replied, "that there are three things in your Order which are particularly offensive in the sight of the Most High Majesty: the multiplication of land-estates, unnecessary building projects and a secular style of singing."[49]

As a matter of fact, Bernard himself and his collaborators in the chant reform of *circa* 1147 may have provided a bit of stimulus for such excesses, by introducing into the Cistercian repertory of liturgical song melodies of a frankly trouba-dourish stamp. Indeed, the proper Office composed for Saint Bernard himself, and adopted in 1175,[50] fairly cries for a sustained pitch of warm, lyrical intensity. Is it extraordinary that a melody redolent of schwärmerei be sung with a certain degree of schwärmerei?

In retrospect, we can easily situate these and similar plaints in their historical and cultural context. We find identical expressions of alarm in other monastic circles—as at Farfa, in Italy, around 1122, when the chronicler Gregory of Catino complained about the flashy renditions by the newcomers, whose musical tastes lay in the direction of novelties and campfire tunes;[51] or, later in the century, at Saint Gall,

---

48. Cap. 20, pp. 334-6 of the edition by Fr Bruno Griesser, SOC, indicated above, Note 34.
49. *Ibid.*, p. 335.
50. Canivez, *Statuta*, Anno 1175/2, 1:82.
51. *Historiae Farfenses*, n. 41, in MGH SS 11, p. 583.

Switzerland, where Notker V included in his *Instituta Patrum* a prohibition against "histrionicas voces, garrulas, alpinas sive montanas, tonitruantes vel sibilantes, hinnientes velut asina, mugientes seu ballantes quasi pecora, sive femineas. . . ."[52] It sounds a bit like the barn-yard concert in the song "Old Mac Donald Had a Farm, Ee-I-Ee-I-O." No less dogmatic were non-monks such as John of Salisbury, who could write the astonishing lines:

> Music defiles the services of religion; for the admiring simple souls of the congregation are of necessity depraved —in the very presence of the Lord, in the sacred recesses of the Sanctuary itself—by the riot of the wantoning voice, by its eager ostentation, and by its womanish affectations in the mincing of notes and sentences.[53]

Nothing would be easier than to fill many pages with similar examples of "musical criticism." Abuses there certainly were, but these have to be viewed against the cultural revolution which was taking place. For a person of the twentieth century, it is quite impossible to experience the reactions of a man of the twelfth century, for whom the simple simultaneous sounding of a *la* and a *do* (harmonic interval of a minor third) represented the ultimate in musical experience of the adventurous sort. Much of the medieval music which, for us, comes across as wondrously noble, subtle, and perfectly proportioned, doubtless produced in many of its first hearers reactions not unlike those of that celebrated first night audience of the *Rite of Spring*.

Metrum et finem—semper auscultando, Lines 7-12

The next several lines of the *Institutio* deal with points touching on ensemble singing. Ensemble singing always poses a problem, even when the ensemble consists of no more than

---

52. As cited in Van Dijk, "Saint Bernard and the *Instituta Patrum* of Saint Gall," *Musica Disciplina* 4 (1950) p. 101.
53. *Policraticus* I, 6; tr Erik Routley, *The Church and Music* (London, 1950) p. 101.

two singers. Put yourself, in imagination, into an acoustical environment characterized by ample volumes, many resonating surfaces, stone walls unadorned by tapestries or any other kind of sound-absorber, and you will have something of an idea of the acoustical environment familiar to most Cistercians of the twelfth century. Consider further that, at Clairvaux, at the time of Bernard's death, the monks actually gathered in choir must have totalled several hundred, since the entire personnel of the monastery was close to seven hundred (if the author of the fifth book of the *Vita Prima* is to be believed).[54] Since the *Institutio* almost certainly had its origin in Clairvaux, it is understandable that several lines are devoted to the problem of the brethren keeping together.

Metrum et finem versus simul intonemus et simul dimittamus (line 7). A reasonably accurate paraphrase would read: "We start each half-verse together, and end it together." Most readers know already that the psalm-verses were generally divided into two half-verses (occasionally, in longer texts, the first half-verse was itself punctuated mid-way by a melodic inflection called, in standard current terminology, a flex). In our modern terminology, *metrum* would normally be considered the *cadence* marking the end of the first half-verse, and *finem versus* would refer to the final cadence at the end of the second half-verse. From the context, however, it seems fairly clear that the author extends *metrum* to mean the entire first half-verse, and *finem versus* to mean the entire second half-verse; and each half-verse is to be begun and ended by all the brethren in perfect unison. In other words, "We start each half of the psalm verse together, and end it together."

Punctum nullus teneat (line 8). The word *punctum* calls for exegesis. Since the term has been variously used by various scholars in various periods, its exact meaning in the present context is problematical. Clearly, we must rule out *punctum* as referring to a simple note in the jargon of the twentieth century palaeographer. Subject to correction, I suggest that

54. Vita Bern V, iii, 20; PL 185:363.

punctum as here used probably refers to the final cadence of the psalm-verse. Many of the readers of this article are familiar with the traditional mnemonic aid used for psalm-tones and similar formulas: "Sic facies flexam, sic vero metrum, sic autem punctum," where *punctum* refers to the final cadence of the formula. Such a meaning fits admirably into the present context, where the meaning would be: "Do not latch on to the final syllable or note of the cadence of your psalm-verse, but simply sing it and let it go." The reason for not dragging out the final note is obvious to anyone familiar with traditional conventions of psalm-singing. The verses are alternated between two choirs, and as soon as one choir ends its verse, the other choir launches into the next verse without pause. The only pause occurs within the interior of the verse, at the end of the first half-verse (mediant cadence). This is the next point dealt with by the *Institutio: Post metrum bonam pausam faciamus* (line 9). "After the first half-verse, we make a good pause." Just what constitutes a "good pause" will always be a matter of conjecture. But the general drift of the statement is clear enough. Psalm-singers often tend to rush their tempo; and so often as a tendency in the direction of speed obtrudes itself, the mediant pause inevitably becomes skimpier and skimpier, until, at times, it disappears altogether. Thus, when Stephen of Lexington, during his last year as abbot of Stanley, in 1228, made a visitation of the Irish houses, he found it necessary to include in one long visitation card a reminder that the Office of the Dead (which was chanted over and above the Canonical Office) should be sung with at least some kind of pause after the mediant cadence: "cum aliqua pausa in metro";[55] and we have already referred to a similar prescription in the visitation card drawn up a few years later, when Stephen, now abbot of Savigny, made the visitation at Longvillers.[56] Peter the Venerable's parallel prescription about the length of the mediant pause is well known to musicologists. In the very first of his *Statuta*,

55. P. 101, n. 27 of the edition referred to above, Note 29.
56. Above, Note 33.

he calls for a "moderate pause" at the mediant: *mediocrem
. . . repausationem.* He goes on to explain his "moderate
pause" by way of contrast to the exaggerated pause he had
heard in some monasteries—a break so long that it permitted
of two, yes, even occasionally *three* repetitions of the *Lord's
Prayer* during the silent pause. On the other hand, Peter's
"moderate pause" must have been longer than was customary
in other quarters, since he also states that the introduction of
a moderate mediant pause will lengthen the Office, but the
extra time entailed will be time well spent.[57] (Incidentally, in
this same statute, Peter exempted his own community at
Cluny from making even a moderate pause at the mediant,
since the local liturgy was already so monumental that there
simply was not time left for observing such a pause.) Tenta-
tively, we are probably justified in surmising that Peter's
"moderate pause" must have been more or less equivalent to
Bernard's (or Pseudo-Bernard's) "good pause."

Nullus ante alios—punctum tenere (lines 10-11). The meaning of the text is too clear to require commentary: "No one
is to presume to begin before the others, or to rush ahead of
the others; neither is anyone to presume to take a slower
tempo and drag behind the others, or to hold the final notes
or cadences (*punctum*) longer than they should be held." The
exact meaning of *punctum* might bear further discussion, but
the general meaning of the sentence is clear. *Simul cantemus,
simul pausemus, semper auscultando* (lines 11-12). "We sing
together, we take breath and make the pauses together, and
we keep together by *listening.*" In other words, *listening* is
the key to ensemble singing.

Paragraph on Intonations and Reprises (lines 13-19)

Here the subject matter is that of intoning the various types
of chant in Office and Mass. At a time when organ accompa-
niment was unknown, and pitchpipes not yet invented, into-

---

57. G. Charvin OSB, *Statuts, Chapitres Généraux et Visites de l'Ordre de Cluny*
(Paris, 1965) p. 22; PL 189:1026.

nations were perilous moments. A mistake in the intervals or
in the general pitch might easily mislead the rest of the choir,
and produce disasterous results. Accordingly, *Quicumque
incipit antiphonam aut psalmum aut hymnum aut responsorium aut alleluia, unam aut duas partes solus dicat, aliis tacentibus* (lines 13-15)., "Whoever intones an antiphon, psalm,
hymn, responsory, or alleluia, sings one or two syllables
[? —*partes*: perhaps "one or two incises" is meant]; this is
done *deliberately*, while the others listen." The aesthetic
effect would be horrendous by present norms, when we
expect the intonations to establish the tempo and mood of
the formula in question. Whereas the practice described
seems to make the intonation rather independent of what
follows: something sung with great deliberation (*tractim*),
and with the others listening intently so as to be sure they
have the right pitch and interval relations. *Similiter teneatur
—dictum est* (lines 17-19). What is true of intonations is also
true of reprises: "The same norm is observed when the cantor
reintones an antiphon, alleluia, or responsory. This is the
general practice in all analogous cases, so that no one repeats
what has just been sung by another." In the case of the
antiphon, present day usage is different from what the *Institutio* prescribes: at the end of the psalm, everyone launches
into the antiphon; so also after the alleluia-verse in the Mass,
the entire choir repeats the alleluia; and, after a responsory-
verset (sung by soloist or soloists), the reprise is taken up by
everyone. Not so in earlier days. One has a suspicion that the
long-suffering Cantor occasionally had to correct the pitch
for the antiphon at the conclusion of a psalm in which the
choir had gravitated towards the lower regions of the tonal
range (dropping pitch is a problem in the twentieth century,
was a problem in the twelfth century, and will be a problem
in the twenty-second century); or, again, a badly sung respon-
sory-verset, or alleluia-verset, might have made it safer for the
Cantor alone, rather than the whole community, to follow up
the verse with the reprise or the alleluia.

Paragraph on Pauses after Cadences of Certain Types of Chants (lines 20-22)

Dum hymnos—festivis diebus. "When we sing hymns, or an alleluia, or a responsory, we make a break at the end of phrases, and with longer breaks on feast days." The practice alluded to is one abhorrent to the present day gregorianist, or, for that matter, to any sensitive present day musician or music lover. In times past, it was quite normal for the pause allowed between phrases to vary with the solemnity of the feast. The greater the feast, the longer the pause. There are legends, for instance, of so devotional a chanting of the *Salve Regina* in some communities, that this antiphon (with its collect) lasted at times a full quarter-hour. We moderns rightly tend to think of the time allowed for breath between major sections of the melody as being relative to the overall rhythm. The general tempo and pauses within the interior of the chant emerge from the music itself, and in no way depend on extrinsic factors such as the difference between a Sunday and a Solemnity.

So much, then, for the *Institutio Sancti Bernardi quomodo cantare et psallere debeamus.* Humble and limited though it is, it deserves a place in some future *corpus* of writings and documents related to Cistercian chant. Hopefully, these brief notes will meet the eye of some musicologist who will one day provide a detailed commentary on the text, such as will give us a still clearer idea of Cistercian choir discipline and practice.

Chrysogonus Waddell OCSO

Gethsemani Abbey
Trappist, Kentucky

RELIGIOUS AWAKENING

SAINT BERNARD AND THE EAST

RELIGION IS MAN'S RELATING himself to *that* which he perceives to be the Ultimate Reality. Christians perceive this Ultimate Reality as God, those outside of Christianity perceive him as the Absolute, the All-Embracing Reality, the All-Mind, the Universal or Cosmic Consciousness.

Religious awakening takes place when man's perception of the Ultimate reaches the experiential level. Man originates from the Ultimate, his religious awakening arises when he realizes his original state of being, when he links himself with the Divine. Religious awakening occurs when man's empirical ego, or "self," breaks its hard crust, as a chick breaks through its shell, and touches the Ultimate which transcends but at the same time permeates all beings. This break-through occurs when man, with his inward eye or intuition, transcends all dualities, all tensions of "opposites," and penetrates into the Oneness of Being, or rather when man lets himself be penetrated by the Oneness of Being.

For a Christian, religious awakening takes place when he experiences the Father begetting his eternal Son in the depths of the Christian's own soul, and this soul being born back to the Father. Both birth and rebirth are realized in one act: the act of the Father who is the Life-giving-Spirit and the act of the soul who is the Life-receiving-spirit. Religious awakening is the ever-renewed-coming of the Trinity into the soul, and the souls's ever-renewed-welcoming of the Trinity who is

209

Father (Life), Son (Wisdom) and Holy Spirit (Bliss.) Bernard of Clairvaux spoke of religious awakening as the "visit of the Word to the soul"; St Theresa and St John of the Cross called it the realization of the indwelling of the Trinity in the center of the soul.

Eastern masters call religious awakening "Enlightenment." It is *wu* in Chinese, *satori* in Japanese and *bodhi* in Sanskrit. In Sanskrit *bodhi* and *buddha* come from the same root—*bud* which means "to be aware," "to awake." Thus Buddha is the "Awakened One," the "Enlightened One."[1] Enlightenment is the discovery of a new mode of consciousness. In this new consciousness man realizes himself being permeated by the Infinite Being and becomes one with it. A personalized presentation of enlightenment, or religious awakening is the Buddha sitting in or on the Lotus-flower which indicates the Absolute penetrating the relative universe.

Religious awakening has been the subject of ultimate importance for both the East and the West for thousands of years. This interest has continued from generation to generation in the East. There has always been a direct line of transmission of these experiences. Presently in the West there is a renewal of concern for religious awakening. It is the core of the movement for spiritual renewal. The forthcoming General Chapter of the Cistercians of the Strict Observance (April, 1974) has as its theme the practical demands for the experience of God in monastic life today. The success of this Chapter will depend on its ability to show what this experience of God is, where it lies, and what means can be used to attain it.

In the following pages an attempt has been made to present the religious awakening of Saint Bernard of Clairvaux, the Mellifluous Doctor.

According to Eastern masters there are eighteen major religious awakenings, and countless numbers of minor ones, before perfect enlightenment.[2] Bernard of Clairvaux was a mystic when he was a novice in the monastery of Cîteaux

---

1. Daisetz Teitaro Suzuki, *The Field of Zen* (New York: Harper and Row, 1970) p. 21.
2. See Lu-K'uan-Yu, *Ch'an and Zen Teaching* (London: Rider, 1961) p. 21.

(1112-1113).[3] His religious awakenings were many: some were small, some were great. These experiences he related in his many literary works such as, *On Loving God,*[4] *On Consideration,*[5] *On Precept and Dispensation,*[6] and especially in his *Sermons on the Song of Songs.*[7] Nowhere else did his religious awakenings display themselves with such depth, vitality and spontaneity as in his reflections on the *Song of Songs.* All these reflections are an overflowing and expression of his religious awakening to the Infinite God. But the account of what he called the "visit of the Word" expresses his religious awakening at its highest peak. In this experience Bernard left his senses and imagination, his sense of separate ego, and realized the oneness of his self with God. The "visit of the Word" experience could be said to be the "sun," around which all the other experiences were centered as so many satellites.

Bernard described the effects of the "visit of the Word" in such tangible terms as the arousing of the slumbering soul, the softening of the stony heart, the illuminating of the dark corners of the soul, the heating up of what is cold, the expulsion of vices, the infusion of grace which expands the mind and the heart. In one word, love and truth.[8]

Bernard did not, however, explain the nature of this "visit of the World". He could not say exactly what it was. The reason for his inability to express it in words is not far to seek. To express is to define, and to define is to confine, to limit. In the "visit of the Word" he experienced indefinable and unlimited Life, Wisdom and Bliss. In his *Sermons on the Song of Songs* and elsewhere he expressed this in a number of ways. This we shall see as we go along.

The spiritual masters of the East indicate some characteristics whereby we can identify religious awakening, or enlightenment, or new consciousness or *Samadhi.* They are:

3. Jean Leclercq, *Saint Bernard Mystique* (Paris: Desclée, 1948) p. 484.
4. OB 3:119-54; CF 13.
5. OB 3:393-493; CF 37.
6. OB 3:253-294; CF 1:103-50.
7. OB 1-2; CF 4, 7, 31.
8. SC 74:5-7; OB 2:242-4.

1) The mind of the meditator is completely absorbed in the object upon which he is meditating. It is a state of fusion, or unity, of the meditator and the object meditated upon.

2) The meditator always experiences an intensely blissful sensation, which is both physical and psychic. The intensity and profundity of this blissfulness exceeds any other blissful state which the average human being experiences; it is something greater than the rapture of human love.

3) The meditator invariably experiences the presence of a great "illumination." This is not a vision of a luminous nature, but the clear and bright awareness of the meditator's own consciousness, an experience impossible to describe. The very universe itself seems to vanish into one great whole of transparency and light.

4) In advanced stages of meditation no thought arises in the meditator's mind, not even a thought of the object with which the meditation began. This "thoughtlessness" of consciousness is not torpidity or insensibility; it is a stabilized, illuminated awareness devoid of any thought-in-motion. In our daily run of activity thought is awareness in action or in motion, whereas in religious awakening it is awareness at rest.[9]

The characteristic of religious awakening in a rather advanced state called "cosmic consciousness" is summarized in the following statement of a Canadian psychiatrist, Dr R. M. Bucke:

The prime characteristic of cosmic consciousness is a consciousness of the cosmos, that is, of the life and order of the universe. Along with the consciousness of the cosmos there occurs an intellectual enlightenment which alone would place the individual on a new plane of existence— would make him almost a member of a new species. To this is added a state of moral exaltation, an indescribable feeling of elevation, elation, and joyousness, and a quickening of the moral sense, which is fully as striking and more important than is the enhanced intellectual power. With these

9. Cf Garma C. Chang, *The Practice of Zen* (New York: Harper, 1970) p. 203.

come what may be called a sense of immortality, a consciousness of eternal life, not a conviction that he shall have this, but the consciousness that he has it already.[10]

I believe that the observations of the Eastern masters on religious awakening can help to bring Bernard's own experience into clearer focus. For this reason I endeavor in the following pages to study Bernard alongside the Eastern masters. However, before going further let me clarify a few important points.

You are perhaps asking, "How is it possible to reconcile the religious experiences of a Bernard who is so thoroughly representative of the West, or Christianity, with those of the non-Christian East? This is a good question. For years scholars have attempted to answer it. There is a whole range of opinions on the subject, from complete identification to absolute negation. Anselm Stolz is of the opinion that "outside the Church, there is no mystic;" whereas René Dumal thought that, "there are mystics everywhere and they are the same."[11] In between these two opinions are those who think that religious experiences are different on the level of doctrine and conceptualization, but in the depths they are the same; the one experienced in religious awakening is the Ultimate Reality. At the risk of over-simplification I would accept the ancient saying, "Truth is one, sages name It differently." Ramakrishna's appetite for religious experience was insatiable. He was fascinated by the personality of Jesus. He had the Bible read to him. He went into ecstasy before a painting of the Madonna and Child. One day, while he was walking in the temple garden, the figure of Christ approached him, embraced him, and entered into his body.[12] A Taoist

10. As quoted by William James, *The Varieties of Religious Experience* (New York: Macmillan, 1971) p. 313.

11. As quoted by Henry de Lubac, *La Mystique et les Mystiques,* ed. A. Ravier (Paris: Desclée, 1965) pp. 12 ff.

12. Theodore de Bary, *Source of Indian Tradition,* 2 vols. (New York: Columbia University, 1969) 2:85. Cf. also Christopher Issherwood, *Vedanta For The Western World* (New York: Viking, 1969) p. 17; and the classical biography of Ramakrishna's disciple Swami Saradananda, *Sri Ramakrisna: the Great Master,* tr. Swami Jagadananda (Mylapore-Madras, 1952) pp. 295-6.

who was once reproached because he allowed himself to be influenced by Zen Buddhism said, "There exist no two 'Ways' under heaven, and the sages are all of the same heart." [13]

On the other hand, some of the spiritual masters of the East have their reservations in our regard. Christians, such as Bernard of Clairvaux, Teresa of Avila, and John of the Cross, have expressed their religious experience in symbols, particularly in the symbol of "spiritual marriage," which seem to be esoteric, unsuitable for expressing genuine religious or mystical experience. It must be born in mind that although the symbol of "spiritual marriage" expresses a high mystical state, namely the unity of wills between the experiencer and the Reality experienced, for Bernard it was not the highest. Mystical experience only reaches its highest peak when there is no distinction between the Lover, the Beloved and the Power to love. At this stage of experience these three are one, for God is "All in all." This Oneness is the "visit of the Word." In the following pages I will attempt to analyze this experience.

A comparison between Bernard's insights and those of the Eastern Masters is intensely interesting. A grasp of what these men relate will help to awaken our own minds to the Ultimate Reality within which all partial realities have their being. We will realize the essence of this Reality by a direct intuition superior to discursive reasoning, and so will be able to identify with it. We will know who we are, and knowing this, we have only to be. To a great extent, this is an appeal to an insight which we already possess. The value of exploring what the masters have articulated lies in the heightened awareness of our own consciousness and in an intensified appreciation of our own value, for unless their experience is also essentially ours, the beauty of their wisdom will have no appeal.

THE VISIT OF THE WORD

1. *I confess to you*
    that I have received the visit of the Word
    and indeed not once but many times;

13. As quoted by Henry de Lubac, *La Mystique*, p. 19.

but although he has often come to my soul
I have never been able to ascertain
the exact moment of his entrance.

2. I have been conscious of his presence within me.
I can afterward recall that he has been present,
sometimes I have even a presentiment of his coming;
yet I have never perceived him either in the act of entering
or in the act of retiring.

3. Certainly he does not enter through the eyes
for he has no color, nor through the ears
since he has no sound, nor through the organ of smell.

4. For his mingling is with the mind
not with the atmosphere.
Neither does he gain admission through
the avenue of the mouth, because he is not anything
that can be eaten or drunk.
The sense of touch is especially powerless to attain him
since he is altogether intangible.
By what then does he enter?
Or perhaps it would be more correct to say
that he does not enter at all,
inasmuch as he is not any of the things
which exist outside of us?

5. But neither can he be said to come from within me.
I have ascended to what is highest in me
and behold I have found the Word to be higher still!
I have descended to explore the lowest depths of my being
only to find that he was deeper still.
I looked to the exterior, I perceived him beyond what is
outermost; and if I turned my gaze inward,
I saw him more interior than what is inmost.

6. Then I realized the truth of what I read that
"In him we live, we move, and
have our being."

7. Blessed is the soul in whom he is,
who lives for him and is moved by him! [14]

14. SC 74:5, OB 2:242-3.

In Bernard's terminology "visit" means the presence, the union of the Word in and to the soul, and the soul's awareness of this presence and union. This visit is granted because of the soul's longing to be united with the Word. In his *Thirty-first Sermon* on the *Song of Songs* after describing various ways in which God reveals himself to the saints in heaven and to men of both the Old and New Testaments Bernard wrote:

There is still another mode of contemplating the Divinity, differing from those mentioned in that it is more interior. In this manifestation God vouchsafes to visit in person the soul that seeks him, provided, however, that it devotes itself with all its desire and love to this holy quest. . . . But take care, Brothers, that you do not understand me as conceiving the union between the Word and the soul to be something corporeal and perceptible to the senses. I am speaking only the language of St Paul who said that "he who is joined to the Lord is one Spirit." The union of which I speak is a spiritual union because "God is Spirit," and he desires the beauty of the soul which he observes to be walking in the spirit and not making provision for the flesh with its concupiscence. More especially, if he beholds her inflamed with his love. Such a spouse, then, so disposed and so beloved, can by no means be content with that manifestation which is given to the many by the things that are made, nor yet with that which is vouchsafed the few in visions and dreams. She will not be satisfied, unless, by a special privilege of grace he descends into her from the height of heaven so that she may embrace him with her intense and strongest affection in the very center of her heart.[15]

This visit of the Word is given to different souls in different ways, and to the same soul differently in different times, depending on their longing and their needs. Sometimes the Word comes as a doctor to cure, at other times as a father to nourish, and at still other times as a bridegroom tenderly yearning to take the soul in his arms, delighting in its love.

15. SC 31:4-6; OB 1:221-3; CF 7.

This last kind of visit, granted from time to time even in our present pilgrimage, crowns all the heart's desire:

> It is necessary that grace and the savor of the divine presence should vary in accordance with the varying desires of the soul, and that the infused relish of heavenly sweetness should please the spiritual palate in different ways and degrees. How often the Word changes his countenance, and with how great a multitude of sweetness he kindly transformed himself in the presence of his beloved one. Thus one time he appears as a beautiful Bridegroom, soliciting the secret embraces of the soul. At other times, he reveals himself in the role of a Physician with oils and unguents for the sake of such tender souls as still have need of lotions and ointments (these are designated as the "young maidens," a name expressive of delicacy). . . . Occasionally also, as a wayfarer, he associates himself with the wayfaring spouse and relieves the labor and weariness of the journey with his delightful conversation. . . . Sometimes again, he presents himself as a wealthy father of a family, whose house abounds with bread. Or, rather as a magnificent king who appears in order to support the timidity of his poor Spouse and to excite her religious desires by showing her all the riches of his glory and the wealth of his winepresses, and finally, to lead her even into the privacy of his bedchamber. For he trusts her, and among all his possessions there is nothing which he thinks ought to be concealed from her whom he redeemed from poverty, whom he has found faithful under trials, and whom he now embraces as worthy of his love.[16]

We shall see shortly how Bernard responded differently to the Word's visits during the different stages of his spiritual life.

THE WORD

For Bernard the Word is both the Incarnate Word who has become like unto man, and the Word whose image and like-

---

16. SC 31:7; OB 1:223-4; CF 7.

ness man bears within himself. Jean Leclercq noticed that, "in most instances when Bernard spoke of the Word he meant the Word Incarnate. His main preoccupation has been with Christ, the Word made flesh even though Bernard spoke only of the Word."[17]

In Bernard, as in all early Cistercian masters, two aspects seem to be highlighted. First, they had great devotion to the humanity of Our Lord, so much so that some scholars claim that devotion to the Incarnate Word is a characteristic of Cistercian spirituality. Secondly, this devotion seems to be regarded by Bernard as a ladder to attain to a higher contemplation of God, namely, that of the Divinity.[18]

To Bernard the road back to God supposes the love of Christ. Christ himself is the indispensable Way by which man returns to the Father.

> For God [Bernard wrote] was then unimaginable and inaccesible. He was altogether beyond the reach of sight and sensible perception. But now he would be better known. He would make himself an object to be perceived by our eyes as well as by our intellects. How so, do you ask? By showing himself to us lying in the manger, reposing on his Virgin Mother's lap, preaching on the mountain, passing the night in prayer, suspended on the Cross. And whichever of them I reflect upon, I am thinking of my God, and I know that in them all he is my God.[19]

The Incarnate Word is the pivotal point for the reorientation of love. In his *Twentieth Sermon* on the *Song of Songs* Bernard said:

> I think this is the principal reason why the invisible God willed to be seen in the flesh and to converse with men as a man. He wanted to recapture the affections of carnal men who were unable to love in any other way, by first drawing them to the salutary love of his own humanity, and then gradually to raise them to a spiritual love of his Divinity.[20]

17. Jean Leclercq, *Saint Bernard Mystique*, p. 106.
18. Cf Anselm Le Bail, "Saint Bernard," *Dictionaire de Spiritualité*, Vol. 1 (Paris: Gabriel Beauchesne, 1937) col. 1481 ff.
19. S. Nat. BVM, 11; OB 4:282.
20. SC 20:6; OB 1:118; CF 4:152.

Therefore, constant meditation on the mysteries of Christ is true wisdom, true philosophy, the source of salvation, the royal road.[21]

Despite the fact that Bernard had tender devotion to the mysteries of the Incarnate Word, he always perceived the Eternal Word through the transparency of the humanity of Christ. Reflecting on the Incarnation of the Word he wrote: "In the Incarnation I behold eternity shortened, immensity contracted, sublimity levelled down, profundity made shallow. I contemplate there the light without splendor, the Word without speech."[22]

The "Word without speech" is certainly the inward thought of the Father which is one with the Father. It is the Word that the Father spoke in his eternal silence: "For while gentle silence enveloped all things and night in its swift course was now half gone, your all-powerful Word, O Lord, leaped down from heaven, from the royal throne into the land that was doomed."[23] Reflecting on these words of Wisdom, Bernard wrote:

> He came, as we well know, not at time's beginning, not in the midst of it, but at its end. Wisely did Wisdom ordain that when evening had come and the day was declining and the light of the knowledge of God was dim and love was waxing cold before the prevalence of weakness. . . . When all things were in silence and night in the midst of its course, then, came your Almighty Word, O Lord from the royal throne. When the fullness of the time was come, God sent his Son.[24]

St John wrote:

> In the beginning was the Word, and the Word was with God, and the Word was God. He was in the beginning with God. All things were made through him and without him nothing was made.[25]

21. SC 43:4; OB 2:43; CF 7.
22. Miss 2:9; OB 4:27.
23. Wis 18:14.
24. Adv 1:9; OB 4:167-8.
25. Jn 1:1 ff.

Bernard exclaimed: "What could be more fragrant than that revelation of St John, which allowed me to perceive the eternity, the generation and the Divinity of the Word? "[26] Then he wrote: "The Word is Truth, is Wisdom, . . . Wisdom from Wisdom, Truth from Truth, Light from Light, God from God."[27] The Word that visited Bernard is without color, without form, without shape, He is totally spiritual and visible.

> Whenever you hear or read that the Word and the soul converse together, and contemplate each other, do not imagine them speaking with human voices nor appearing in bodily form. The Word is a spirit, the soul is a spirit, and they possess their own mode of speech and mode of presence in accord with their nature. The speech of the Word is his loving kindness; that of the soul, the fervor of her devotion.[28]

It is the word that fills the cosmos and becomes the cosmic fullness of which St Paul spoke.[29] He is the center of the whole cosmos. He is immersed in and gives life to the created world. He is the unity of all that has been created. This Word always speaks to us, but only those who are alert and observant at the time of his visit can hear:

> With a vigilant soul and a sober mind he shall perceive the Beloved; he shall perceive the Word while he is yet afar off. He shall know at once when he is drawing near, and when he is actually present. He shall feel his eye shining upon him like a sunbeam, and this consciousness shall make him glad, and finally he shall hear him uttering words of exalation.[30]

One last word should be added about the Divinity of the Word. The Word who visits Bernard is God, but in order to know what the Word is we should know what Bernard under-

---

26. SC 67:7; OB 2:193.
27. SC 80:2; OB 2:278.
28. SC 45:7; OB 2:54; CF 7.
29. Col 1:15.
30. SC 57:3; OB 2:121-2.

stands by "God." For him God is pure Being. Therefore the Word is also pure being. He wrote:

> God is HE WHO IS. No other name would be so suitable to the Eternity which is God. Should you call him good, should you call him great, should you call him blessed, should you call him wise, should you call him any other name whatsoever, you sum all up when you say that HE IS. For him "to be" is to be all perfect. Though you should assign him a thousand such attributes, you would not have gone beyond his simple essence. [31]

THE EASTERN CONCEPT OF THE WORD

To the Hindu mind, the expressed visible universe is the form behind which stands the eternal, the inexpressible, the *Sphota* or the *Logos,* the Word. This eternal *Sphota* is the power through which God creates the universe. For the Christian the Word was made flesh and has spoken many words. But for the Hindu the *Logos* has only one word—*OM.* Swami Vivekananda says: "This *Sphota* has one word and only one possible symbol, and this is *OM.* This *OM* and the eternal *Sphota* are inseparable; and therefore it is out of this holiest of all holy words, the mother of all names and forms, the eternal *OM,* that the whole universe may be supposed to have been created. And as the symbol can never be separated from the thing signified, *OM* and the *Logos* are one. And as the Logos, being the finer side of the manifested universe, is nearer to God, and is indeed the finest manifestation of Divine Wisdom, this *OM* is truly symbolic of God."[32] Swami Pradhavananda says, "From Vedic time until the present day the word *OM* (pronounced: A-U-M) has been accepted both as one with God and as the medium, the *Logos* connecting men with God. It is God, and by its aid men may realize God. It has been a symbol and an aid to meditation for spiritual aspirants."[33]

31. Csi V, 6, 13; OB 3:477.
32. As quoted by Swami Prabhavananda in Christopher Issherwood, *Vedanta for the Western World,* p. 149. See also *The Upanishads,* Vol. IV (New York: Harper, 1959) p. 28.
33. Issherwood, *Vedanta,* p. 29.

CONSCIOUSNESS OF THE PRESENCE OF THE WORD

We stated earlier that religious awakening is a discovery of a new mode of consciousness. Bernard used the phrase, "I am conscious of the presence of the Word." It might throw some light on this statement if we consider "consciousness" as it is understood by the Eastern masters. They understand two types of consciousness: (1) the consciousness of something or of some one, and (2) pure consciousness which has no object. Pure consciousness is consciousness itself; it is knowing as such without any object. It is called also pure awareness; it is that consciousness which *we are* rather than a consciousness that we *have*.[34] Thomas Merton called it "superconsciousness" and explains that, "It is the one in which one experiences Reality not mediating an object, a concept or a symbol, but directly, and the one in which, clinging to no experience and to no awareness one is simply aware."[35]

Consciousness of the first kind is knowing *about* things, whereas pure consciousness is knowing things as they are. In Zen terminology this latter kind is called "Suchness." To know *about* things is to know horizontally or on the surface; to know things *as* they are is to know vertically, to penetrate into things. This is called wisdom or intuition. Wisdom has to do with knowing our mind, life, the beyond, the Divine. It goes beyond empirical knowledge.

Pure consciousness is the reservoir of infinite possibilities. Our consciousness *of* things evolves out of the pure consciousness. It is something superficial, touching only the fringe of Reality. It is nothing but an insignificant floating piece of island in the ocean circling the earth.[36]

If we only read Bernard's statement that, "I am conscious of the presence of the Word" we are inclined to think that he

34. Ernest Wood, *Zen Dictionary* (Tokyo: C. Tuttle, 1972) p. 30.
35. Thomas Merton, *Mystics and Zen Masters,* (New York: Farrar, 1967) p. 237.
36. D. T. Suzuki and Eric Fromn, *Zen Buddhism and Psychoanalysis,* (New York: Harper, (1970) p. 14.

has the consciousness of the first kind—consciousness *of*. But if we read on in the text we will find that this "consciousness of" is only at the "gross level" which leads him gradually to a finer and finer level of consciousness until he has reached the finest level in which he is no longer conscious of himself or of the Word, but only of the Ultimate Reality. God becomes his life, his moving force and his being: "In whom I live, move and have my being." This will become clearer if we analyse Bernard's religious awakenings in the light of the steps traced out by the Eastern masters.

In training their disciples for the attainment of enlightenment Zen masters bring home the fact that there is one Great Light, one Absolute, and, further, this great Light is in darkness, and this Absolute is within all changing forms. In other words these are two opposite yet cooperating aspects of the one Reality—light and darkness, absolute and relative—and the achieving of consciousness of that Reality lies beyond the sway of these opposites.

Several ways have been devised to present the unity of these opposites. The Tibetan esoteric iconography of the Buddha embraced by a Divine Mother symbolizes the interpenetration of the positive and negative aspects of all contraries in the field of relativities (*samsara*) for the realization of the undivided whole on the plane of Absolute Reality. In the old tradition of India one can find several such symbols, such as the Great Lord (*Elephanta*), the *Shica Shakti* and the like. Heinrich Zimmer observed that, "This is a convention that has developed with particular emphasis in the Hindu and later Buddhist traditions, where, though the outward symbolization in images is strikingly erotic, the connotation of all the forms are almost exclusively allegorical."[37]

This way of representing the oneness of dualism, although fundamentally genuine, did not appeal to the more refined Zen masters who distinguished the Absolute from all relativities in their own way. They devised what has been called the

---

37. Heinrich Zimmer, *Myths and Symbols in Indian Art and Civilization* (New York: Harper) p. 137.

"Five Steps." It is a set of five stages or rungs of meditation leading to full enlightenment, or full realization of the Ultimate. These "Five Steps" have to do with "paired opposites" of every kind. Some examples of these opposing pairs are:

Absolute	Relative
Infinite	Finite
Universal	Particular
One	Many
Unmanifested	Manifested
Eternal	Temporary
Permanent	Transient
Yang	Yin
Heaven	Earth
Sun	Moon
Wisdom	Love
Consciousness	Life
Formless	Form
Activity	Rest
Dynamic	Passive
Host	Guest
King	Minister
Real	Apparent[38]

The "Five Steps" are all necessary steps for the disciple to pass through if he is to attain full enlightenment. Under the guidance of the masters, the disciple, after several years of initiation in meditation, begins to see, to intuit the interaction of the "Five Steps." By way of an example, take the pair, Host and Guest. The steps of progressive perception would be:

1. Guest within Host
2. Host within Guest
3. Resurgence of Host
4. Guest returning to Host
5. Host in Host

---

38. An Oriental Christian could add: Yahweh-Israel, Christ-Church, etc.

These "Five Steps" are also called the philosophy or spirituality of Buddhism. One by one let us examine them and see if they help us grasp Bernard's stages of consciousness of the Word.

1. *Guest within Host*

The first step of being aware of Ultimate Reality begins when one discovers or accepts the fact that there is the Host. This Host overshadows the Guest. In Biblical terms we would say that "the Spirit hovers over the water."[39] Spiritually speaking, this Host is a great spiritual reality. If we like we can call him God who rules the universe, or the Kingdom of God within. At this step this Reality is still too dark for the Guest to see. To the Guest he is still hidden and so unable to be seen; he is imperceptible. Master Tozan Ryokai expresses this step in this way:

> In the third watch of the night
> Before the moon (enlightenment) appears
> No wonder when we meet
> There is no recognition.
> Still cherished in my heart
> Is the beauty of early days.[40]

The Soto Zen School[41] and D. T. Suzuki of the Rinzai school[42] let this step be represented by the following symbol:

a ⟶ b

39. Gen 1:2.

40. This verse and the following four verses of Tozan Ryokai are the translation of Isshu Miura in *The Zen Koan* (New York: Harcourt, 1965) p. 67 ff.

41. Lu-K'uan-Yu, *Chan and Zen Teaching,* Second Series (London: Rider, 1961) p. 151 ff.

The dark part in the figure symbolizes the hidden Host, or Ultimate Reality, and the light, or white, symbolizes the Guest. The Guest's consciousness of the Host is still very little, almost unnoticeable. The darkness in the hidden Host is too great. He is still unable to appear and is therefore imperceptible. Suzuki's line is straight, or rather flat, that is to say, the consciousness or knowledge the Guest has of the Host is still too logical, too dim. There is no life, no "personality," no experimental contact with the Host, no real awakening.

Bernard did not express his different states of consciousness in these terms, but a close look at his many experiences gives us a picture identical to that described by the Zen masters. At his first step Bernard awakens to the reality of God, of the Word, but in a dim, weak way. In most instances there has been no warmth, no truly personal contact with the Word. He wrote:

> I am not ashamed to admit that very often I myself, especially in the early days of my conversion, experienced coldness of heart while deep in my being I sought him whom I long to love. I could not yet love him since I had not yet really found him. At best my love was less than it should have been, and for that very reason I sought to increase it, for I would not have sought him had I not already loved him in some degree. I sought him therefore that in him my numbed and languid spirit might find warmth and repose, for nowhere could I find a friend to help me, whose love would thaw the wintry cold that chilled my inward being, and bring back again the feeling of spring-like bliss and spiritual delight.[43]

2. *Host within Guest*

The second step of consciousness begins when one discovers and accepts the fact that one is only a Guest, a shadow of the Host. One therefore should act accordingly, namely,

42. D. T. Suzuki and Eric Fromn, *Zen Buddhism and Psychoanalysis*, p. 63 ff.
43. SC 14:6; OB 1:79; CF 4:102.

one should recognize the Host as a permanent Reality, whereas I, the Guest, am only transient. As a result of this, one should realize that those things one has been pursuing—personal ambitions, pleasures, power, possessions,—are transient, and must be relinquished for the sake of the permanent thing.Tozan Ryokai's verse expressing this situation is:

> A sleepy-eyed *grand dame*
> Encounters herself in an old mirror.
> Clearly she sees her face
> But it doesn't resemble her at all.
> Too bad! With a muddled head
> She tries to recognize her reflection! [44]

The Soto school and D. T. Suzuki presented the situation with the same circle and line, but with the color and the arrow in reverse:

b ⟵————————— a.

The Host has now become the "light" which overshadows the Guest, who at this stage considers himself to be a sinful and ignorant person. With the grace and joy of the first "conversion" the soul now starts to recognize himself. This recognition is negative. A Christian in this state of consciousness would cry, "Have mercy on me, O Lord, for I am a sinful man! "

In Zen many strong expressions are used in this second step to describe the man. For instance, he is a "withered log," "an unconscious skull," a "wooden horse," a "stone girl,"[45] an

44. See above, no. 40.
45. A wooden horse and a stone girl symbolize a mind completely stripped of its feelings and passions like a dead body.

"incense-burner in a desert temple." All these epithets indicate that the man's attachment dies away. No doubt this is how people often regard the religious, the monk.

This second step of consciousness is what Bernard called the "knowledge of self," and a "judgment about God." Self-knowledge is a judgment of self in faith and in sincerity, because it is a question of judging oneself before God according to the truth. The knowledge of God in the face of one's misery makes one acknowledge that God is all-merciful, all-loving and all-gracious. This knowledge is certainly a religious awakening, an experience of God, a consciousness of the Word, as Redeemer. Bernard wrote:

> As for me, brothers, as long as I look upon myself, my eye is filled with bitterness. But if I look up and fix my eyes on the aid of divine mercy, this happy vision of God soon tempers the bitter vision of myself. . . . This vision of God is not a little thing. It reveals him to us as listening compassionately, as truly kind and merciful. . . .[46]

3. *The Resurgence of the Host*

In this third step the Guest starts to realize that he himself is something of a Host. This is called "the resurgence of the Host." The Guest begins to live the life of the family of the Host. His responsiveness to the Host now is positive. He now realizes that he is living right in the heart of the Host's house. He feels more and more at home, and feels so near to the Host that his concern is the Host's concern. Tozan's verse reads:

> Within nothingness there is a path
> Leading away from the dust of the world.
> Even if you observe the taboo
> On the present emperor's name
> You will surpass that eloquent *one* of yore
> Who silenced every tongue.[47]

46. SC 36:6; OB 2:7; CF 7.
47. See above, n. 40.

The Tsao-Shan school and D. T. Suzuki depicted the situation as follows:

Note in the above picture the fact that the black dot—the
Host—has now moved to the center. This indicates that the
Host is now the center of the Guest's attraction. The Host
becomes the ground from which grows all the Guest's energy
and consciousness. The second point of the picture is that
Suzuki's straight lines now become curves. This indicates that
the relationship between the Guest and the Host is no longer
a mere intellectual knowledge, a cold acquaintance, but a
wisdom, an affective and cognitive intimacy. The relationship
now becomes life and bliss.[48]

In this third stage of consciousness Bernard realized that
the Word came to him as a Bridegroom; the Word is now
making him his own home. The Word's concern is now his
concern. Bernard feels as though he heard the Word's fascinating invitation, saying, "Behold the Bridgroom comes, go
out to meet him! " He was delighted to leave himself in order
to go out and meet the Word. This meeting is realized not by
mere intellectual knowledge, but by a knowledge which the
Biblical man equates with the union of man and woman in
marriage.[49] Bernard writes:

48. Suzuki and Fromn, *Zen Buddhism and Psychoanalysis*, p. 64. The inter-
action of these two curves is expressed by another koan which reads: "The
Coming-from within the Going-to, and the Going-to within the Coming-from." Cf.
Isshu Miura, *The Zen Koan*, p. 70.
    49. Cf Gen 4:1. See also Louis Boúyer, *Introduction to Spirituality* (New York:
Desclée, 1967) p. 272.

It is by conformity of love, brothers, that the soul is wedded to the Word, when, namely, loving even as she is loved, she exhibits herself, in her will, conformed to him to whom she is already conformed in her nature. There, if she loves him perfectly she becomes his bride. What can be sweeter than such a conformity? What more desirable than this love by which, O happy soul, no longer content with human teachers, you are enabled of yourself to draw near with confidence to the Word. You can cleave to him stead-fastly, consult him familiarly in all your doubts, be as courageous in your desires as you are capacious in your understanding? This is in truth the alliance of spiritual marriage. But it is too little to call it an alliance; it is rather an embrace. Surely we have then a spiritual embrace when the same likes and dislikes make one spirit out of two. Nor is there any occasion to fear lest the inequality of the persons should cause some defect in the harmony of wills, since love knows nothing of reverence. Love means an exercise of affection, not an exhibition of honor. . . . Love is all-sufficient for itself. Wherever love comes, it subjugates and renders captive to itself all the other affections. Consequently the soul that loves, simply loves and knows nothing else except love. The Word is indeed One who deserves to be honored, admired and wondered at, yet he is better pleased to be loved.[50]

4. *Guest Returning to Host, or Arrival at Mutual Interpenetration*

As the disciple's practice of meditation progresses on these lines the effects grow stronger and stronger every day. This involves an increasing responsiveness to the Spirit. The Host and the Guest no longer move around one another, but progress toward interpenetration which is the goal. We would say in Christian theology that the soul is now more responsive to actual grace and the motion of the Holy Spirit. Tozan's verse reads:

> When two blades cross points
> There is no need to withdraw.

50. SC 83:3; OB 2:299-300.

That master swordsman
Is like the lotus blooming in the fire.
Such a man has in and of himself
A heaven-soaring spirit.[51]

Tsao-Shan and D. T. Suzuki expressed the situation in this manner:

Note in the picture that the circle is now all white. This indicates that the consciousness, or the mind, is stripped of all thought and is similar to a dead body before its resurrection.[52] The two arrows, now within the circle, indicate that the interaction, or movement, of the Host and the Guest is no longer mechanical, but creative and inexhaustible. The circle represents the cosmic wheel (*Dharmacakra*) in its never-ending revolution.[53]

In this fourth step of consciousness Bernard realized the "mutuality" and "reciprocity" of love between himself and the Word. Similarity is one of the characteristics of love and this is at the heart of Bernard's experience. To him God is not a supreme impersonal God but a supremely personal, or trans-personal God. God is so personal that he "desires" to share his being and his love reciprocally with man. God is not simply a supreme good to be desired, but a "desiring" God. Reflecting on the angelic salutation (Luke 1:28): "Hail Mary, full of grace, the Lord is with you! " Bernard wrote:

"Mary was so full of the Divinity dwelling in her corporeally, so full of the Holy Spirit as to conceive by him."[54] He

51. See above, n. 40.
52. Lu-K'uan-Yu, *Ch'an and Zen Teaching*, Second Series, p. 161.
53. Cf Suzuki and Fromn, *Zen Buddhism and Psychoanalysis*, p. 64.
54. Miss 3:2; OB 4:37.

felt that God "went forth from his tent and rejoices as a giant
to run his course, with ardent affection, in search of the Virgin
whom he loves, whom he has chosen, whose beauty he desires."[55] God expresses his own love so that he might over-
whelm us with gifts, gambling on our becoming his prize.
There is here a mutual giving, a mutual interpenetration. Commenting on this mutual giving and interpenetration as expressed by the soul, "My Beloved is to me, and I am to him,"[56]
Bernard wrote:

> There can be no doubt that the mutual love of the Bride-
> groom and the bride burns as a fire in the furnace. And in
> that reciprocity of affection we behold the supreme happi-
> ness of the one and the amazing kindness of the other. This
> is a secret which no one can pretend to understand fully
> except those who by the perfect purity of their souls and
> bodies have deserved to experience something similar in
> themselves. For it is a mystery of love. Hence it is not by
> discourse of reason we are to attain it, but by conformity
> of will.[57]

5. *Host in Host, or Unity Attained*

We now come to the final step—the Host in Host, or Unity
attained. Here the oneness between the Host and the Guest is
realized. Here God is "all in all." There does not seem to be
much difference between this last step and the preceding one
except the fact that in the fourth step the Guest has not
completed the act of attainment. He is still on the way to the
goal, whereas in this last step he has completed the journey.
The seeker attains his object, for he reaches his destination.
Tozan's verse reads:

> Who dares to equal him
> Who falls into neither being nor non-being!
> All men want to leave

55. *Ibid.*
56. Song 2:16.
57. SC 67:8; OB 2:193-4.

The current of ordinary life,
But he, after all, comes back
To sit among the coals and ashes.[58]

The Soto School and D. T. Suzuki depicted the situation as follows:

Note the fact that the circle now turns all black. This indicates that the true Reality, or the sameness of the Host and the Guest, the Real and the Apparent is but one, a manifestation which is very difficult to perceive, but experience will teach us what it is. Note also the fact that Suzuki used the Chinese symbol of Yang and Yin in the fourth stage to indicate the intimate penetration between the Host and the Guest, but I think this symbol is more suitable to this final step, for these symbols express the absolute oneness of the paired "opposites." In Chinese philosophy this absolute oneness is expressed in the following formula:

A round of Yang
Plus a round of Yin
equals TAO.[59]

In this formula Tao means the Absolute from which the paired opposites originate. Yang stands for movement or activity, whereas Yin stands for rest or serenity.

Maharishi Mahesh Yogi has a formula of his own to express this absolute oneness. He wrote:

58. See above, n. 40.
59. Fung-yu-Lan, *The Spirit of Chinese Philosophy,* tr. E. R. Huges (Boston: Beacon, 1967) p. 81.

One hundred per cent of the Unmanifested, or the never-changing Absolute plus one hundred per cent of the Manifested, or the ever-changing Relative, equals one hundred percent of Life in Creation.[60]

The reason for this, according to Maharishi, is that Being is the absolute existence of unmanifested nature. It has a tendency to manifest or "vibrate," resulting in the creation of *Prajna* (i.e. breath, transcendental Wisdom), through which the whole creation evolves. The manifested creation and the unmanifested Being, although appearing to be different, in reality are one and the same. Creativity lies in the nature of the Absolute Being, Creation is its play, and evolution is its expansion in beingness.

In this final step Bernard found himself completely lost in the Word. Here is unity of love, here is the *consummatum est*. There is nothing more here for the soul to expect. Bernard wrote:

In this contemplation the soul is sometimes rapt in ecstasy, and withdrawn from the bodily senses, and so completely absorbed in admiration of the Word that it loses consciousness of itself. This happens when under the attraction of the Word's ineffable sweetness it steals away, as it were, from herself, or rather is ravished and slips away from itself to enjoy the Word.[61]

And he exclaimed:

A great thing is love! If it returns to its Principle, if it is restored to its Origin, if it finds its way back again to its Fountainhead, so that it may thus be enabled to flow continuously.[62]

This is the state of a man who has reached the level of transcendental consciousness, or "cosmic consciousness" in

60. Maharishi Mahesh Yogi, *Transcendental Meditation* (New York: Mentor, 1968) p. 36.
61. SC 85:13; OB 2:315-6.
62. SC 83:4; OB 2:300.

which he can rest while engaged in activities. William of St Thierry, an intimate friend of Bernard, noted that "Bernard's soul was flooded with such peaceful grace that, while he gave himself completely to the work at hand, his mind was completely taken up with God."[63]

HE DOES NOT ENTER THROUGH THE EYES

Here Bernard describes the spiritual nature of the interchange between the Word and the soul. This interchange is beyond sense perception and the natural mode of knowledge. He wrote:

> Whenever you hear or read that the Word and the soul converse together, and contemplate each other, do not imagine them speaking with human voices nor appearing in bodily form. The Word is a spirit, the soul is a spirit, and they possess their own mode of speech and mode of presence in accord with their nature. The speech of the Word is his loving kindness, that of the soul, the fervor of devotion.[64]

Thus, to be perceptive of the Word the eye of the mind and the affection of the heart are needed because:

> The Word of God is not a sounding but a piercing Word, not pronounceable by the tongue but efficacious in the mind, not sensible to the ear but fascinating to the affection. His face is not an object possessing beauty of form but rather it is the source of all beauty and all form. It is not visible to the bodily eyes, but rejoices the eyes of the heart. And it is pleasing not because of the harmony of its color but by reason of the ardor of the love it excites.[65]

Bernard admitted the limitation of human language and invited us to investigate the truth of the Spirit in a spiritual way. He wrote:

---

63. Vita Bern, PL 185:238C ff; tr. G. Webb and A. Walker, *St Bernard of Clairvaux* (Westminster, Md.; London, 1960) p. 41.
64. SC 45:7; OB 2:54; CF 7.
65. SC 31:6; OB 1:223.

Although the language in which visions are described seems to refer directly to the body, yet what is meant is something spiritual and hence the causes and significance must be investigated spiritually.[66]

It is important to go through the more opaque level of the senses and sense objects to the more subtle level of the spirit in order to reach pure consciousness and union with the Word:

> If it should ever be the lot of any of you to be so transported for a time into this secret sanctuary of God, and there be so rapt and absorbed as to be neither distracted nor disturbed by any necessity of the body, importunity of care, or remorse of conscience, or perhaps by that which is more difficult to avoid, the inrush of corporeal images from the senses or the imagination, such a one indeed, when he returns to us can glory and truly say: "The King has brought me into his nuptial chamber." [67]

There is no doubt that the senses can be best used in the service of others or that they are of value when treating things of the earth, but when dealing with the things of heaven they are powerless:

> He is great who is satisfied to use the senses as if they were the wealth of those citizens [of this world] and to employ them for his own salvation and that of others. And he is no less great who uses philosophy to establish the senses as a step toward invisible things. The latter is more pleasant, the former more beneficial; the latter more delightful, the former more courageous. But he is greatest of all, who, scorning the use of sensible objects insofar as is possible to human frailty, has accustomed himself occasionally to soar in contemplation to the sublime, not by gradual steps but by sudden ecstasies.[68]

In early Buddhist philosophy, there are three levels of consciousness to be considered from the point of view of objects.

---

66. SC 32:1; OB 1:226; CF 7.
67. SC 23:16; OB 1:149-50; CF 7.
68. Csi V, 2, 3; OB 3:468-9.

There is the material, the limited object, that is to say, objects perceivable through the senses and there is the immaterial, objects which are unlimited and perceived only by the mind. In the former all the senses may participate, but in the latter only the "form-free" mind, the mind free from all perception of what is individual, may function. Between these two are the intermediate objects which are not perceptible to the lower senses such as smell, taste, or touch, but which certainly are perceptible to the higher senses insofar as these are free from all entanglement with the ego, that is, free from selfish craving, and therefore capable of being completely merged into the object, capable of becoming one with the object in order to experience it from within. These objects are designated as "pure forms," untarnished by any kind of entanglement with the ego. These "pure forms" belong to the essence of our mind, and the essences of things. Lama Govinka observed that:

> The sense-world is designated as purely the domain of sensuous desires, for its objects are bounded in their individualness, discrete in their existence exterior to the subject, and hence give rise to that state of tension (dualism) called craving. Those objects belonging to the realm of non-form, of immateriality, possessing no limiting boundaries, are beyond all multiplicity and every kind of isolation or I-entanglement. With this is excluded all possibility of tension and of craving.[69]

Govinka admitted, however, that:

> the tension in the realm of sense-perception is not a necessary state but only a product of illusion. If the mind is directed toward supra-mundane knowledge, the sense objects are perceived and investigated with proper discrimination, and instead of arresting and binding the forces of consciousness they will reflect them, throw them back upon their source, thus intensifying their power.[70]

An anecdote may be appropriate here to suggest how we might transcend the sense object in order to enter the realm

---

69. Lama Anagarika, *The Psychological Attitude of Early Buddhist Philosophy* (New York: S. Weiser, 1971) p. 82.
70. Ibid., p. 83.

of the spiritual experience. This is a story about the "The Sound of One Hand."

The master of Kennin temple was Mokurai (Silent Thunder). He had a little protégé named Toyo who was only twelve years old. Toyo saw the older disciples visit the master's room each morning and evening for *sanzen* or personal guidance, during which they were given koans to keep the mind from wondering. Toyo wished to do *sanzen* also.

"Wait for a while," said Mokurai. "You are yet too young."

But the child insisted, so the teacher finally consented.

In the evening little Toyo went at the proper time to the threshold of Mokurai's *sanzen* room. He struck the gong to announce his presence, bowed respectfully three times outside the door, and went in to sit before the master in respectful silence.

"You can hear the sound of two hands when they clap together," said Mokurai. "Now show me the sound of one hand."

Toyo bowed and went to his room to consider this problem. From his window he could hear the geishas. "Ah, I have it! " he proclaimed.

The next evening, when his teacher asked him to illustrate the sound of one hand, Toyo began to play the music of the geishas.

"No, no," said Mokurai. "That will never do. That is not the sound of one hand. You haven't got it at all."

Thinking that the music interrupted his meditation, Toyo moved his abode to a quiet place. He meditated again. "What can the sound of one hand be? " He happened to hear some water dripping. "I have it," imagined Toyo.

When he next appeared before his teacher, Toyo imitated dripping water.

"What is that? " asked Mokurai. When Toyo told him, he replied, "That is the sound of dripping water, but not the sound of one hand. Try again."

In vain Toyo meditated to hear the sound of one hand. He heard the sighing of the wind. But that sound was also rejected.

He heard the cry of an owl. This also was refused. The sound of one hand was not the locusts.

More than ten times Toyo visited Mokurai with different sounds. All were wrong. For almost a year he pondered what the sound of one hand might be.

At last little Toyo entered true meditation and transcended all sounds. "I could collect no more," he replied later, "so I reached the soundless sound."

Toyo had realized the sound of one hand.[71]

The realm of the spirit is not perceptible to sound or sight, or to any other sense object; it belongs to the domain of the mind.

BECAUSE THE WORD'S MINGLING IS WITH THE MIND

"Certainly he does not enter through the eyes; nor through the organ of smell, because his mingling is with the mind." By "mingling with the mind" Bernard indicates the light which is infused into the mind by the Word. He wrote:

If, when the conscience is thoroughly cleansed and stilled, you experience a sudden expansion of the mind with an infusion of heavenly light ... there beyond doubt are the Bridegroom's eyes looking in through the window.[72]

For Bernard as for Biblical authors the mind can also be taken to mean the "heart" of man. He was well acquainted with the Biblical vocabulary in which psychic activity is usually associated with various organs of the body, the chief of which is the heart. In the Biblical idiom the heart is considered the seat of intelligence, and therefore heart and mind are mutually inclusive. To the Semitic, the heart indicates a wide range of faculties including all that is interior to man. The heart stands not only for sentiments, but also for memories, thoughts, reasoning and planning. The Semitic frequently uses heart where we would say mind or awareness.[73]

71. Paul Reps, *Zen Flesh, Zen Bones* (New York: Doubleday, n.d.) pp. 25-6.
72. SC 57:8; OB 2:124.
73. Read, for example, Mt 12:34; Mk 7:21; Jn 12:40; Acts 7:23.

Of the heart as a reception room for the visit of the Word
Bernard wrote:

> So great, Brothers, is the efficacy of this touch, that the
> moment it is received, it causes the heart to expand with an
> abundance of spiritual nourishment. Those of you who are
> most given to prayer understand what I am saying from
> their own experience. How often we draw near to the altar
> with dry and cold hearts? But when we are persevering in
> prayer, suddenly there is an infusion of grace, and our heart
> expands and our whole interior is deluged with an over-
> flowing of love.[74]

Likewise, according to Chinese philosophy, mind and heart
stand as a unity. In point of fact, both mind and heart are
symbolyzed by only one letter, the letter *Li*. *Li* is a trigram
($\equiv\equiv$) consisting of two continuous lines ($\equiv$) and a broken
line in between them (-----). The continuous lines stand for
Yang, or the active principle, whereas the broken line stands
for the negative, the receptive principle. When the two lines
which represent mind and heart meet, there is enlightenment,
and man is integrated as a whole.[75]

In Zen the word "mind" has several meanings. There is the
Buddha-mind. This is the enlightened or awakened mind; it is
not the thinking mind or its thoughts. Then there is the
ordinary mind which is objective, because, even when considering abstractions, it *sees* within, which involves the duality
of seer and seen. Thirdly, there is a looking into one's own
mind which is quite similar to looking into a mirror. It is not
so with the Buddha-mind. In the Buddha-mind we have only
pure consciousness knowing pure consciousness.[76]

In Zen thought, the mind, defined as intellect, is to be
transcended or to be put aside, and this for the same reason
as in the Christian experience. But here we are dealing with
an experiential or sapiential knowledge which involves an
immediate or intuitive contact and not a speculation. Knowing, in this sense, and thinking are not to be confused. Perhaps another Zen story would be useful, which can be

74. SC 9:7; Ob 1:46; CF 4:58.
75. *Cf* Lu-K'uan-Yu, *Ch'an and Zen Teaching,* Second Series, p. 151.
76. Ernest Wood, *Zen Dictionary,* p. 83.

applied to a Christian preparing himself for the visit of the Word:

Nan-in, a Japanese master during the Meji era (1868-1912), received a university professor who came to inquire about Zen.

Nan-in served tea. He poured his visitor a full cup, and kept on pouring.

The professor watched the tea overflow until he no longer could restrain himself. "It is full. No more will go in! "

"Like this cup," Nan-in said, "you are full of your own opinions and speculations. How can I show you Zen unless you first empty your cup? "[77]

HE DOES NOT ENTER AT ALL

Being unable to identify the Word's entrance into the soul through the senses Bernard admitted that "perhaps it would be more correct to say that he does not enter at all, inasmuch as he is not any one of the things which exist outside of us. In other words, "The Word is within us; he does not enter, because he has always been there." The theme of the "Kingdom of God within" was prominent in Bernard's spirituality, as also in that of St Augustine and St Teresa of Avila.[78] In answering a question put to him by some Benedictine monks concerning the Gospel text, "Your reward is great in heaven," Bernard wrote: "Heaven does not refer to any visible or material heaven, nor is our reward to be found in any passing changeable thing, but the reference is to some spiritual heaven for which, you say, you don't even know where to look."[79] By spiritual heaven Bernard, of course, means our heart, our interior heaven. He offered a number of Biblical texts to that effect, such as: "The Kingdom of God within us." (Luke 17:21); "Christ dwells in our heart by faith."

---

77. Paul Reps, *Zen Flesh, Zen Bones*, p. 5.
78. *Confessions of St Augustine*, Bk X, ch. 27; tr. F. J. Sheed (New York: Sheed and Ward, 1957). St Theresa of Avila, *Interior Castle*, "Fourth Mansion," ch. III, 3; tr. A. Allison Peers (New York: Doubleday).
79. Pre XX, 61; OB 3:293; CF 1:149-50.

(Eph 3:17); "The suffering of these times is not worthy to be compared to the glory that shall be revealed *in* us." (Rom 8:18). Elaborating the last text of St Paul, Bernard remarked that, "Paul does not say that glory will be revealed *to* us, as if it were something outside of us which we must realize."[80] In this Biblical vein of thought Bernard concludes:

> If you ponder these and many other similar passages in Scripture you will learn that the Kingdom of God and his justice are to be sought within our own souls rather than outside or above them. For the realities which are "within" us in virtue of the subtlety of their invisible nature, are also "above" us in virtue of their excellence, and "outside" us in the immensity of their majesty. But these matters are very deep.[81]

I have stated earlier that for the Eastern masters the All-Mind stands for God. So the All-Mind within can stand for God within. Bernard's notion of the Kingdom and his experience of God within is similar to the Eastern experience of the Mind within. Hui-Neng wrote:

> This physical body of ours is a city. Our eyes, ears, nose and tongues are the gates. There are five external gates. The mind is the king who lives in the domain within. We should work for enlightenment within the essence of mind, and not for it apart from ourselves. He who is kept in ignorance of the essence of mind is an insignificant being. He who is enlightened as to the essence of mind (within) is a Buddha. . . . Within the domain of our mind, there is a *Tathagata* of enlightenment who sends forth a powerful light which illumines the six gates of sensation thus purifying them. This light is strong enough to pierce the six *Kama* Heavens of desire and when it turns inwardly it eliminates at once the three poisonous elements, purging away our sinfulness which might lead us to hell.[82]

The search for God within is expressed in the immortal phrase of "The Voice in Silence":

80. Ibid., CF 1:150.
81. Ibid.
82. The Sutra of Hui-Neng tr. A. F. Price and Wong Mou Lam (San Francisco: Shambala Publ., 1969) pp. 39-40.

Avert your face from the world of deception; mistrust the senses; they are false. But within the body—the shrine of your sensations—seek in the Impersonal, the Eternal Man,[83] and having sought him out, look inward: where you are the Buddha.[84]

NEITHER CAN HE BE SAID TO COME FROM WITHIN

I have ascended to what is highest in me
and behold I have found the Word to be higher still!

I have descended to explore the lowest depths of my being
only to find that he was deeper still.

If I looked to the exterior
I perceived him beyond what is outermost;

And if I turned my gaze inward,
I saw him to be more interior than what is inmost.[85]

Here Bernard expresses the experience of the Word as the All-embracing Reality. Going beyond his presence to himself and transcending the zenith of his consciousness, he found immediately that the Word is deeper than the inmost point of his spiritual being and, leaving the world at its outermost reaches, Bernard searched, only to find that the Word is beyond.

In Eastern spirituality this kind of grasp of the All-embracing Reality is called *Prajna,* or transcendental Wisdom. Bernard himself borrowed a phrase from the Book of Wisdom to express his experience: "O Wisdom all powerful, reaching from end to end mightily. O power all wise, disposing all things sweetly! "[86]

---

83. The "Eternal Man" means the "Eternal Person," "The Tao." Cf. Suzuki and Fromn, *Zen Buddhism and Psychoanalysis,* p. 36.
84. As quoted by Christmas Humphreys, *Zen Buddhism* (New York: Macmillan, 1970) p. 18.
85. SC 74:5; OB 2:243.
86. Wis 8:1.

Wisdom is one in itself, but it is manifold in its effects and operations. Wisdom is length because of its eternity; breadth because of its love; height because of its majesty, and depth because of its understanding.[87]

In graphic terms Bernard's experience of the all-embracing reality of the Word can be presented through the paradigm of the Cross:

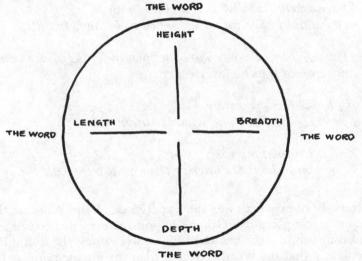

In exhausting the analogy of dimension where the limits of the perceived world are crossed, Bernard seems to hint at the unity of his experience which corresponds to the circle of Eastern symbolism. The silence of the point, the fullness of the circle, the dimensions of the cross are all part of the fecundity of the Word that arises from consciousness of his presence.

In order to comprehend this great reality of the Word in all its immensity, Bernard suggested two things: first, to have a supreme awe of and, second, to have an intense love for this Word. Awe corresponds to height and depth, whereas love corresponds to length and breadth. He said:

87. Csi V, 13, 29; OB 3:492.

We should stand in supreme awe before that Being from whose vision nothing escapes and whose arm is omnipotent. Our love for this God must be expansive beyond the dimensions of length and breadth, for is there anything so amiable as this Love itself by which you both can receive love and can love in return. The soul that posseses these two favors in their perfection can employ them as two arms to comprehend God, to embrace him and hold him fast. [88]

In his lengthy study on *The Christian experience and Oriental spirituality*, J. A. Cuttat observer that there is a common use of the symbol of the Cross as a means for religious awakening. He also draws attention to Bernard's experience which we quoted above as being in the form of the Cross. [89]

The intersecting point of the two axes of the Cross, or the square, is a symbol commonly used in all the religions of the East. This symbolic point of crossing lines has been considered to be analogous to the center which is common to both man and the universe. Concentration on this intercepting point contains within itself a form of notional knowledge that is massive and diffuse rather than distinct and a dynamic of motion that heads outwards beyond the horizons of consciousness with a centrifugal force. When the aspirant recollects himself and brings himself to the consciousness of the point of intersection between the horizontal and vertical axes, then the pure spirit, becoming more and more disincarnated, will ascend from this point along the vertical axis to the top of the cross and beyond. In this meditation there occurs a subtle transference from a directional motion to a qualitative motion, from a spatial image to a notional insight.

Typical of this whole class of symbolism are the elements of the Shri-Yantra which consists of a square outer frame, an enclosed arrangement of concentric circles, a stylized lotus-petal pattern and a concentric composition of nine interpenetrating triangles:

88. Ibid.
89. J. A. Cuttat, "Experience Chrétinne et Spiritualité Orientale," *La Mystique et Les Mystiques* (Paris: Desclée, 1965) p. 926.

POINT

In
the stillness
of
a point
beating and
pulsing
beyond
the reaches
that matter knows
there echos
a fullness
of reality and
other
consciousness
whose name is
word
whose age is
beyond
whose knowledge is
the music of
being
rushing beyond
the waters of
void
and the pain of
"no."

I
would touch
this point
with the thunder
of my
thought
but I cannot
reach
a word
closer
than my
name.

Shrī-Yantra

The outer square represents a square sanctuary which carries the notion of temple or enclosure. This sanctuary is the seat of the Divinity, and should be thought of as the center of the heart of the devotee. Here resides his own "Chosen Divinity," who finally is to be understood as symbolizing the nucleus of his own existence—his eternal, divine or higher self.

The abstract linear design (the triangles) indicate the "Primal Pair." There are nine interpenetrating triangles, five pointing downward and four pointing upward. The downward pointing triangles are the negative symbol, corresponding to the Yin symbol, and the upward pointing triangles are the positive, corresponding to the Yang symbol in Chinese philosophy.

Together the nine signify the primitive revelation of the Absolute as it differentiates into graduated polarities and represents the creative activity of the cosmic positive and negative energies. Most important is the fact that the Absolute is not represented. Precisely, it cannot be represented, for it is beyond form and space. The Absolute must be visualized by the concentrating worshipper as a vanishing point or dot, "the drop" (*Bindu*), amid the interplay of all the triangles. This *Bindu* is the power point, the invisible, elusive center from which the entire diagram expands.

Note that, whereas four of the negative triangles link with their positive counterparts, the fifth, or the inmost, remains over to unite with the invisible point. This fifth triangle pointing now nowhere is the focus of creative energy, the manifestation of the Unmanifested, Pure, Quiescent, the Great Original.

The Shri-Yantra symbolizes life, both universal and individual, and carries the meaning that this life is an incessant interaction of cooperating opposites. This is the archtypal mystical marriage represented by an abstract imaginative diagram. Through a static pattern of geometric figures it offers a clue to the secret marriage of the soul with God.[90]

90. Heinrich Zimmer, *Myths and Symbols in Indian Art and Civilization*, p. 146.

Commenting on the Shri-Yantra symbolism, Anieta Jaffé wrote:

> In term of psychological symbolism these two sets of inter-penetrating triangles, one pointing upward, the other pointing downward, express the union of opposites: namely, the union of the personal, temporal world of the "ego" with the non-personal, timeless world of the non-ego. Ultimately, this union is the fulfillment and goal of all religions: it is the union of the soul with God.[91]

Over the past ten years Joshu Sasaki Roshi, a wise and mature Japanese Zen master has been helping many Christians come to religious awakening by using Zen technique. His desire has been to develop a kind of Christian Zen.

Joshu Roshi belongs to the Rinzai School of which the characteristic has been the *koan* exercise. With his great insight Joshu Roshi has devised a Christian *koan* called the "Cross-koan." It runs as follows:

> How do you realize God
> when you make the sign of the Cross?

A few words on the *koan* are in order. A *koan* is a kind of problem which is given by a Zen master to his disciples to solve. It is an utterance, which is seemingly paradoxical, coming from the master's state of pure consciousness, or from the one who is the pure consciousness. For example, the "I AM WHO AM," the utterance of Yahweh to Moses; the "Before Abraham was I am," the utterance of Our Lord to the Jews. According to a Mahayana legend, Buddha uttered the following words when he came out of his mother's womb: "Heaven above, earth below, I alone am the most honored One." Joshu Roshi's word was, "Christ is the Cross! Christ is God! To realize the Cross is to realize God! "

These utterances are called *koans. Koan,* a Japanese word, originates from the Chinese *Kung* = public, and *An* = document. It is a document given to us, and it is public since there is no secrecy involved; it is open to all. To those who have

---

91. Anieta Jaffé, "Symbolism In The Visual Arts," *Man and His Symbols,* ed. Carl G. Young (New York: Dell, 1970) p. 267.

eyes to see, the utterance presents no difficulty. If there is a
hidden meaning, it derives from our opacity and not from the
koan. The *koan* is within us. Take, for example, Joshu
Roshi's *koan*: "How do you realize Christ when you make
the sign of the Cross? " This *koan* is within us, because Christ
is within us. What Joshu Roshi did was no more than to point
it out for those who attended the *sesshin* or Zen retreat, that
they might see it more plainly than before. When the Cross-
koan is brought out of the unconscious into the field of
consciousness, one may say that it has been understood.

To effect this awakening Joshu Roshi told his students to
make the sign of the Cross, to make it again and again, to
make it hundreds of times a day, until the students and the
Cross of Christ became one. It is then that one realizes Christ
within oneself.

The present writer has had the privilege of attending a Zen
retreat, along with a number of Christian monks, under the
guidance of Joshu Roshi. If I might speak a word concerning
my experience I would say that it was one of the most trea-
sured experiences in my whole spiritual life.[92]

Joshu Roshi believes that there is great similarity between
Buddhism and Christianity. He believes that if we go down
deep enough we will find the two currents crossing one another and flowing from the same source. He warned us, however, not to use many Buddhist terms when speaking of
Christian Zen, such as Voidness, Emptiness, or Nothingness.
"Although in Buddhism," he said, "Voidness is not negation
but fullness, still it is not appropriate to use a term such as
this in Christianity. Christianity has its own vocabulary to
express the same reality, and that is the Cross of Christ. As in
Buddhism for those who are not enlightened, Void is just
void (i.e. nothingness) but for those who are enlightened
Void is fullness; so too in Christianity for those who are not
enlightened, the Cross of Christ is death and shamefulness,

92. For a detailed description of this Zen Retreat at St Joseph's Abbey, Spencer, Mass., see M. Basil Pennington, "A Christian Zen Retreat," *Review For Religious* 31 (September, 1972) 710 ff.

but to those who are enlightened, the Cross is life and glory. The empty tomb is the Resurrection."

Returning to Bernard, we have no doubt that his experience of the Word's immensity in the form of the Cross was the fruit of his constant meditation on the Cross and the Passion of Christ. He confided his experience to his brothers at Clairvaux, saying:

> As for me, Brothers, from the very beginning of my conversion to God, I applied myself with diligence to collect together, and to bind into a bundle, and to place between my breasts, all the cares and sorrows which our Lord had to endure. . . . Wisdom consists in meditating on these sufferings of our Saviour. In them I have placed the perfection of justice, the fullness of knowledge, the richness of salvation and an abundance of merits. From these I sometimes drank a draught of redeeming bitterness, and sometimes I extracted therefrom the soothing oil of consolation. They united me to our Lord.[93]

Etienne Gilson made note of the fact that Bernard had a great love for the Passion of Christ. Gilson remarked, however, that this love for the Passion was only a vehicle leading toward a higher love. He wrote:

> The sensible affection for Christ was always presented by Bernard as love of a relatively inferior order. This is so precisely because of its sensible character, for love is of a purely spiritual order. By right, the soul should be able to enter directly into union in virtue of its spiritual powers with a God who is purely spirit. We have it from Bernard that he was much given to the practice of this sensible love at the outset of his conversion; later on he was to consider it an advance to have passed beyond it; not, that is to say, to have forgotten it, but to have added another dimension which outweighed it, as the rational and spiritual outweighs the carnal. Nevertheless, this beginning is always a summit.[94]

---

93. SC 43:3-4; OB 2:42-3.
94. Etienne Gilson, *The Mystical Theology of St Bernard*, tr. A. H. C. Downes (London: Sheed and Ward, 1955) p. 80.

Gilson's observation is certainly in line with Bernard's own view. For Bernard, meditation on the Passion and the Resurrection always prepares the soul for the visit of the Word. Bernard wrote: "If we wish to have Christ as a frequent guest, we must ever have our hearts fortified with unfailing testimonials both of his mercy in dying and of his power in rising from death. . . . Where he (Christ) perceives that the grace of his Passion or the glory of his Resurrection is the subject of diligent meditation, there straightway he is present with eagerness and joy." [95]

It was clear to those who attended the Zen retreat under Joshu Roshi that it was the Resurrection, that is, the everlasting life of Christ here and now that the Roshi desired to awaken in the mind of the students. He said "I would like to spend the rest of my life in teaching you Zen. I like Christianity. But I would not like it without the Resurrection. I want to see your own resurrection. In the morning show me your resurrection."[96] And Bernard wrote: "The soul longs to add to the fruits of the Passion which she has plucked from the tree of the Cross the flowers of the Resurrection whose fragrance especially allures the Beloved to visit her again."[97]

REALIZATION OF THE ULTIMATE TRUTH

Then I realized the Truth of what I read that
"In him we live, we move and have our being."[98]

To realize the truth means to awaken to the truth, or to be enlightened. Here Bernard describes in a few words his awakening to the truth of God, who is his power, his life and his being. This experience is not of many ideas or many truths but only the one great truth of God. Here the universe of the many is obliterated. Here one finds that one lives, moves and has one's being in God the Ultimate Reality. "When one has attained this supreme illumination," said Sri Ramakrishna,

95. Dil 8-9; OB 3:125-6; CF 13.
96. M. B. Pennington, "A Christian Zen Retreat," p. 712.
97. Dil 7; OB 3:125; CF 13.
98. SC 74:5; OB 2:243, quoting Acts 17:28.

"one lives always in God. With eyes closed one sees God, and with eyes open one sees God, for, transcending the senses, one sees him as Becoming All."[99]

Enough has been said about religious awakening or enlightenment. Here one additional note should be enough to bring us back to where we began. To awaken to religious truth, to be enlightened, is to acquire a new viewpoint on life and things. It is an intuitive looking into the nature of things in contra-distinction to an analytical or logical understanding of them. In practical life it means the unfolding of a new world hitherto unperceived by our ordinary mind. All the world's opposites and contradictions dissolve. All become united and harmonized. It is the remaking of life itself.[100] If it is genuine, its effects on moral and spiritual life are revolutionary; they are enhancing and purifying as well as exacting. When a Zen master was asked what constitutes Buddhahood or enlightenment, he answered, "The bottom of a pail that broke through." It means a complete change takes place after enlightenment. The story of "No Water, No Moon" illustrates this point:

When the nun Chiyono studied Zen under Bukko of Engaku she was unable to attain the fruits of meditation for a long time. At last one night she was carrying water in an old pail bound with bamboo. The bamboo broke and the bottom fell out of the pail, and at that moment Chiyono was set free! In commemoration, she wrote a poem:

> In this way and that I tried to save the old pail
> Since the bamboo strip was weakening and about to break
> Until at last the bottom fell out.
> No more water in the pail,
> No more moon in the water.

Here water and pail were dissolved, and so also the moon on the water. All detachment disappeared. That is to say, there is neither enlightenment, nor the one who is enlightened.

99. As quoted by Swami Prabhavananda in Christopher Issherwood, *Vedanta For The Western World*, p. 217.

100. D. T. Suzuki, *Zen Buddhism*; ed. William Barrett (New York: Doubleday, 1956) p. 85.

Everything became one. There is no more lover nor Beloved, but only the power to love, or pure consciousness.

When Bernard realized or awakened to the truth that God is One in whom he moves, lives and has his being, he felt, as the Zen nun expressed it, like "a dewdrop that slips into the shining sea." He was embraced by the Word as a bird embraced by the air, and a fish by the ocean. His attitude was one of a lover haunted by the Beloved who uninterruptedly affects him in every dimension of his being.

Here the Word is not merely making a visit. The dwelling is permanent, a sort of fusion. The Word can depart from the soul only by bringing it with him. More than that, he is not other than the soul; he is one with it, the oneness not of a juxtaposition but of a penetration. There is a profound change in the manner of being. In Paul's experience, which Bernard knew well, "It is now not I who live, but Christ who lives in me."[101] There is no longer any barrier between the Word and the soul, no barrier between the absolute and the relative. This overcoming is a great mystic achievement. In this state the soul becomes one with the Absolute and becomes aware of its oneness. Absorbed in God the soul becomes one with him, like the center of a circle which coincides with the center of another concentric circle, a pure mirror facing another mirror without any least thing between them. Reflecting on the words of St Paul, "If any man does not love our Lord Jesus Christ, let him be anathema," Bernard wrote, "Surely, he is most deserving of my love, from whom I have my existence, my life and my understanding."[102]

In this state of consciousness the soul dies the great death, and yet is all alive in the marvels of the Godhead. Bernard wrote:

> I can be guilty of no absurdity when I describe the ecstasy of the Spouse as a kind of death, not the death which terminates life but that which gives us freedom. . . . For as

101. Gal 2:20.
102. SC 20:1; OB 1:114; CF 4:147.

often as the spouse is transported out of herself by some holy and irresistible attraction, just so the mental exultation and ravishment seem to be so great as to lift her above the common and usual modes of thinking and feeling. . . . Would to God that I could often endure a death of this kind. . . .[103]

In Eastern religions, the one who realizes enlightenment, the one who realizes the Absolute is compared to water that is poured out into other water, a fire that is poured out into another fire. The Upanishad reads: "As pure water when poured into water remains unchanged in substance, so is the self of a thinker who knows. Water in water, fire in fire, ether in ether, no one can distinguish them; likewise a man whose mind has entered the Self."[104]

Inayat Khan tells a Hindu story of a fish who went to a queen fish and asked: "I have always heard about the sea, but what is this sea? Where is it? "

The queen fish explained: "You live, move, and have your being in the sea. The sea is within you and without you, and you are made of sea, and you will end in sea. The sea surrounds you as your own being."[105]

This was the state in which Bernard found himself. He expressed it in this way, "Rightly, therefore, does the Spouse, renouncing all other feeling, abandon herself entirely to love alone, since in the interchange of love she has to correspond to a Bridegroom who is Love itself. For even when her whole being has been dissolved and poured out in love for him, what after all is her love compared with the never failing outflow from Love's own fountain? "[106]

Now, the realization of oneness with God involves oneness with all, not only all men but with all God's creation, so that the realization includes every thing. Once realizing that God was the being of his life, Bernard started to awaken to the fact that the presence of God permeates the whole universe

---

103. SC 52:4; OB 2:92.
104. *The Upaniahds*; tr. M. Muller, II, 17, 334.
105. Paul Reps, *Zen Flesh, Zen Bones*, p. 175.
106. SC 83:6; OB 2:302.

and the whole of creation. To him now God is in the stone and the tree as much as in heaven and in the inmost center of the soul. He is all about us, just as much as within us. From now on the world is charged with the grandeur of God, full of God. To Henry Murdac, a close friend, Bernard confided this experience. "Believe me who has experience, you will find much more laboring in the woods than ever you will among books. Woods and stones will teach you what you can never hear from any master. Do you imagine you cannot suck honey from the rocks and oil from the hardest stone, that the mountains do not drop sweetness and the hills flow with milk and honey; that the valleys are not filled with corn? So many things occur to me which I could say to you that I can hardly restrain myself."[107] Centuries later Shakespeare expressed the same insight in poetical form:

> Tongues in trees,
> Books in the running brooks,
> Sermons in stones
> and good in everything. [108]

Bernard loved the creatures of God's hand so much that he felt at one with them. He felt their every pulse beating through his veins, so to speak. They became life to him. He not only saw creation as beautiful and full of splendor and nature as an open book, but he saw in every flower, in every wild wood, in every stone, the deepest mystery of life and being. He felt the divine love which reaches the mysterious depths of cosmic life. This is the fruit of a mind which awakened to the reality of God. D. T. Suzuki wrote:

When one's mind is religiously awakened, one feels as though in every blade of wild fern and solid stone there is something really transcending all human feelings, something which lifts one to be a real equal to that of heaven. One has a specific gift that detects something great in all

107. Ep 106, PL 182:242; tr. B. S. James, *The Letters of St Bernard of Clairvaux* (London: Burns and Oates, 1953), Letter 107, p. 156.
108. *As You Like It,* Act 2, Scene 1.

the ordinary things of earth, something that transcends all quantitative measurement. He plunges himself into the very source of creativity and, there drinks from life all that life has to give. He not only sees by taking a look, but he enters into the source of things and knows them at the point where life receives its existence.[109]

Here is another anecdote on the mystery of how God's world is inclusive of our own.

One day Osho went for a ramble in the mountains. On his return to the monastery, the head monk said to him:

Osho, where have you been?"

"I have come from a ramble in the mountains," Osho replied.

"Where did you go, Osho? " the head monk inquired.

"Going, I followed the fragrant grasses; returning, I pursued the falling blossoms," answered Osho.

"How very springlike the feeling! " exclaimed the head monk.

"Still better is the dripping of autumn dew from the full-blown lotus flowers," returned Osho.

"I am grateful to you for your answer," said the head monk.[110]

This is the new way of looking at things and the world of God. In Zen it is called *satori* or looking directly into the essence of things—suchness. Bernard and all of us are sup-posedly living in the same world, but who can tell whether the thing we popularly call a stone which may be lying in our garden or in the garth of our monastery is the same for us as it was for Bernard? Bernard sought "oil from the hardest stone," and "saw the mountains drop down sweetness." Do we?

THE INEFFABLE JOY OF RELIGIOUS AWAKENING

Blesses is the soul in whom he is.
who lives for him, and is moved by him![111]

109. Suzuki and Fromn, *Zen Buddhism and Psychoanalysis*, p. 2.
110. As quoted by Isshu Miura in *The Zen Koan*, p. 55.
111. SC 74:5; OB 2:243.

"Blessed is he" is the exclamation of joy which Bernard uttered after he came out of a deep experience of God, after being momentarily lost in the divine immensity. It is the last word, the summing up of all that he could say about the ineffable blessedness which the soul enjoys through being united to the Word in a most intimate friendship. In his *Eighty-third Sermon on the Song of Songs* Bernard said,

> This is truly a blessed state when the soul is united with God the Word in a nuptial union. This is nothing but the final crown of all our love for God in this life. Happy the soul to whom it has been given to experience an embrace of such surpassing delight! This spiritual embrace is nothing else than a chaste and holy love, a love sweet and pleasant, a love perfectly serene and perfectly pure, a love that is mutual, intimate and strong, a love that joins two, not in one flesh, but in one spirit.[112]

But how short-lived, how rare and how incommunicable is this blessedness. Bernard wrote:

> ... it is better for the soul to be transported out of itself and united with the Word. But when does this happen, and how long does it last? It is an exchange of love most delightful to experience, but it is as rare as it is delightful, and as short-lived as it is rare! ... Perhaps there are some of you who would now like an explanation of what it is like to enjoy the Word in this way.... Had I been privileged sometimes to experience that favor, do you suppose it would be possible for me to describe the ineffable?[113]

The sense of well-being and happiness brought about by religious awakening is not a mere consciousness of something; it is a fusion, in the innermost depths of the soul, from which an awareness of some ineffable good and an experience of deep joy overflows. D. T. Suzuki observed that:

> The feeling of exultation which inevitably accompanies *satori* is due to the fact that it is the breaking up of the restrictions imposed upon one as an individual being. This

112. SC 83:6; OB 2:302.
113. SC 85:13; OB 2:316.

breaking up is not a mere negative incident but a quite positive experience fraught with significance because it means an infinite expansion of the individual. The general feeling, though we are not always conscious of it, which characterizes the routine functions of consciousness, is that of restriction and dependence, because consciousness itself is the outcome of two forces conditioning or restricting one another. *Satori,* on the contrary, consists essentially in doing away with the opposition found between any two terms. *Satori* is to realize the Unconscious (or the Transcendental) which goes beyond opposition. To be released from this tension, therefore, causes one to feel raised above conflicting forces and intensely exalted. Thus the individual man, who is a wandering outcast, maltreated everywhere, not only by others but by himself inexplicably finds that he is the possessor of all the wealth and power that is ever attainable in this world by a mortal being—if this experience does not give him a high feeling of self-glorification, what could? [114]

In his *Varieties of Religious Experience,* William James put together an extensive and authentic collection of Christian experiences, which, of course, includes the revelations of such people as Teresa of Avila and John of the Cross, and all of these give witness to this feeling of exaltation.[115] Let me quote some experiences of the Eastern masters. Notice the terminology of astonishment and exultation.

Imakita Kosen, one of the best-known masters gives a fairly complete description of his experience:

One night when I was engaged in *zasen* (meditation) the boundry between before and after was suddenly cut off. I entered the blessed realm of the exceedingly wonderful. I found myself, as it were, on the ground of the Great Death, and no awareness of the being of all things and of the ego remained. I felt only how in my body a spirit extended itself to ten thousand worlds, and an infinite splendor of

114. D. T. Suzuki, *Zen Buddhism,* ed. William Barrett (New York: Doubleday, 1956) p. 107.
115. William James, *Varieties of Religious Experience* (New York: Macmillan, 1970) pp. 299-336.

light arose. After a short while I breathed again. In a flash, seeing and hearing, speech and motion, were different from every day. As I sought the supreme truth and the wonderful meaning of the universe, my own self was clear and things appeared bright. In the excess of delight I forgot that my hands were moving in the air and that my feet were dancing.[116]

Hsueh-yen Tsu-chin wrote:

The experience was beyond description and altogether incomprehensible, for there was nothing in the world to which it could be compared. . . . As I looked around and up and down, the whole universe with its multitudinous sense-objects now appeared quite different; what was loathsome before, together with ignorance and passions, was now seen to be nothing else but the outflow of my own inmost nature which in itself remained bright, true and transparent. This state of consciousness lasted for more than half a month.[117]

Tsu-yuan, the renowed founder of the Engakuji temple of Kamakura, wrote:

All of a sudden the sound of striking the board in front of the head-monk's room reached my ear, which at once revealed to me the "original man" in full. There was then no more of that vision which appeared at the closing of my eyes. Hastily I came down from the seat and ran out into the moonlit night and went up to the garden house called Ganki, where, looking up to the sky, I laughed loudly, "Oh, how great is the *Dharmakaja*! (the Absolute!) Oh, how great and immense for evermore! "

Thence my joy knew no bounds. I could not quietly sit in the meditation hall; I went about with no special purpose in the mountains, walking this way and that. I thought of the sun and the moon traversing in a day a space

116. As quoted by Heinrick Dumoulin in *A History of Zen Buddhism* (Boston: Beacon, 1969) p. 273.
117. D. T. Suzuki, *Essays in Zen Buddhism,* Second Series (New York: S. Weiser, 1971) p. 116.

4,000,000,000 miles wide. "My present abode is in China," I reflected, "and they say the district of Yang is the center of the earth. If so, this place must be 2,000,000,000 miles away from where the sun rises; and how is it that as soon as it comes up, its rays lose no time in striking my face? " I reflected again, "The rays of my own eye must travel just as instantaneously as those of the sun as it reaches the latter; my eyes, my mind, are they not the *Dharmakaja* itself? [118]

Hakuin Ekaku (1686-1769) more than any one Zen master has left us many detailed descriptions of his own religious awakenings. These can be found in Heinrich Dumoulin's *A History of Zen*. The following is Dumoulin's summary account of Hakuin's experience:

Once with great joy he read a verse by the Chinese master Hsi-Keng. As a ray of light in a dark night illumines the way, so light fell upon his soul. In rapture he shouted loudly for joy. In another instance he wandered during the rainy season in the vicinity of Ise. The rain fell in torrents and the waters reached to his knees. There he suddenly understood the deep meaning of some verses of Hsi-Keng which he had read earlier. He was so enraptured that he could not stand upright, and he fell into the water. In amazement a passerby looked at him and helped him to his feet. Hakuin laughed aloud for joy, so that once more the passerby took him for a madman. In the enlightenment state he is as though beside himself. Immeasurable jubilation wells up in his heart and breaks out in involuntary shouts and spontaneous dancing. [119]

In his *Zen Buddhism*, Christmas Humphreys, a Western scholar practised in Zen, describes his experience:

I was having tea with a cat on my lap. I suddenly felt very happy, (an unusual state of my intensely active and imaginative mind). Then, as it were, I felt about me a steady

---

118. D. T. Suzuki, *Essays in Zen Buddhism*, First Series (London: Rider, 1970) p. 257.

119. Heinrick Dumoulin, *A History of Zen Buddhism*, pp. 242 ff.

rising tide of enormous joy, I wanted to sing, or to dance to the music. The warmth of the tide was glorious as of a large affectionate flame. Never before had I attained to this discriminative consciousness which functions on a plane where all discriminations seemed absurd. The tide ebbed slowly and I was left exhilarated, rested and refreshed.[120]

The context of a deep religious experience is what gives rise to the great variety of ways of experiencing it. One must expect the surroundings of one's life style, and the associations of one's personal faith to enter into the drama of the moment. Thus it is that for Christians of the Western tradition the moments of prayer are also moments of intensification of their faith, and so you find constant reference to the great themes of Revelation, such as the indwelling of the Trinity, the Incarnation of the Word, and the revelation of unbounded love expressed by the Passion and Death of Christ. These themes are familiar and often encased in an aurora of the "heroic" when used to describe states of prayer, but this is not necessary and is often misleading. A feeling of awe is natural but it should not overcloud the simple, innocent familiarity of religious awakening. My own experience of God is deeply connected to these mysteries of faith. Though the expressions of Eastern mysticism have helped to release in me an awareness of the riches of Biblical revelation and give me a key to the naturalness of growth in the consciousness of God, it is still ultimately in terms of the indwelling Trinity that I am personally inclined to locate the highest moments of my consciousness.

Perhaps a personal description of a prayer experience would not be entirely out of place and might serve to indicate the variety of forms such awakening to God may take. I also think it will demonstrate how even a slight taste of this consciousness brings with it a sense of joy that is always ineffable.

The particular antecedents to my experience were, first of all, several years of searching for God and familiarity with the thought of St Bernard, or in his terms, "longing after the

---

120. Christmas Humphreys, *Zen Budhism* (New York: Macmillan, 1970) p. 118.

Word," and then a period of about a year of intense application in an effort to "solve" the Zen *koan* which says, "Empty hand, yet holding a hoe; walking, yet riding a water-buffalo." One day in January about two o'clock in the morning I was on my way to my cell in the dormitory. As I walked through the door that leads to the dormitory, suddenly there seemed to be something sweeping into me and elating my whole being—such a sensation as I had never experienced before. I felt like I was being carried above the ground although I was fully alert and knew that my two feet were on the floor. A whole realm of undifferentiated consciousness overwhelmed me. I felt a complete break from my past manner of thinking and feeling. Nothing remained of myself. An ineffable sense of release, of well-being, of clarity of mind inundated me. This state of being placed me in an exalted mood of supreme delight which stayed with me more or less clearly for about two days until one night I awoke from sleep and suddenly I was given a glance at the truth of the Blessed Trinity— Father, Son and Holy Spirit, the truth of the One God in Three Persons. An infinite splendor of light enveloped me, awakening my entire being from the inmost to the outermost. My faith in the Blessed Trinity became an intuition. I saw, or I must say, I understood as clearly as an apple on the palm of my hand, the essence of the Godhead and its Three Persons in their "relatedness" and what theology has called the "appropriations." I experienced the Godhead as being one immense ocean of Life, of Light and of Bliss. It is so calm so serene and so transparent. The truth about the Father dawned upon me when I saw the wave of this immense ocean rose. The flood of life rose and rose until it reached a "marvelous peak"! As this "marvelous peak" broke through, the truth of the Only-begotten Son dawned upon me. This breaking-through gave rise to a sense of incommunicable bliss and rest, which opened me to the truth of the Holy Spirit, the delightful moving energy itself of the Father and the Son.

For the first time in my life I was given a glimpse into the joy of the Blessed Trinity's life within, which filled me with an extraordinary transparency and delight. For my own sake, as a memory of this happy event, I attempted to depict it in the form of a *semiye* drawing and a poem.

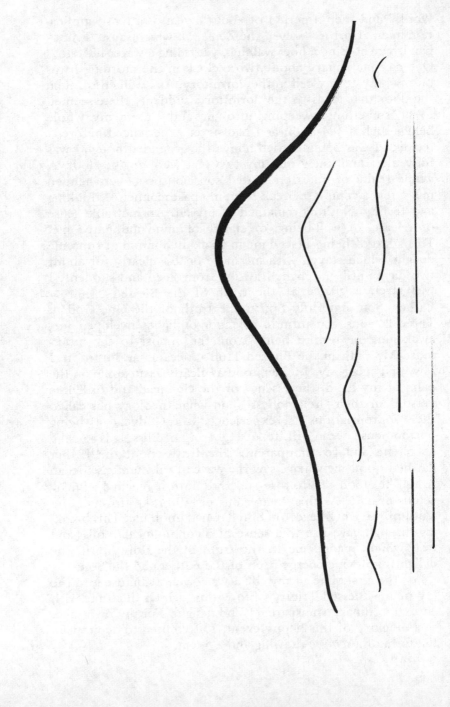

THE TRINITY'S BLISS

BEING, Principle of Life, of Light and Goodness
Actualizes Itself by pouring these out.
As this pouring reaches Its "Marvelous Peak,"
The only-eternal-Son is born.

BEING eternally begotten from God
The Son, in turn, poures Himself all-out.
When this pouring breaks down the unutterable Abyss
The uncommunicable Bliss is "proceeding."

BEING aware of Itself as the Love of Both
The eternal BLISS moves Himself as divine Spirit,
Who joins the Begetting and Begotten together
In an ineffably piercing Embrass.

THIS is an eternally repeating Process (ion),
As ever-renewed-Coming, an ever-Freshness;
It goes on within Itself all at once,
Outside of time, and in spaceless sphere.

As GOD is like the Ocean of moving Delight
the "waves" as seen as rising within It
Indicate man's measure of "religious awakening."
Those "lying flat" are ones who still in deep sleep.

We must experience the moments
Of the "meeting" of the paired-opposites:
Of Light and Darkness, or something alike
To realize within us this TRINITY's BLISS.

SUMMATION

Space does not allow me to deal here with the methods for
religious awakening suggested by Bernard and the Eastern
masters. An adequate presentation of this method would
require another essay as long as this one. By way of summing
this up, I have presented on the following page a diagram
which serves as a synopsis of all I have said. The diagram
shows Bernard's five stages of religious awakening, and the
five positions of the Host and Guest, or the "Five Steps"
toward full enlightenment as used by both the Soto and the
Rinzai schools of Zen Buddhism.

The diagram can also be used as a "Method in a Nut shell"
for religious awakening. The key point to the method consists in
MEDITATION. Meditation here does not mean discursive reasoning or process, but a "dwelling upon." For Bernard meditation is the "dwelling upon" the Word of God; for the Eastern masters, it is the "dwelling upon" either a symbol or a
koan. The most important thing is the "dwelling upon."

On the diagram you see first the words of the *Song of
Songs* meditated upon or dwelt upon by Bernard;[121] then, the
symbols used by the Soto school, then the *koans* used by the
Rinzai school. The key to success, or to religious awakening,
lies in our constant application to meditation on these words
and these symbols. The technique can best be applied with
the guidance of a master, or with the help of those who have
experience. But until you find one, you can "do-it-yourself."
The blank spaces on the diagram can be filled with any sacred
text of your choice, such as the followings:

> I am the vine, you the branches
> Abide in my love
> and you will bear much fruit.[122]

or,

> Who believes in me (i.e. adheres to me)
> A stream of living water
> will spring from his inmost being.[123]

---

121. SC 68: 1 ff; OB 2:196ff.
122. Jn 15:5.
123. Jn 7:38. Other suggested texts: Gen 1:2; Ps 80:11; Mt 26:26; 1 Cor 10:16;
Rev 3:20.

THE FIVE POSITIONS OF THE LOVER AND THE BELOVED
(Or The Five Steps Towards Full Enlightenment)

1	2	3	4	5
The Lover		a ———▶ b	Guest in Host	—
The Beloved		b ◀——— a	Host in Guest	—
"My Beloved is to me,		a ⟳ b	Resurgence of Host	—
I am to Him		a ⟳ b	Guest returns to Host	—
Who feeds among the Lilies."			Host in Host	—

(1) SC 68: 1; (2) The Soto school's symbol; (3) D. T. Suzuki's (of the
Rinzai school) symbol; (4) Five koans expressing the "Five Steps"
leading to full Realization; (5) spaces to be filled by the reader.

Dwelling upon the Word of God certainly will lead us toward religious awakening provided we apply the instruction and invitation of Bernard who wrote that those who have not yet enjoyed such an experience should desire it ardently:

> We do not hesitate to proclaim boldly that every soul among us, if it is vigilant like the spouse, shall also, like the spouse be saluted as his love, consoled as his dove and embraced as his beautiful one.[124] ... Every human soul, no matter how burdened with sins, no matter how entangled with vices, no matter how enslaved to the enticement of pleasures, ... no matter how worried with anxieties, disquieted and suspicious; ... yes, I say, even though the soul should be in such a state of despair, ... it can still discover in itself something which is not only capable of establishing it in the hope of pardon and in the confidence of mercy, but also of animating it with courage to aspire even to the nuptials of the Word, to enter boldly into an alliance of friendship with God and fearlessly to draw the sweet yoke of love with him. ... For what may it not safely presume in the case of One with whose image it beholds itself adorned, and by whose likeness it perceives itself ennobled? ... Only let it strive henceforth to prove and preserve the nobility of its nature by innocence of life; or rather let it study to enhance and decorate with the appropriate colors, so to speak, or worthy actions and affections that heavenly beauty which is its birthright.[125]

Joseph Chu-Cong OCSO

St. Joseph's Abbey
Spencer, Massachusetts

124. SC 57:11; OB 2:125.
125. SC 83:1; OB 2:298-9.

I would like to thank Fr Robert Morhous OCSO for reading this manuscript and for his many insightful suggestions.

APPENDICES

We give here a translation of the four *Letters* of Pope Alexander III, all dated from Anagni, the eighteenth of January (the fifteenth day before the Kalends of February) 1174, in which he proclaimed to the Church of France, to the King, to the Cistercian Order and to the Abbot and monks of Clairvaux the solemn canonization of St Bernard. The translation is based on the text found in Mabillon's edition of the *Sancti Bernardi opera omnia* (PL 185:622-5) and which is reproduced in *Acta Sanctorum* (Aug. 4:244-5) and in Marinque's *Annales Cisterciences* (3:2-3). To these we add a fifth letter sent by Tromund, the abbot of Chiaravalle, to Abbot Gerard of Clairvaux to report on his labors and those of his collaborators which helped bring about the canonization. This interesting letter is also found in Mabillon (PL 185:826-7).

ALEXANDER III TO THE CHURCH IN FRANCE

Alexander, bishop, servant of the servants of God, to his venerable brothers, all the archbishops and bishops, and to his dear sons, the abbots and other prelates of the Church in the kingdom of France.

When we were at Paris some time ago some important men worthy of esteem spoke to us of the canonization of the former abbot of Clairvaux, Bernard of blessed memory. They indeed desired it, and suggested to us with filial petitions that in the council which was about to be celebrated at Tours we should without delay grant their good and praiseworthy desire. Although we were favorably inclined toward the idea, many petitions were pouring in from different regions seeking similar favors. Since we could not see how we could

269

fittingly satisfy everyone, it was decided, in order to avoid scandal, to put off even this petition, since we had to refuse others for the time being. Recently, however, the same petitions have been again presented through the untiring devotion of the brothers at Clairvaux and other high-ranking persons. We have reconsidered the holy and venerable life of that blessed man, how he so shone with singular graces that from him not only radiated holiness and religion but also he illumined the whole Church with the light of his faith and doctrine. Indeed there is hardly a corner of Christendom that does not know what fruit he bore in the house of the Lord by his word and example. Even beyond Christendom among barbarian peoples he brought religious life and established monasteries and brought back an infinite number of sinners from the broad downward path of a worldly life to the straight way of the spiritual life.

In a special way, however, he supported the holy Roman Church—over which by the authority of God we preside—in the midst of her sufferings from grave persecutions, by the merit of his life and the zeal of the wisdom which he received from on high. So it is fitting, indeed, that he should be remembered by us and all the sons of the Church and venerated with lasting devotion. By the frugality of his life he belongs to the order of confessors. But at the same time it is clear he underwent a long martyrdom, for he mortified him body to the point that the world was crucified to his and he to the world so that we are confident he obtained the merit of the holy martyrs.

And so all these things having been reverently considered and set forth in the council of our brothers, confiding in the mercy of God whom he perseveringly and faithfully served, and presuming on the merits of the blessed apostles, Peter and Paul, and of this most blessed Confessor, we have commanded by the authority of the Apostolic See, that he be inscribed in the catalog of the saints and we decree that his feast is now to be publicly celebrated.

You, therefore, who are accustomed to receive the decrees of this Apostolic See and to give greater glory to God in honoring his saints, may you so celebrate the memory of this Saint on earth that by his prayers and merits you may receive a due reward in heaven.

Given at Anagni, the fifteenth day before the Kalends of February (in the year 1174).

ALEXANDER III TO THE KING OF FRANCE

Alexander, bishop, servant of the servants of God, to Louis, the Illustrious King of the Franks, health and apostolic benediction.

Your Majesty knows, we believe, that those things that are pleasing and acceptable to you and are to God's honor we, with a large and willing heart, seek to bring about. This is above all the case in those undertakings which especially honor God and proclaim the glory of his saints. For we know indeed that whatever is done by apostolic authority for the glory of the Church and the honor of the heavenly kingdom is most pleasing to you.

Wherefore, because Bernard of blessed memory, the former abbot of Clairvaux and a man always dear to God, was pleasing and acceptable both to you and to the whole of your kingdom, we have decreed for the glory of God and the exaltation of the Church in your whole kingdom that he be canonized and honored among the most blessed confessors with a festal celebration so that by the mercy of God and the blessed apostles, Peter and Paul, his merits might be proclaimed and his holy life might not be forgotten.

We therefore admonish Your Most Christian Majesty[1] to embrace with the arms of joyful devotion this gift of heavenly grace given to your kingdom during your reign, and with your accustomed piety reverence him enjoying his heavenly beatitude whom you loved because of his venerable sanctity while he was still in the shadows. Out of reverence for him

---

1. Literally the Latin text reads: "the pious Lordship of Your Most Christian Serenity."

we wish to commend to you the monastery of Clairvaux which he founded and in which his venerable body lies so that you may merit to have him always as a patron.

Given at Anagni, the fifteenth day before the Kalends of February.

ALEXANDER III TO THE CISTERCIAN ORDER

Alexander, bishop, servant of the servants of God, to his beloved sons of Cîteaux, La Ferté, Pontigny, Clairvaux, Morimond, and all the abbots of the Cistercian Order, health and apostolic benediction.

As often as a suitable opportunity presents itself to us that we can in some way respond to you according to the merits of the faith and devotion which you have for the Church of God in our times, we gladly embrace that opportunity. Above all in those things which proclaim your special virtue we do not hesitate to seek your benefit. Now at this time the petition for the canonization of the former abbot of Clairvaux, the blessed Bernard, which had been previously presented and which was set aside at the time of the celebration of the Council of Tours because of possible scandal to others seeking the same thing, is again brought to our attention by the will of God who has done us a good turn in providing that this work of piety should be brought to completion by our hands.

We have considered with careful concern the life and holiness of the most blessed Confessor; in particular, how magnificent he was in himself in his special holiness and religious life and how useful and abundantly fruitful was his faith and doctrine to the whole Church of God and especially for your Order.

Confiding then in the mercy of God and of the blessed apostles Peter and Paul and presuming on the merits of this holy Confessor, with the counsel of our brothers, we by the authority of the Apostolic See have ordered him to be inscribed in the catalogue of the saints and the day of his death to be publicly celebrated in the Church.

Wherefore because this so shows forth the glory and honor of the supreme Creator that it redounds also to your edification and consolation, it is for you most of all to give thanks to almighty God who in modern times willed to raise up in your Order a man of perfection and praiseworthy holiness. Receive therefore with special devotion this magnificent gift and in celebrating him in a special way honor God who is wondrous in the glorification of his saints.

Given at Anagni, the fifteenth day before the Kalends of February.

ALEXANDER III TO THE ABBOT AND COMMUNITY OF CLAIRVAUX

Alexander, bishop, servant of the servants of God, to his beloved sons, Abbot Gerard and the whole community of Clairvaux, health and apostolic benediction.

Just as the religion and piety you show towards God is in no wise unknown to us, so too, the strength of your devotion and the brightness of your faith is always certainly manifest. For you could not, nor from now on, by the power of God, can you show yourselves unworthy of the grace of holiness which you have inherited from your holy Father. To his merit, spiritual grace abounded in him, and there was no lack of efficacious works to give good example. You know and recall with filial veneration how Bernard of blessed memory, the first abbot of your monastery and its outstanding founder, was indeed acceptable to God for the virtue of his religious life and pleasing to the Church of God for the fullness of his devotion and faith. And so rightly you should have been considered guilty if you had been negligent in imitating and venerating him.

It has pleased us therefore that you have been solicitous concerning him as for a devoted Father and you have made praiseworthy petitions for his canonization.

We who, because of the many signs of your devotion, son and abbot, and the religion and filial zeal of your whole house, always have it at heart to acquiesce to your requests and to favor their fulfillment, have mercifully granted your petition so that we confirm our favor and benevolence toward you.

Therefore, calling to mind the life of this most blessed Confessor, how he shone with faith and religion and doctrine and how much he illumined the Church of God with the extraordinary brightness of his light, with the counsel of our brothers and confidence in the mercy of God and of the blessed apostles Peter and Paul and presuming on the merits of this Saint, we have ordered he be inscribed in the catalogue of the saints and the day of his death henceforth be celebrated as a feast.

Wherefore, because it is for you above all to imitate his life and honor his glory, seek in all things and be eager to walk in the footsteps of this holy Father and to celebrate the feast of his holiness so that you who have merited to be sharers of his way of life may be held worthy to be companions in his blessedness.

Given at Anagni, the fifteenth day before the Kalends of February.

ABBOT TROMUND OF CHIARAVALLE TO
ABBOT GERARD OF CLAIRVAUX

To the Reverend Father and Lord, Gerard, Abbot of Clairvaux, from brother Tromund, called abbot[2] of Chiaravalle, salvation and increase of ready devotion.

May your Paternity have as much merit before God and as much favor before men as the outcome of both our labor and of our work proclaim in manifold ways, because in both, being borne up on both sides, we feared neither the danger of the labor nor the obstacles to the work. On the other hand,

---

2. Mabillon has a note in his text to the effect that this "should rather read *monachus* (monk)." But his opinion here arises from a confusion of Abbot Tromund of Chiaravalle with Tromund, who had been in the Roman Curia and later entered Clairvaux, where he served as secretary to Abbot Henry. See S. J. Heathcote, "The Letter Collection attributed to Master Transmundus," ASOC 21 (1965) 86-9.

from the day of his departure from our earth there has been no end to fear and anguish until the solicitude over the work was ended and tha labor was completed. However, blessed be God above all things, who rescued us from all, and with the happy completion of the business called us back, well and happy, to our own affairs.

And now, behold, our most blessed confessor, Bernard, who in every way is worthy of veneration and who already belonged to the college of the saints, has been formally inscribed. As from his mother's womb it was his lot to be among the saints, so he has obtained this title of holiness with them by the beneficence of Mother Church. This was brought about by his wonderful merits and by the laudible zeal of your filial piety, by the efforts of the brothers whom you designated to work with me for this, and also by your many friends both inside and outside the Curia who helped us in attaining this favor. Henceforth, we will celebrate for him and through him a feast with the angels. It will no longer be necessary to sing mournful songs for him,[3] who we believe is singing solemn hymns in heaven in the angelic choirs.

We set aside a similar project on behalf of St Malachy on the advice of the Pope who intimated to us in our opening conversation that seeking the two together might cause a lack of interest which could frustrate our aim in regard to the one. You must therefore be grateful that in your days it was granted to the one and patiently bear with the fact that it was deferred in regard to the other. Let us give thanks to him who established the times and the changes in the heavenly lights so that the rising of the morning and evening stars is not the same although the glory of his brightness shines forth in both.

The Lord Abbot of Casamari himself and his monks and his monastery were with us and helped us from start to finish. The Lord Abbot of Fossa Nuova and the Bishop of Veroli,

---

3. The reference here is probably to the fact that the community in accordance with the usages of the Order were accustomed, up to the time of the official recognition of Bernard's sanctity, to offer the Requiem Mass on his anniversary.

when they were asked, gave us the favor of their help and counsel. Br Frank, Br Peter and Br Stephen stood by us and the undertaking in everything. Br Guy, through his own many labors and those of his [brothers] and through brother's considerable expenditures, enabled us to find our way through the various byways in that a more than usual ill will on the part of those who would waylay us beset the direct pursuit of our undertaking. Br Roch worked a bit, sustaining us and the business itself with faith and prayer. Because I was admonished by the tenor of your letter to use your stipends to further our cause, I did so but in all was guided by Roman parsimony as I do not go along with Gallican prodigality.

May the Lord grant to all of us together that in memory of the labor and work we may preserve your good favor and that of the brethren at Clairvaux here on earth and receive the mercy of God in heaven.

We would advise that the Mass which the Pope sang on the solemnity of this Saint not be changed. We are sending the collects for it to you.

I would like to thank Fr Robert Morhous OCSO for reading this manuscript and for his many insightful suggestions.

LIST OF ABBREVIATIONS

Note: For references to Sacred Scripture the abbreviations found in the Revised Standard Version are employed. The standard abbreviations for the *works* of Bernard of Clairvaux and William of St Thierry which are used in this volume are listed separately below.

AA SS — *Acta sanctorum.* New ed. Joanne Carnandet. 64 vols. Paris and Rome: Palmé, 1865.

Anal. Boll. — *Analecta Bollandiana.* Brussels: Societé des Bollandistes, 1882—.

ASOC — *Analecta Cisterciensia* (formerly *Analecta Sacris Ordinis Cisterciensis*). Rome, 1944—.

CF — Cistercian Fathers Series. Spencer, Massachusetts/Washington, D.C., 1970—.

CHOC — Commission d'Histoire de l'Ordre de Cîteaux.

CS — Cistercian Studies Series. Spencer, Massachusetts/Washington, D.C., 1969—.

DHGE — *Dictionnaire d'histoire et de géographie ecclesiastique.* Ed. Baudrillart et al. Paris: Letouzey, 1912—. (14 volumes to date - up to Eg).

J—L — *Regesta Pontificum Romanorum.* Ed. Jaffé-Loewenfeld. 2 vols. Leipzig, 1888; repr. Graz, 1956.

MGH SS — *Monumenta Germaniae historica. Scriptores.* 30 vols. Berlin: Weidmann, 1826-1903; 32 vols. Hannover: Impensis Bibliopolii Hahniani, 1926-1934.

n.	note
OB	*S. Bernardi opera.* Ed. J. Leclercq, C. H. Talbot, H. M. Rochais. Rome: Editiones Cistercienses, 1957—.
PG	*Patrologiae cursus completus, series Graeca.* Ed. J. P. Migne. 161 vols. Paris 1856-1866.
PL	*Patrologiae cursus completus, series Latina.* Ed. J. P. Migne. 216 vols. Paris, 1844-1864.
RAM	*Revue d'ascetique et de mystique.* Toulouse, 1925—.
RB	*Benedicti Regula.* Ed. R. Hanslik. Corpus Scriptorum Ecclesiasticorum Latinorum 75. Vienna: Hoelder-Pichler-Tempsky, 1960. Tr. L. J. Doyle. *St Benedict's Rule for Monasteries.* Collegeville: Liturgical Press, 1948.
repr.	reprinted.
RBen	*Revue bénédictine.* Maredsous, 1890—.
S Ch	Sources chrétiennes. Paris: Cerf, 1943—.
SMGBOZ	*Studien und Mitteilungen zur Geschichte des Benediktinerordens und seiner Zweige.* Munich, 1880—.

THE WORKS OF BERNARD OF CLAIRVAUX

Csi	*De consideratione libri V,* OB 3:393-493; *St Bernard's Five Books on Consideration,* CF 37
Ded	*S. in Dedicatione Ecclesiae,* OB 5:370-98; *Sermons for the Dedication of the Church,* CF 34
Dil	*Liber de diligendo Deo,* OB 3:119-54; *On Loving God,* CF 13.

Div	*S. de diversis,* OB 6-1; *Occasional Sermons,* CF 46, 49.
Ep	*Epistola(e),* OB 7, 8; Letter(s).
Gra	*Liber de Gratia et de libero Arbitrio,* OB 3:165-203; *Grace and Free Choice,* CF 19.
Palm	*S. in Ramis Palmarum,* OB 5:42-55; *Sermons for Palm Sunday,* OB 22.
S.	*Sermons/Sermones*
SC	*S. super Cantica Canticorum,* OB 1, 2; *Sermons on the Song of Songs,* CF 4, 7, 31.
Sept.	*S. in Septuagesima,* OB 4:344-52; *Sermons for Septuagesima,* CF 22.

THE WORKS OF WILLIAM OF ST THIERRY

Cant	*Expositio super Cantica Canticorum,* PL 180:473-546, S Ch 82; *Exposition on the Song of Songs,* CF 6.
Contemp	*De contemplando Deo,* PL 184:365-80, S Ch 61; *On Contemplating God,* CF 3:36-64.
Nat am	*De natura et dignitate amoris,* PL 184:379-408; *The Nature and Dignity of Love,* CF 15.
Vita Bern	*Sancti Bernardi vita prima,* PL 185:225-68. *St. Bernard of Clairvaux.* Tr. G. Webb and A. Walker. Westminster, Maryland: Newman; London: Mowbrays, 1960.

CISTERCIAN PUBLICATIONS
Titles Listing
1977